Life's Cheat Sheet:
Crucial Success Habits School Never Taught You

Sign up for Jeff's e-zine at *www.lifescheatsheets.com* to get free materials to apply these concepts and to get advance notice on the follow-up *financial habits* book as soon as it's available.

Company and Group Partnership Opportunities

This is my long-term anti-bailout solution for young adults, but obviously everyone can benefit from these success habits. I am partnering with several organizations to get this information out so it spreads quickly and helps turn the country around. If you act now, you can be one of my key partners in teaching these critical skills.

If your company, school, association, or non-profit partners with me, I will coordinate with you to print a customized *Special Edition* of this book that will allow you to replace this page with highlights of your organization and its brand in each copy produced for your organization. We can also partner concurrently with a charity of your choice, donating a part of the proceeds to it while benefiting your organization from the associated goodwill and spreading your brand to all of the charity's subscribers. You can feature our partnership in your marketing materials, which will demonstrate your concern for educating and equipping people with the skills to succeed in life, and I will prominently list you as a key partner in my marketing materials.

There are many great ways you can offer your customers extra value and make an impact on them with this book. You can give the customized book as a premium, as an added bonus with a purchase, with a mail-in coupon after a purchase, as a free gift for making a phone call in response to a solicitation. Or you can give it to your customers as a free gift without making a purchase, or at a reduced price with a purchase or contact to your organization. Use your creativity. Alternatively, you could give it to your staff for staff development or give it to your key clients. If you're in a role like financial advisor, banker, or relationship marketer, you could give it to any clients who are parents as a gift to their kids. This way, you can develop younger, multi-generational clients. Why not use the book to motivate subordinates or relationship marketers in your down-line?

I will also speak to your organization and participate in conferences that you sponsor. In addition, I can help key partners design contests with challenges to departments, small groups, or individuals to see who can best apply the skills and gain the most disposable income. You can give out prizes and incentives to further encourage them to implement this knowledge and teach others.

As you can see, there are countless ways to use this book to help grow and strengthen your organization. I have negotiated affordable volume pricing that can dramatically reduce your cost per unit in order to fit your budget. Help your organization expand its exposure to a much larger audience, help adults learn crucial success skills, and help the country turn around. Give me a call at 1-866-475-4675 or send me an e-mail at *jv@prestigemediagroupllc.com* today to take advantage of this opportunity.

LiFE'S CHEAT SHEET

Crucial Success Habits
School Never Taught You

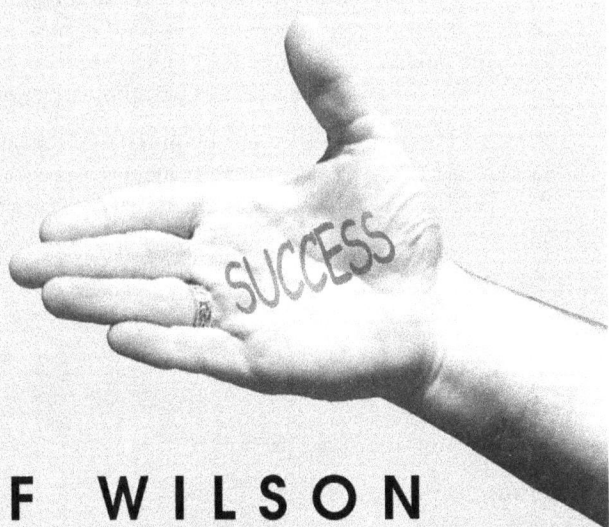

SUCCESS

JEFF WILSON

Prestige Publishing books may be purchased for educational, business, or sales promotional use in bulk. For details about this program, write to the address below "Attn: Bulk Sales." Find more information on the website at www.prestigemediagrou-pllc.com, e-mail jv@prestigemediagroupllc.com, or call toll free at 1-866-475-4675.

Prestige Publishing
An affiliate of Prestige Media Group, LLC
P.O. Box 350986
Toledo, OH 43635
Phone: 419-842-8112
E-mail: Info@lifescheatsheets.com

Printed in the United States of America

Cover and interior design by: 1106 Design, Phoenix, AZ
Copy Editors: Beth A. (Rowe) Wilson, Doran Hunter

Library of Congress Control # 2010931724

ISBN-13: 978-0-9845965-0-8

Disclaimer and Legal Notice (damn attorneys)

Throughout this book, you will need to consider all of the other factors in your life at that time to make the best decision for your particular situation. The author has given suggestions based on typical circumstances, but if your situation is different, change your decisions accordingly. Use this information as you see fit and at your own risk. Readers are urged to consult a variety of sources and educate themselves about these areas before taking any risks. The advice and strategies contained herein may not be suitable for every case.

Please remember that the information in this book may be subject to varying state and local laws or regulations that may apply to the user's particular situation. Adherence to all applicable laws and regulations, federal, state, and local, and all other aspects of doing business in the U.S. or any other jurisdiction, is the sole responsibility of the reader.

All trademarks such as eBay.com, Amazon.com, etc., service marks, product names, and company names are assumed to be the property of their respective owners, and are used only for reference. There is no implied endorsement by those entities. Likewise, the fact that an organization or website is referenced in this work as a potential source of further information does not mean that the author or the publisher (Prestige Publishing and Prestige Media, LLC) endorses, has confirmed, or warrants the information provided in this book or in those references.

This book is sold with the understanding that the author and publisher are not engaged in rendering legal, accounting, tax, or other professional services with this book (especially for less than $20). There is no engagement agreement, no attorney-client relationship, and no other professional relationship with you. If legal, accounting, or other expert assistance is required, you should seek the services of a competent professional to assist you.

The author and publisher make no representations or warranties with respect to the accuracy or completeness of the contents of this work and specifically disclaim all warranties, express or implied, including without limitation warranties of fitness for a particular purpose or merchantability. No warranty may be created or extended by sales or promotional materials.

Please note that much of this publication is based on personal experience and represents the opinions of the author as of the date of publication. The author and publisher shall in no event be held liable to any party for any direct, indirect, punitive, special, incidental, or other consequential damages arising directly or indirectly from any use of this material, which is provided "as is," and without warranties.

If you do not agree with these terms, return the book. Finally, use your head. Nothing in this book is intended to replace common sense.

Advance Praise for *Life's Cheat Sheet*

Anyone with high personal aspirations will benefit from and appreciate Jeff's common sense "cheat sheet" that flies in the face of the pervasive "entitlement mentality" that so many of us have fallen victim to. Life won't hand you success, but you can and should hand this book to anyone that is seeking it.

—**Jim Cockrum**, International Internet Business Expert,
Author of *The Silent Sales Machine (www.SilentJim.com)*

This guide to real-world life skills should be a "must read" for all high school and college students and graduates. Written in easy-to-understand language with humor, relevant examples, and lots of references, this book constitutes a "handbook for success" that can be used by readers for years to come. If you want to guide your life in a positive direction, rather than simply react to the events of the day, this book is for you!

—**Thomas G. Gutteridge,** Dean, College of Business Administration,
The University of Toledo

Crucial success habits is a great start for this series. After reading this one, we can't wait for the next one on financial habits.

—**Lillian Miller, MD** and **Robert Miller, PhD**
Physician/Practice Partner and Research Scientist

As much as I like to see the 100s of investors in our audience each month, some seem paralyzed in the education mode unable to take the next step and actually invest in properties. Jeff's book can make you finally 'take action,' jump-start your life, and get ahead in your investing career now. Can't wait for MORE.

—**Anna Mills,** Realtor and Real Estate Investor
President, Toledo Real Estate Investors Association (REIA)
Past President, Ohio and National REIA

Life's success skills is a great topic to lead this series. It challenges young adults to think without limitations and expand their goals, outline a plan to accomplish them, and accelerate their completion by taking action to get ahead of the crowd.

—**Tom Schmidt,** President and CEO,
Ed Schmidt Auto Group

I applaud Jeff's purpose, which is to keep young adults from entering the rat race many adults find themselves in by showing them how to avoid the paycheck to paycheck trap. His book and teachings should be a part of our primary education in this country. I will be buying three copies, one for each of my children to use as their roadmap to success.

—**Scott Meyers** *(www.selfstorageinvesting.com)*
President, Alcatraz Storage and Real Estate Investor
Author of a complete guide to buying self storage facilities

Jeff's book shows young adults how to broaden their thinking to achieve bigger goals than they thought possible, map out a strategy for achieving them, then kick start their life by completing steps on the path toward finishing their most important goals right away.

—**Pamela Rose** *(www.pamelaroseauction.com)*
AARE, CAI and International Auctioneer Champion
President of Pamela Rose Auction Company, LLC

Jeff has been an entrepreneur since high school; in his "What Would Jeff Do" chapter endings, he gives some great practical step-by-step actions you can take to apply these habits on your journey to success.

—**Teresa Knisely,** Independent Consultant
Executive Regional Vice President, Arbonne International

Foreword

*L*ife's Cheat Sheet inspires young adults to learn real-life street-smart skills, showing them how to control their mind, think big, and take daily action to achieve results beyond their dreams. It's amazing to realize that these skills are not required subjects for multiple years in all schools before graduating. Jeff's book fills these critical gaps in curriculum.

It shows young adults, and really all adults, how to streamline their success by steering their life toward their dreams. It's filled with long-term foundational skills everyone needs to master and continuously improve. It's also designed to have parents partner with their children to help them hone these skills, which will allow them to bond and support their children as they experience new, challenging situations.

I see why he calls it the long-term, anti-bailout plan the country needs since it teaches young adults to "grab the bull by the horns" by learning and applying these key life skills. This can be a new solution to one of our country's biggest problems. These techniques show young adults (possibly your children and grandchildren) to not count on others but to help themselves, which will help the country come out of one of the worst recessions we have experienced in decades.

With his business and charity partnering options, everyone should pick up a copy.

Some of the book's features I like include:

- written in simple, common language
- sprinkles in humor to keep readers' attention
- provides many additional resources
- includes actual experiences to easily apply the concepts
- ends chapters with "What Would Jeff Do" action steps
- challenges readers to pay-it-forward by teaching others
- features a Frequently Asked Question (FAQ) format
- set up as a series to continue to build more skills

Jeff gives simple techniques for mind control, outlines key skills to accelerate success, and concludes with essential life planning for everyone. It gives readers a daily routine for a healthy and focused mind so they can maintain clarity and achieve their life's goals. He encourages them to get out of their comfort zone regularly so they can grow daily. Everything he teaches helps convert dreams to reality. It's a pocket guide to reference throughout life and a brilliant start for the series.

With all of Jeff's decades of experience running businesses and his lengthy list of degrees and licenses, I don't think anyone can question his qualifications for providing great habits for achieving your success. Start learning and applying as many of these techniques as you can. *Life's Cheat Sheet* is a great template for success. I'm anxious to see what financial habits he shares in the next book in the series.

—**Mark Matteson** (www.MattesonAvenue.com)
Best-selling Author of *Freedom From Fear*
International Speaker and Management Consultant
President and Chief Excitement Officer
Pinnacle Service Group, Edmonds, WA

Contents

About the Author

Jeff was born a poor, Russian immigrant girl from the old country GOTCHA! Now that I have your attention… Jeff grew up in Fayette, Ohio, a small town with just one stoplight 35 miles west of Toledo, Ohio. He was and continues to be a very driven person, letting little stop him once he sets his mind to something. Having bought his first rental home at a sheriff's auction as a 17-year old high school senior in 1981, Jeff rarely does the "normal" thing.

For over 25 years since high school (15 of those while in college at night, during the day, and on weekends), Jeff ran and owned companies, filling roles of CFO, COO, CEO, In-House Counsel, and turnaround specialist, helping those companies reach record sales and profits several years. He also provided financial planning services, served on multiple boards, and volunteered and did pro bono work for over 25 entities. Jeff has also taught at three colleges and gave estate and financial planning seminars. Having consulted with a number of companies, led and assisted with start-ups, company growth, and business turnarounds, he now wants to share some of the wisdom gained from all of his unique experiences.

Jeff has an ever-growing list of credentials that no longer fit on a business card, including JD (attorney licensed in Ohio and Michigan), MBA, MHCA, CMA, CBM, BS, and AA in management, marketing, computer science, finance, and law; he has also completed advanced training in real estate investing and obtained licenses in insurance/financial investing. As a real estate investor, he remains active in foreclosure/bank-owned, bankruptcy, and probate properties, residential homes, self-storage facilities, and mobile home parks. Jeff still plays competitive volleyball and golf, emcees and sings at local events, and regularly spends time with his family.

Preface
Why could reading this book change my life forever? (Glad you asked)

As we find ourselves in a financial and housing crisis as well as a recession ("mortgage meltdown," "foreclosure boom," "bankruptcy nightmare" among other headlines), the subjects in this book, and the follow-up *financial habits* book, could not be more fitting. I didn't realize when I started writing this that these skills would become even more obviously critical to everyone.

Let me help paint the picture we are facing:
Foreclosures = 1 out of 8 houses in a stage of foreclosure
Bankruptcies filed up 30–50% for the last 3 years
Housing values declined up to 50% in many areas
Unemployment = 10–15% in most states
Jobs eliminated = over 4 million in 2009
Social Security depleted by 2037; Medicare depleted by 2017
Baby Boomers retiring and starting to draw retirement
College costs rising 5–10% per year
Inflation = 3–5% vs. savings rates = 1–2% (before tax)
Gas prices rising, Income tax increasing… OH MY!
Regardless of the true values, we're in deep doo-doo.

Sorry, that was not meant to depress you (so don't go jump off anything; it takes too long to clean up), but understand that you need to step up and start planning if you ever want to have some freedom from a job and do the things you dream about. If you don't have a wealthy family or a "sugar daddy," you need to become proficient at these success and financial skills to have a chance at a decent life. Also realize that the average life spans for both men and women continue to increase, so you will need to have more investments available to fund your retirement. The point is that you need to start preparing now.

The government is not going to be able to take care of you because it is running out of money taking care of too many people already. People are living longer and fewer are paying into the retirement program. Medical costs are escalating at double digits per year, significantly outpacing inflation and salary increases. Unions have become so powerful that they have made some U.S. businesses uncompetitive, forcing them to cut jobs. Many other companies will file bankruptcy because they cannot afford to compete. And many pensions are gone because when companies file bankruptcy protection, their first move is to cut pension benefits.

After nearly 15 years of full- and part-time college, and having finished a full doctoral program in business, finance, and law, I recognized that the life lessons in this book are not taught much in school. I want you to benefit from my street skills and experiences. Without these lessons, you will have to figure them out on your own, struggle, and may make costly mistakes.

One of the many reasons I decided to write this was that when my oldest nephew graduated high school I recognized that it would be helpful for him and other young adults to know what I had learned, at his age. I want young adults to have this reference which shows them the shortest path to understanding all of these challenges. This is a huge void in our school system and may be the most important area in each student's life.

China requires their children to take a minimum of eight to ten years of the English language because they see that it is that valuable to their future. Even though these success and financial skills are clearly as important, we don't require schools to teach (or students to take) these subjects for even one year. This must become a multi-year requirement.

I challenge parents, grandparents, and others to give this book to their kids, grandkids, other young adults. Follow up with them to see if they are working through it. See if they have questions you can answer or send me an e-mail and we can get you an answer. The point is that everyone needs to get involved in developing success and financial literacy skills for young people. Older adults can also benefit from these additional skills. Based on our economy, there is an enormous need right now.

You'll find that life is a big set of choices. I am giving you the Cliff Notes version for making good choices before you are faced with them and have to wing it like most people do. The key is to take immediate action once you've covered a chapter. I can't make you; you have to make a conscious choice to do it. Any one of the hundreds of hints in this book can save you the price of the book quickly. So, what are you waiting for? Take action and starting reading right now.

Acknowledgements

Thanks to those who have supported me including:

My grandma **Maxine Powers,** who left us too early, but taught me to do what I know I should even when others don't think so, and also my Grandpa **Ralph Powers** who, along with Maxine, supported my loony thought of buying my first house in high school with encouragement and a mortgage.

My parents, **Joe** and **Bonnie,** for hanging in there when I zigged even though they thought I should have zagged like everyone else, and for all of the support my whole life growing up, especially when I really needed to have the drapes open to see outside. Congratulations on your 50th wedding anniversary on August 27, 2010. That is a real feat in today's world. Stop and savor the moment. This is one of my gifts to you.

Diane Rowe, my mother-in-law, for regularly checking in to chart my progress on this project, even while undergoing cancer treatments, and encouraging me along the way. You always thought I could do it.

My sisters, **Angie Abraham** and **Suzy Sommers** (not from *Three's Company*), and their families for staying close and supporting me over the years through lots of challenges and for the frank input that is exchanged regularly.

Aaron Abraham, my nephew, and his friend, **Jake Carlson,** for their input on chapters and Aaron's idea for the book cover.

Morgan Allen and **Mike Miller** for being good friends that check in every so often and help keep our friendship alive.

Everyone who helped with my survey to name the books: **Sylvania Southview** teachers and administration: **Dave Minard, Paul Moffitt, Shelley Bielak,** and **Samantha Stevens. Owens Community College, Assistant Professor Susan Wannemacher,** and other instructors. **The University of Toledo, Susan Shultz,** and other instructors. Everyone who answered my online **Survey Monkey** questions.

Competitive volleyball and golf leagues and my other sports that helped me get some of my pent up frustrations out before going all postal on someone.

All of the contracted professionals, fellow authors, marketers, publishers, and promoters that taught me the ropes and provided their services to make this whole project come together.

The many books and courses that taught me all of my disciplines. Also, all of the teleseminars, webinars, boot camps, etc. that filled me with the knowledge to do what I want.

Richard Dickson, the President at my first real "corporate" job who took a big risk and put the wet-behind-the-ears kid in charge by naming me Financial and Information Systems Director at the ripe old age of 21 because he "had an instinct that kid can do it."

Yoga/meditation music and James Taylor music DVDs that gave me a "Calgon, take me away" break when I needed it. Some people can't tell the difference between Jim (that's what he asked me to call him) and me when I sing his songs.

People in all those daily grind jobs who taught me what I don't want to do or feel like for the rest of my life. What you do with your life is your decision, not your employer's.

Jerks (and more racy synonyms) for building my resolve, increasing my stamina, boosting my ability to stand up and fight whoever and whatever for what's right, and enhancing my "Robin Hood" complex (help those who have been dealt a bad hand). The crap that I have been through has toned me into a lean, mean, fighting machine.

Dedication

Beth Wilson, my wife, closest friend for over 15 years, and Editor-in-Chief, where do I begin? For tireless, laser-sharp editing (still has the record for the most corrections in one chapter); for brainstorming along the way; for supporting this project and our household while I spent tons of time on this; for boosting me when I was feeling down; for being flexible; for hanging in there while I faced countless struggles after law school; for working through her challenges and personal growth to become partner, shareholder, and board member at the law firm of Cooper and Walinski; for always knowing I would figure it out and complete this project; for being the Ying to my Yang; for reeling me in when my ideas were "a little too out there"; and for being the one there daily as I worked through the speed bumps to make this a reality.

Also, my little buddies and closest canine friends, **Katie** and **Lexi** (our Bichon-Maltese sisters), who were sleeping, playing, eating, singing, and barking in my office and throughout the house each day as I put this together. Their company helps improve my demeanor when I miss the lunch breaks with coworkers and other interactions I used to get at a "regular" job.

Things are looking up; can't wait for what's in store next.

I've sprinkled quotes like those below throughout the book to share some of those that have inspired me. I hope they do the same for you.

"Whether you think you can or think you can't, you're right."
—Eleanor Roosevelt

"Be willing to be different."
—Warren Buffet

Why Are These Subjects So Crucial To My Life?

Q. Why do I need to be proactive early in life?

I speak to young adults in my books, but these principles apply to anyone at any age. I focus on young adults because I want to help them avoid making costly mistakes before learning these important principles. But it is never too late to take charge of your life and pursue success. I'm giving you my "cheat sheets," including street skills I've learned during more than 25 years "in the jungle," that I wish I would have known when I was in my teens, 20s, and 30s.

As a young adult, you need to take the reins of your life and steer it in the direction you want it to go. Otherwise, life can pass you by and you will be no closer to your goals. Start to fulfill your true desires now (I use goals and desires interchangeably to describe what you want).

Find some quiet time and really think about what you want from life. You probably want material things like a nice car, a big house, or a cool boat, but go much further and consider intangible things like spending less time at work and more time with friends and family, playing a sport or musical instrument, having great health, taking exotic vacations, etc. This book will show you how to program your mind to go after what you want daily, set clear goals, and build other key life skills. Since goals of prosperity and wealth are high on many readers' lists, they are covered in much more detail in my follow-up *financial habits* book. Push your mind to think without boundaries and limits in all areas of your life. Decide what you want, and I will show you how to get it.

Q. I couldn't ever lose my home, right?

If you are not proactive and assertive about your life's ambitions, you could find yourself among the millions of Americans who are losing their homes. ("Dude, Where's My House?" was one of the possible titles for this book, inspired by the Ashton Kutcher movie "Dude, Where's My Car?"). I don't mean to make light of the problem. This is the situation for many and it's very sad.

Can you imagine being homeless? Many of the people in foreclosure I've talked to could not believe that they would ever be kicked out of their own house. Stop right now and picture vividly what that would be like. I was in Cleveland, Ohio, during the winter when it was 30 degrees below zero with the wind chill off the lake. I walked by a homeless man sleeping on the sidewalk, wearing what were probably all of his clothes. He looked dirty, hungry, cold, and lonely. My heart cries out every time I picture that sight. It makes my stomach queasy just trying to put myself in his shoes and wondering what I would do. I recommend that you volunteer in shelters and listen to the people there who have become homeless, struggling to survive on the street. Empathizing with them can drive you to take action.

Perhaps this example seems extreme. But there are less severe scenarios you may face if you aren't proactive. You don't want to live paycheck to paycheck, worried that the check you write for groceries will bounce. You don't want to only be able to wish for the luxuries that others seem to have, while driving a "beater" car and never being able to take a vacation.

Don't depend on others or outside factors falling into place to get you the life you want. Take stock of all your options, choose those that match your goals, and start acting on them right now. Take steps to achieve your goals each and every day, and never let your life get to the point where you are simply living in survival mode. Plan ahead, stay focused, and make your life everything you want it to be.

Q. I'm done with school, how do I get these skills now?

Assuming your school does not offer regular training on these topics, put yourself through your own self-directed educational program by going over and over these principles until they are programmed into your subconscious mind and become automatic. You will gain control over your schedule and won't have to trade hours for money until you run out of hours. You will take control of your future and live life to the fullest.

Q. Why learn these success skills now?

I focus on young adults because you will run into many challenges and opportunities in the coming years, and I want you to be knowledgeable beforehand. If you have read through these chapters, done the action steps, and quizzed your family and friends as I outline, you will be ready to successfully work through these situations.

By learning these concepts and building skills in these areas, you are more likely to handle your interactions well and not have to learn by doing things wrong the first time and having to correct mistakes. Doing your homework before you are faced with these situations is a shortcut to getting ahead.

Q. Why didn't I get these subjects in school?

Most schools are required to follow a curriculum that meets state and federal standards. They focus on subjects that are covered in standardized tests and prepare students for college but often fail to cover practical topics that are necessary to prepare people for real life, beyond academics.

Q. Why do we need to form good habits daily?

Much of what you learn will become habit as you go through the information and action steps. Forming good habits is a key to getting a jump-start on the accelerated path to meeting and exceeding your success and wealth goals. You will continue to get better at these skills as you practice them and learn from experience. But change is inevitable and new opportunities arise, so you need to keep abreast (yes, I said abreast, as one word, silly) of changing circumstances and modify your habits accordingly. For example, many people are eliminating their land line telephone and using a cellular phone as their primary telephone. That conversion will require a change in habit to get used to and get the benefit from. Once these skills become habits, you will use them automatically, unconsciously. You will gain confidence in your abilities and accomplish more than you originally thought possible. Never stop building these skills.

Q. What are key methods of building knowledge daily?

Successful people never stop learning and are always on the lookout for ways to take advantage of new information. Realize that people learn in different ways. Some people learn most effectively when people explain to them in person, by listening to CD's, by watching DVD's, or on their own with home study materials to name a few. They typically use multiple senses concurrently (sight, sound, smell, and touch) and enhance their learning through repetition, practice, and by teaching the subject to others because one learns and retains things better when he has to communicate them to others. Knowing your learning style allows you to learn more quickly and efficiently.

Ask questions until you have a good handle on what you are considering. Questions clarify and give you a better understanding before you make a decision or commitment. Screw that "dumb question" thought looming in your head. The more curious you are, the better your understanding will be. I had a guy in law school tell me that I had asked dumb questions in one class. I ranked #1 in my class and he was in the bottom, so you do the math.

In the learning process, everything builds on everything else. So if you get a good grasp of your subject from the beginning, you'll have a solid foundation to build on and you won't have to cram everything in just before you need it. Plus, getting into this habit now will save you from the agony of procrastination. Believe me, it's no fun to have to burn the midnight oil the night before a presentation.

Q. Why take control of my future now?

You may be thinking you will just wait and learn these skills when you are older, more established, start making more money, and have more expenses to control. Hit the delete key on that thought. You need to have these skills and form good habits in each of these areas before you really need to use them and are faced with important decisions. Don't wait until you have a dire need because it will severely increase your stress load and you may make a poor decision. For example, when you sign a mortgage for the first time and realize how much you now owe, you will be more confident because you have assessed the issues in advance and know how things work.

Q. Why is the *financial habits* book so important?

The *financial habits* follow-up book will add a key set of skills to the habits you will learn in this book. They complement each other and are both needed to succeed in reaching your life goals. Financial statements, budgeting, credit scores, credit cards, passive income, automatic saving, investments, diversification, etc., will add to your success habits and show you how to move forward with confidence. You will learn ways to earn more, stretch all of your income to get more for less, and decide what is most important when it comes to achieving your longer-term goals. All of these areas equip you to make good decisions as you become the CEO of your life and take charge of your direction.

Q. Should I care about an emergency fund now?

Even though this is a financial habit, building an emergency fund is a success habit also and can't wait until you get to Chapter

17 (explained in more detail) or the follow-up *financial habits* book. One of the big reasons for all of the foreclosures and bankruptcies is that these families didn't have emergency funds.

Even though you may not currently have the need, I strongly recommend you build the fund now. Without having the emergency fund to buy you time if you lost your job or business, you could then lose your car or home like many others already have which would amplify your problems.

Q. How can I have fun with this and grow from it?

I recognize these topics might lack some excitement, but just plow through them realizing these are the skills that will allow you to reach your life goals and "Big Why." Your Big Why is your overall purpose in life. You may not know what that is yet, but as you go through life, pay attention to what you are drawn to and feel strongly about. Look at how you can make a difference by focusing on what stirs your emotions and build that area into your goals.

If you learn something new each day, in a month you will have progressed by at least 30 steps. That knowledge will increase your confidence and self-esteem as well as reduce your worrying and stress level. You will also gain the respect of others. You will be happier, more carefree, and won't need to be a slave to a job. You will feel more comfortable encountering new opportunities that will help you reach your goals more quickly.

You must be willing to persevere and persist when others give up or succumb to temptation to take an easier route. Be willing to go against the grain and be unique. Ignore naysayers and, unfortunately, it is common to have several.

Since I am a challenge junkie, I suggest you turn the action steps and exercises into a challenge you need to conquer. This will help you apply your new habits in the field, which, in turn, will help you retain them better. Now, let's get started and have some fun!

P. Programming Your Mind

A. Accelerate Success with Crucial Skills

L. Life Planning 101

Blueprint to Success System

Section 1:
Programming Your Mind

This first section of Chapters (2–8) gives you techniques for controlling your mind and a daily routine for utilizing your mind to accelerate your progress every hour of every day. You will find that your mind is more responsible for your success than anything else, so learning to put it to use for you daily is very important to your future. You will start by becoming aware of what is going on in your mind throughout the day and then learn techniques for controlling it to help you get where you want to go.

"Nobody will believe in you until you believe in yourself first."

"What you think about will come about."

"The size of your success is determined by the size of your belief."

CONTROL YOUR MIND, CONTROL YOUR FUTURE

You have two distinct parts to your mind, the conscious and subconscious. The conscious mind (CM) gives direction and deals with day-to-day decision making, plus it has the power of reason. It questions information it is being fed and decides whether it will accept it as true or reject it as false. In contrast, the subconscious mind (SM) does not have the power of reason; therefore, it accepts what it is fed as true and goes to work to find ways to make it a reality.

Q. Why do I need to learn how to program my mind?

Experts agree that what you tell your self each minute of each day is one of the most important factors in your success. Researchers have shown that most people have 40,000 to 50,000 thoughts per day and as many as 80% of those thoughts have a negative component. Many of these are quick thoughts, so you can have several in a few seconds. Since most of your thoughts are negative, reprogramming your CM and SM to be more positive has been shown to cause profound changes. If you can get your SM to be working toward your goals all day and night, even when you are sleeping, it makes sense that you will have a much better outlook and a stronger likelihood of reaching your goals.

What I am referring to as your "SM" some call your spiritual self, inner voice, inner self, or intuition. Some experts would draw detailed distinctions between these, but we will treat them as the same. Generally, your SM functions as your "worker bee" all day by screening out lots of unneeded information. And when your SM is functioning optimally, it feeds you only the information you need to make the choices that lead to your goals.

If you are a little hyperactive like me, meditation and connecting to this subconscious level is more difficult, but practice will make you better. The key is to reach this deeper level and listen to its direction. Techniques in this book will help you tune in to your inner self, form good habits, and overwrite bad habits that hold you back from achieving your potential.

Q.   How do I control my SM?

People accomplish what they *believe* they can rather than what is truly possible. Your belief system is very powerful and ultimately controls your behaviors. Therefore, if you change your beliefs, you change your behaviors. (Read the rest of this section slowly, it gets a little hairy.)

When we are born, we start recording our thoughts as emotions ("I'm cold, I'm hungry, I'm tired…," etc.). As we understand pictures, we add them to these emotions, and then we label these pictures with words as we learn them. As adults, we use these three dimensions (emotions, pictures, and words) to form thoughts that feed the self-talk that goes on in our mind all day. Self-talk is what your mind says to you as you encounter experiences throughout the day (no you're not a freak, it happens to everyone).

Self-talk triggers these pictures that bring out the related emotions. Every thought formed by these dimensions leaves a record of what we *perceive* is happening and these perceptions form our personality. Perceptions are personal to you based on the accumulation of your prior experiences. Through different sets of prior experiences perceptions will be different; therefore, siblings from the same family form different personalities.

The key becomes controlling what we think and our perception of reality. Once we accept something as our reality, it continues to confirm our belief, whether or not it is accurate. Our SM cannot accept conflicting beliefs, so once we accept something as our reality, we gather additional information that supports our belief to alleviate the stress caused by any conflict. If this belief is not reality, the acceptance of the belief can work against us because our internal defense system will continue to believe what we've told it is our reality, and it cannot reason its way to actual reality. This is why we need to analyze our beliefs regularly to see if there is a more realistic belief that we should adopt. We tend to fight this because we don't want to see that we are wrong.

The accumulation of perceptions of our experiences, our thoughts, opinions, and self-talk form our beliefs and self image. You can change your self image by controlling your self-talk through goal setting, affirmations, visualizations, and other techniques. We are stuck with this self image until we use our CM to change what is stored in our SM. Remember the SM has no reasoning ability so it accepts what you feed it as true, regardless of the real truth or reality. As you feed it the same thought multiple times, it becomes dominant and we act on these beliefs, as if they are true.

Also recognize that your SM does not differentiate between reality and an imagined thought. For example, if someone calls you fat and you accept that as true, it is recorded in your SM. Now each time your mind goes back through that thought, your SM records it as true and it becomes a more dominant thought. It has established a thought pattern that you will only be able to change using your CM and these techniques to feed it new thoughts.

Affirmations, which become positive self-talk, help to change your SM. It is proven that at least 30 days of hearing new, positive self-talk at least three times per day, along with other techniques I will be explaining, will start to reprogram your SM, overriding conflicting negative self-talk, thereby redirecting your thinking. Techniques for detecting and correcting negative self-talk can be used effectively with affirmations. This reprogramming will build good habits that your

SM will continue to perform as it accepts them as true. The above concepts are explained in more technical detail in *Beyond Positive Thinking* by Dr. Robert Anthony so refer to his book if you really want to fill in the gaps as I've explained it.

At a real estate investing conference, I learned about another effective reprogramming process. Doug Ottersberg, a successful investor and certified hypnotist, showed that he can change habits more quickly through hypnotism. Consider this alternative and decide for yourself. (www.automaticsuccessattractor.com) If nothing else, you might be clucking like a chicken and everyone else would enjoy the show.

Now that you have finished this section, go back and re-read it slowly to try to get a general understanding of how your mind is working. You don't need to understand everything in detail. I will explain the techniques in more detail as I cover them in the next few chapters.

Q. What is the law of attraction I've heard about?

This is not a new concept. The law of attraction and mind control has just become more well-known with the popular movie and book called *The Secret*. The basic concept is that positive thoughts create positive vibrations that attract positive things to you and vice versa with negative thoughts. Please understand that great things don't just automatically happen for you, but using these techniques gives you direction to take actions that cause these positive things to occur. At one point in my life, I proved the negative side of this equation. My negativity brought more problems and conflict to my life. Using these techniques, I have been able to become more positive which led to greater happiness.

Q. What are the primary techniques used in reprogramming?

Positive affirmation statements and goal-specific affirmations will improve specific areas of your life. Visualizations, which are clear, detailed pictures that represent your completed goals, stimulate the mind and your emotions to help you connect to your goals more effectively. Meditation and yoga help clear your mind of clutter allowing you to focus and connect more directly with your subconscious mind without interference from other matters. Gratitude and success journals are additional techniques that build and maintain a positive demeanor, confidence, and self-esteem. These techniques will determine how you treat yourself and affect how you are treated by others.

Taking 20 to 30 minutes daily to read, watch, or listen to positive, motivational materials will help you master these skills. The following chapters outline these in more detail. Jack Canfield's *Key to Living the Law of Attraction* guide also gives good directions on these techniques.

Q. Why is it important to be emotionally tied to my goals?

The stronger your emotions and the greater number of different emotions you can activate in going through these techniques, the quicker you will reach your goals. Emotions activate your mind and cause it to work on your goals more frequently. The more vividly you experience each goal in your mind, the more motivated you will be to reach it quickly.

I use a digital recorder (you can use your cell phone, mp3, or iPod) to record goals and affirmations so I can listen to them in the car or anywhere when I have a few minutes. I recommend that you say them aloud, but even if you don't, they will make a strong impact as you take them in. Getting your SM to accept your goals as true will get your mind to work for you all day. The more you see, hear, and vividly picture these images in your mind, the faster your SM will believe them.

Q. This is "out there"; how do I convince myself to try it?

Not everything in life is going to be black-and-white. But this doesn't cost you any money, unless you buy some additional materials, and it doesn't take a lot of time or effort. What do you have to lose by trying these techniques? At worst, it could be a small waste of time. But it has such a great upside potential that it is at least worth a try.

Many of the techniques should be done in private and in a quiet setting, so you don't need to worry about others making fun of you. In my experience, some of these skills take time to master, but if you just stick with them, you will get better with practice. Once you see some positive results, they will encourage you to continue with the process.

Q. Why does it take 30+ days to reprogram my SM?

Brain researchers and many studies have proven that it takes 30-plus consecutive days (without skipping a day) of hearing a message three or more times (aloud, if possible) to make a positive difference. Give it a full 30 days before evaluating whether the technique has made a positive impact for you. Realize that your beliefs have been ingrained by thoughts that have been fed to your SM for months or years, so your mind has already accepted these as true and it has formed this pattern of thinking. When you put 30 to 45 days up against that time period, it doesn't seem very long to change a bad habit or belief and overwrite it with a good one.

Once your SM is consistently fed your new message so many times, it records it as true and overwrites the conflicting belief. Don't just stop at 30 days, even if it has worked perfectly. Continue to build upon the new, positive pattern you have created so it will be tough to revert back to the negative pattern.

Q. How do I know my SM works for me when I am sleeping?

If you want to analyze or try to remember something, read it a number of times and think about it before going to bed. Your SM will work on it while you sleep. I've dreamed about solutions to problems that I focused on right before going to bed, which shows that my mind was still concentrating on the subject. While I slept, I came up with two alternative solutions for resolving a big case I was defending against a state tax bureau, and then I wrote them down right when I awoke. We used both of them to resolve the case favorably for the company I represented.

Q. How do I counteract fear-based, negative thinking?

Realize that people tend to live in little private mental (not metal) boxes constructed by what they have heard and experienced rather than what they know is possible. They tend to pass this limitation and fear-based thinking on to the people they are around, which allows negativity to spread widely. Sometimes people are more comfortable with negative thoughts and not taking chances. If you think something isn't going to work, then you are not likely even to attempt it and risk failure. Many people tend to fear what they perceive as failure the older they get, so they take fewer risks and miss opportunities for growth.

Surprisingly to many, successful people fail regularly. They are successful because they learn from each of these trials and get better; they don't view them as failures. If you take no risks, you will not grow and experience much of what is available in life. It's the old adage: if you continue to do the same things the same way, you will get what you have always gotten. Is that acceptable? If the answer is no, you need to change your actions and get in the game.

One way to break patterns of fear and risk avoidance is to consciously take calculated risks each day. This gets you out of your comfort zone, which allows you to grow. At the beginning of each day, write down at least three things you are going to do to get out of your comfort zone today. Realize these don't have to be big things. For example, calling someone you have lost track of, talking with a stranger at the grocery store, researching a class at a community college you're interested in taking, calling instructors for guitar lessons, etc. The key is to break your mental shackles and go after things that you would like to do, but have held off on. It's a big world with unlimited possibilities. You just have to look for them and take action to get them. Turn off the TV (you'll hear who got booted from *American Idol* or *Survivor* on the morning news), drop the unnecessary activities, and go for it.

Q. Am I being myself or allowing others to control me?

Do you ignore what you believe others might think of you? Or do you fret and worry about what someone said, how they looked at you, or what someone else told you someone said about you?

Overachievers and perfectionists—and I am guilty of being both—fall prey to this bad habit easily. This is generally referred to as being a "pleaser." Pleasers try to please and impress everyone they are around to the point that they forget to live their life how they want to live it. Instead, they live based on the thoughts they perceive others have of them. Most of the time, pleasers don't know what others are thinking, they just believe they do. Morty Lefkoe teaches a process to eliminate the negative beliefs associated with the need to please others at www.recreateyourlife.com.

But please understand that you will need to conform to some degree to be accepted in the settings and roles you really want to be in. Piercings, tattoos, pants hanging low, ultra-short miniskirts, mohawks, pink hair, cursing, etc. are not going to be acceptable in many settings. So if you want to achieve specific things where those are not the norm, you too will have to adapt to be accepted. This does not mean you should not "let your hair down" and let your true, unique personality show when you are not in professional settings, but there is a time and place for that. Just don't forget that this is your life and you should live it as you see fit.

A Lesson I Learned from "The Street"

When I became a "corporate guy" at 19 years old, I acted like I felt I needed to in order to get respect as a much younger person, and I abandoned many of my convictions. By the time I was 20 years old, I was the Chief Financial Officer who reported directly to the CEO and two boards of directors. I made certain I didn't look immature and learned to control my emotions, regardless of whether I was freaking out inside. I actually had a fellow director twice my age compliment me in a letter of recommendation for being calming to him and others. Go figure.

I felt I had to dress and act a certain way to be accepted in the corporate world. So I gave up much of my personal style and concealed my true personality to portray a more conservative image. Unfortunately, I did not let loose and enjoy myself as much as I deserved. As I look back, I realize that I sort of lost who I was for some time.

It was tough to break out of that corporate mode after more than 20 years of being what I felt I should be in the roles that I held. I had been told you need to do this, act like that, have these degrees, and have X amount of experience, so I did those things to get that great job and reach the goals I had set for myself at that time. After selling my company and finishing law school, I faced more struggles than any other time in my life. I did a lot of soul searching and introspection to determine who I was and what I really wanted. Using some of the techniques described in this book, I realized that it is OK to be myself. I don't have to be a boring "suit" and go along with the crowd to please everyone. I finally stopped being critical of myself for not fitting into that basic mold and listened instead to my unique, inner self.

Most of the people I worked with for years and tried to please have not been in contact with me since I left those companies. So now it seems silly that I allowed them to control how I lived my life when they were not a significant part of my life in the grand scheme of things. My own involvement in personal development for several years has broadened my perspective on what is possible when I follow my inner self and take action. I have read many times that your life will be the same 10 years from now, except for what you read (and act on) and the people you interact with. I'm now seeing the truth in that statement.

What Would Jeff Do?
(Fun action steps to try this stuff out)

1. Start today and listen to the thoughts that go through your mind daily to become aware of what you are saying to yourself.

2. Each day, pick one of your current beliefs. Analyze it and come up with other possible versions of that belief that could be true. Assess whether any of the other possible beliefs are more realistic based on your knowledge now as compared to your knowledge before. Is there a more realistic version of your current belief you should adopt to overwrite the more unrealistic initial one?

3. Try to detect negative self-talk right at the time it occurs. Write down the negative things that you tell or call yourself and become more conscious of those thoughts. Ask yourself whether you would say that to someone you care about. Change that negative to a positive to start reprogramming your thoughts right now.

4. Starting today, take at least 15 minutes a day to read or listen to positive motivational materials. Pay attention to how you feel when you are finished.

5. Read, think, and focus on a project or problem you need to retain right before bed for at least 20 minutes and see if ideas or solutions come to you while sleeping. When you wake up, write them down quickly. You can do the same exercise with information that you need to retain.

6. Write three minor (to start out) risks that you have been avoiding that will get you out of your comfort zone. Commit to taking those three risks before noon, if possible (the earlier in the day, the better). Note how you feel once you are done with each risk. Do this each day going forward and you will grow daily.

7. If you fall into the pleaser category (and most people do to some degree) catch yourself at least once per day thinking a pleaser thought or taking a pleaser action then stop doing it right then. Work on thinking for yourself and pleasing yourself first.

Once you've finished these steps, write me to let me know what happened and what you learned at *stories@lifescheatsheets.com*.

Now, think like Nike and Just Do It!

Build and Maintain a Positive Attitude

Q. Why should I start the day with positive thoughts?

"Control Your Mind; Control Your Future" was one possible title for this book. If you've experienced any situation where you have told yourself something repeatedly and then you made it come true, you realize just how powerful your mind is. For example, let's say you have been getting Cs on algebra tests and you really want to get an A. You put in extra time to study and do the practice problems and say to yourself repeatedly "I am going to get an A on the next test" while you are prepping for it. It's much more likely you will get that A on the next test because you prepared your mind to get it and took steps to ensure it would happen.

If you feed your mind positive thoughts right when you get up, your mind will start the day working for you rather than against you with constant worrying. You'll be less likely to waste mental energy dwelling on negative thoughts and less affected by all of the discouraging messages and images in the media—especially the news. It is harder to override negative thoughts with positive thoughts later in the day after your mind has been filled with negativity than it is to prevent the negative input in the first place.

For the next month, read and listen to the news less often. See if limiting your daily exposure to negative reports of crime, the economy, accidents, political squabbling, and other dire predictions of doom improves your attitude about the world. For this month, replace the time you used to spend listening to or reading the news with reading your list of goals and affirmations, looking at pictures of what you desire, and using the other motivational materials you'll learn about in the next few chapters. See how much better you feel. See whether it gives you more energy to get things done. It worked for me. You don't have to live in a bubble and completely ignore the world's problems, but news media are more focused on sensationalizing bad news than reporting good and bad.

Q.   Are you sure I can control my mind?

Convincing evidence that you control your mind can be seen through a simple exercise I have seen and used in a number of settings.

TRY This EXERCISE WiTh a FRiEND:

1   Start by having your friend make a fist and put her arm out in front of her, parallel to the floor, then have her resist your attempt to push her arm down. Most likely, it will be difficult for you to easily move her arm down.

2   Now with her arm down and eyes closed, have her clear her mind of everything, pause, and then have her repeat out loud "I am a weak and pathetic person" ten times, telling her to really listen as she says it.

3   Now have her open her eyes and make a fist, put her arm back out in front of her, and resist your attempt to push it down. This time, her arm will be weaker and you will be able to push it down more.

4   What happened? She won't be able to explain it, but it's obvious. Feed your mind that you are weak, and your mind believes it is true. Your demeanor will be that of a weak person and people will treat you as if you are weak.

5. Continue the exercise by having her go through the same steps as before, but this time replace the phrase in #2 with "I am a strong and successful person."

6. Now when you try to push her arm down, it will be much more difficult. She'll seem to have become suddenly much stronger. The only thing that changed is what she fed her mind for just a couple of minutes. It demonstrates how easily you control your mind and your actions.

Obviously if you feed your mind uplifting messages regularly, you will feel more confident, project a more confident image, and will be treated as a stronger person.

Another exercise demonstrates how many people think within their own predefined boundaries. These boundaries are based on past experiences and limitations you have been fed and accepted. It stunts the capacity for brainstorming and creativity that exists within you. Stop here, do the exercise, and see if you can figure it out.

```
  •         •         •


  •         •         •


  •         •         •
```

Without lifting your pencil from the paper, draw four straight, connected lines that go through all 9 dots, but just once through each dot.

If you have trouble figuring it out, think about what would allow you to do it and what is restricting you from accomplishing this task. Question the boundaries that you perceive. The answer is provided in the Appendix. This exercise shows how limited thinking stifles original, creative thinking. The same reasoning applies to other challenges that you face in life. Open your mind and increase your problem solving ability by considering new possibilities you didn't allow yourself to see.

Q. How do I improve my attitude daily?

Surround yourself with positive things every day, and you will become a more positive person. Watch happy shows. Listen to happy music. Hang out with positive people. Read uplifting books and articles. Keep a success journal (explained later) to recall positive experiences. Keep a gratitude journal (explained later) to record things that you are thankful for. Post positive pictures in your home and office. Do things that make you happy. Can it really be that simple? Actually, yes. You may not be ecstatic all day every day, but it will help.

Read the book *Happy for No Reason* by Marci Shimoff with Carol Kline. She interviewed lots of people to find her Happy 100 group of people that exude happiness daily. If you read some of the extreme stories of the lives of those people on the list, you will find it easier to be happy with your life, regardless of your struggles. Do some of the exercises. They can be very helpful.

Keep materials that connect with you best and go back through them multiple times. Specific books, chapters, articles, digital recordings, video recordings, pictures, quotes, interviews, etc. can connect with you and really stimulate you into action. Copy and highlight the parts that motivate you the most. Post any physical materials where you can refer back to them many times to continue to take action that will further your goals. When you determine which sources you like best, get additional materials from the same sources to increase your progress.

Post your goals, affirmations, and pictures of your completed desires where you will see them multiple times a day. Do the same with motivational quotes. Put these types of materials on bathroom mirrors, your cupboards, the night stand, the ceiling over your bed, kitchen counters, the refrigerator, your desk or cubicle wall, your briefcase, the dashboard of your car, etc. Your mind will focus on the positive thoughts and work toward finding ways to achieve your goals.

Q. How can I fit motivational materials into my busy day?

If you have a commute, run errands, or drive somewhere regularly, you have a great opportunity to increase your exposure to more positive materials. Treat your vehicle as your traveling school and listen to tapes, CDs, and mp3s with positive, motivating messages. Utilize what would otherwise be a waste of time to enhance your life.

I carry a handheld digital recorder that I record goals and affirmations on to listen to if I am waiting or driving. You can plug in a small set of ear buds and make it your private lesson for the day. Smart phones, iPods, and mp3 players can usually do the same, and you can slip them in your pocket to carry them with you.

Q. Can laughter help my attitude?

Watching a funny movie, comedian, or a program like *America's Funniest Home Videos* (except when they pick a lame video as the winner), can leave you feeling happy, uplifted, and more easygoing. These programs relieve tension and help you release negative energy. They convert your attitude to positive and make you easier to get along with.

Studies have proven that laughter reduces stressors on the body, which improves your overall health and makes life more enjoyable. Loosening up with laughter also allows the creative juices to flow and can help with problem solving. Being tense and under pressure can stunt these abilities. Watching something funny is a much better way to relax than watching a show or news about murder, divorce, tragedy, disease, etc.

Q. What other things can improve my attitude toward life?

Pictures and videos of baby animals just melt me into a sentimental, big ole softy. I would do most anything for them. I would take the place of their mother and take care of them if needed to. Looking at them enhances my attitude and makes me feel good. When they are in real life and not just pictures, the feelings are that much stronger and I forget about other worries. I become a nurturer. One summer at a festival I took care of a baby pygmy goat for its owner for a short time. You couldn't get me to put it down. I have pictures of it with me and really enjoyed the little time I had with it. I still look at the pictures and smile.

Baby animals run, jump, and play around without any worries or cares at all. They don't care about what others think of them. They live in the moment and have unconditional love for their family. What a great feeling to have. I have many pictures of baby animals on my hard drive that I look at to get a positive jolt, and I also use them in e-cards I send.

I have two little Bichon-Maltese mixes lying next to me in my office as I write this, and I have lots of pictures of them around me to make me smile through the day. Many other animal lovers feel the same attitude improvement when they see animals or their images. I have a friend that comes over to get some "animal therapy" by playing with my dogs. If you haven't tried it, you don't know what a positive feeling you are missing.

Go to a pet store nearby where you can play with the animals that are kept in their cages all day and would love some human interaction. Visit your local humane society and spend time with the dogs and cats while they await a new home. Everybody wins. If animals don't connect with you like that, consciously pay attention to those things that do make you feel good and forget life for awhile, then use those to improve your attitude.

Q. How do my past experiences help my attitude today?

Just stop for a minute and think back to the 10 most positive experiences and successes you have had in your life. Jot them down quickly. Really picture each of them one at a time in vivid detail. Stop as you picture each one and feel the feelings you felt when you lived it.

Remember all of the compliments and support you received. Recall the adrenaline rush that ran through your body when you achieved these successes. Maybe it was a sporting event where you scored the winning point. Maybe it was a project that you worked really hard on and nailed the presentation. Maybe it was a test you were worried about but aced. Maybe it was a graduation ceremony celebrating years of hard work. Maybe you took the lead in the school play and remembered all of your lines, getting a standing ovation.

Remembering your successes improves your attitude and demeanor quickly and dramatically and gives you more confidence, even though you are not actually experiencing those events at the time. This exercise only takes a few minutes, but it brings those strong feelings back up and gives you a confidence boost right away. Use this process regularly as you take on new challenges.

Q. Why should I use a success journal to boost my attitude?

A success journal is a record of successes you have had in life. They don't need to be big successes, just times you grew as a person that could also include situations that did not go well but you still learned from. For example, when you learned to ride a two-wheeler bike, got your first job, went on your first date, got all As or a certain GPA, bought your first car, etc. As you get older, your successes will be a little bigger and may include earning a college degree, getting married, or buying a house. When you get to your next challenge where your confidence is being tested, read several entries in your success journal. As you read each entry, picture each setting and stop to feel the way you felt when you succeeded. Once you have read several of them, you will feel your confidence building and will be ready to take on that challenge with a fresh boost of confidence.

A Vice President of a Fortune 500 company I knew had a success journal that he regularly updated for many years. He would refer to the journal whenever he was getting ready to make a proposal to his board or to shareholders and in other situations that made him uncomfortable.

To enhance your experience with the success journal, touch your thumb and forefinger together to form a circle when you initially write and mentally re-experience the success. Then when you are in a situation that is testing you, stop, touch your thumb and forefinger together, close your eyes, and picture in detail a few of your prior successes one at a time. The physical sensation will help you remember the experience, boosting your confidence on the spot.

Q. Should I pay attention to the people I spend time with?

Pay attention to who you are around most, how you feel when you are with them, and how you feel once they have left. Do you feel better or worse? Are they upbeat and positive or downers? Do you realize you will be like the five to ten people you are around the most? You may not realize how much they influence you. Do you want to be like them? If you find you are around a negative person, strongly consider spending less time around them and more time around positive thinkers. Positive breeds positive and vice versa.

Positive people will challenge you to be better, help you reach for your goals, and support you to get past obstacles. Several people I know have become more negative as they have gotten older, so I have had to recognize this and screen out their negative comments. Be around people who are "doers," because they take action and are driven toward their goals no matter what gets in the way. They carry a never-give-up attitude that will rub off on you.

Reduce time around naysayers, slackers, and entitlement thinkers (people who have been getting something for so long that they believe they don't need to earn it but are entitled to it). I know several union workers that have become entitlement thinkers. Now their jobs are getting eliminated and they have become very negative. Don't become part of the pity party. As businesses close and downsize, eliminating thousands of jobs, many more people's attitudes will turn negative like a wave across the whole country. Be aware of this and don't let it affect you.

Q. How do I reduce the negative chatterbox in my head?

Consciously monitor the thoughts that race through your head and catch the negative thoughts right when they start to occur. Replace the negative thought with a positive one, effectively shutting down that negative thought. Get in the habit of monitoring your thoughts for several weeks to start building a new, positive habit. Write down those thoughts as they come to you along with the emotion it brings out. The more you do it, the more positive you will become. People respond better to those who have a good attitude, so you will attract positive things by eliminating negative thoughts.

Q. How do I forgive someone (or myself) for past acts?

Past experiences may continue to make you feel bad or angry when they come to mind, and they take up valuable space in your conscious mind. Your conscious mind can only juggle six to seven items at once, so you don't want a past negative event taking up one of these slots.

Verbal forgiveness is a way to release negative past clutter from your mind. Accept the fact that no one can go back and undo the past. Consider that everyone, even you, makes mistakes. Consider that there may be circumstances you don't know that could help to explain, not excuse, their behavior. Consider whether it benefits you to let go of resentment and anger for what they did.

If you begin to focus on a negative event, verbally say to yourself "I forgive X for what he did to me." The person doesn't have to be present for this to work, but you have to consciously agree to forgive and forget. This doesn't mean you were not wronged or what happened was OK, but it gets the anger and resentment out of your mind. You may need to repeat these steps several times to get it completely cleared.

Hal Dworkin developed The Sedona Method (www.sedona.com) which is a simple set of steps that you repeat to release the things that are cluttering your mind and get them out of your head for good. Getting rid of this mind clutter opens it up to be used for empowering thoughts.

Negative memories cause friction and slow down the achievement of your goals. Getting rid of this mental baggage will lighten your mental load. Cleaning out negative thoughts lets you put all of your energy toward furthering yourself rather than wasting energy on the past.

Q. Why should I use a gratitude journal?

A gratitude (or appreciation) journal is another tool to help you become more positive and thankful. Writing in your journal before going to bed each night is a good habit. I'm a morning person so I do it in the morning if I'm too tired the night before. List the things in your life that you are thankful for and appreciate. When you really step back and look at everything you have, there is a lot to be thankful for. I am not just talking about physical goods, but everything that you want to remain in your life.

Many people take things for granted. For example, my father came from the mountains in Athol, Kentucky, (don't say it with a lisp). They had a very reasonable house on the mountainside, but it had an outhouse as a bathroom, which was normal in that area. Many years ago, when he came to Ohio for his job, indoor plumbing and a typical indoor bath was a luxury that everyone there took for granted—except for him.

I used go from one want to the next before I realized "things" don't make you happy for very long. I bought and sold a nice, extra vehicle every year or two, thinking the next one was really what I wanted. I ultimately realized after doing this for more than 15 years that I get bored with material things quickly, so there is no real lasting positive effect.

The point is that many people are very fortunate, yet they always want more. Journaling about what you are grateful for will make you appreciate what you have now, leave you wanting less, and help you be more thankful. This is a great attitude enhancer that will let you enjoy each day more. The more appreciation and gratitude you show, the more that will come back to you.

Examples of My Journal Entries Note That I am Thankful For:

- A loving, thoughtful wife
- My two little dogs (aka: Jeff's little buddies)
- Unlimited, clean, running water to drink
- A great, warm house during winter in Ohio
- A solid roof over my family during the tornados
- The Toledo Blade getting delivered to my home
- The mail getting delivered to my house each day
- The calming music playing while I am writing

- My computer and its vast abilities
- My little thumb drive and its amazing ability to save so much of my work, etc.

As you can see from my small list, if you list five to ten items each day in your journal, you will start to see abundance in your life right now. Gain an attitude of gratitude. It will reduce your desire to have more things in your life and change your scarcity mentality. This will influence your demeanor and make you more positive. You can also go back and read over your lists when you are at a low point, as with the success journal mentioned previously, and you'll come away with a more positive outlook.

You can further this process by actually telling people, every day, how much you appreciate them. You will be surprised how positively people will react and how good it will make you feel.

FOR EXAMPLE:

- Thank the bagger at the grocery store
- Let the teller at your bank know you appreciate her for being pleasant
- Compliment the coffee shop cashier on her hair style (but guys, no touching, pervs!)
- Thank your co-worker for helping you figure out a problem
- Tell your friend you appreciate her support during your recent break-up
- Give the elderly lady your seat on the bus

It is helpful to do this with your spouse or significant other too. At the end of the day, first write down and then tell them five things you appreciate them for and have them do the same. This can really strengthen your relationships and force you to not take them for granted.

Q. Can my attitude really change the events in my life?

Having a positive attitude will make your day better even if nothing really seems to change at first, and over time you will begin to see positive changes in your life as a result of your attitude. Feeding your mind with positive thoughts regularly will give you a positive attitude and change your behavior for the better. You will approach each new situation differently and handle it with an I-can-do-anything attitude rather than letting it bring you down and defeat you. Even if things don't go as you would like them to, you will respond better and move forward to make the best of it. You will decide to learn from the experience and grow from it. Recall that positive vibrations attract positive and vice versa.

What Would Jeff Do?
(Fun action steps to try this stuff out)

1. Read and listen to less news for the next month (get only the headlines if you must) and keep reading positive materials daily. Watch your attitude improve.

2. Pick a small goal of yours, like getting an "A" on your next quiz, and really focus on doing just that. Put in the prep work and practice time. Make an affirmation, believe it, and recite it multiple times a day for several days before the quiz and see how it makes a difference.

3. Try the mind control exercise, making a fist with your arm out, with several different people. See how words and thoughts control your mind and body. Now recognize how you do that to your mind daily. Begin to replace negative comments with positive statements.

4. Take the mind boundary exercise (connecting the dots). Did you solve it before peeking at the answer? Open your mind to possibilities outside of the norm and you will grow your analytical ability dramatically.

5. During your next "down" time, take in something fun, funny, utilize animals like I do, or find what provides a happy feeling for you. Watch your attitude improve.

6. Write out your 10 most positive, uplifting experiences to date. Add enough details so you can really picture and feel each experience fully. Walk through them and take several seconds to truly re-experience each one. How do you feel now? Start your success journal with these and add as many other positive experiences as you can think of from your life to date. Add to the journal weekly as you have positive experiences.

7. Pay attention to the people you are around and note how you feel while they are present and just after they leave. If the feeling is not good, set a plan to reduce the time you are around them. When you are around them, avoid negative subjects and redirect the subject to something positive to improve your time with them.

8. Start a gratitude journal by looking around at everything you have (health, family, friends, work, skills, etc…) and start appreciating them right now. Write in your journal daily at bed time to give you a great feeling to sleep on. Take this a step further by complimenting or thanking those people you encounter daily who interact with you. Let them know they are appreciated. Don't skip doing this step with your spouse/significant other—take action to build your relationship.

Once you've finished these steps, write me to let me know what happened and what you learned at *stories@lifescheatsheets.com.*

Now, think like Nike and Just Do It!

"Helping someone up won't pull you down."

"People wrapped up in themselves make pretty small packages."

"Praise, like sunlight, helps all things grow."

Visions To Get Where You Want To Go

Q. How do pictures help program my mind?

Put simply, visual images activate and stimulate the creative parts of the mind (the "un-technical" version) as well as your emotions, which allows you to connect to your goals more intensely. The more vividly you create the images, the more intensely you will work toward accomplishing the goals that they represent. When your mind can picture clearly what it is working toward, it continues to focus and drive toward achieving that vision. Professional and Olympic athletes and their coaches have used this technique for many years and have had great success.

More technically speaking, visualizations program your mind's reticular activating system to look for and point out aspects of your daily experiences that will assist you in achieving the vision. This system processes millions of bits of information that go through your mind daily. Programming it with these visions allows it to filter the information and pull out only those bits that will be helpful to make the visions true. This process draws you to the necessary resources and directs you to take the needed actions to make these visions a reality.

Your mind will temporarily see a conflict between the vision of a completed goal and what it currently understands as reality. But, with repeated use of these techniques, it resolves that conflict by suggesting actions and resources to make these completed-goal visions become reality. This creative portion of your subconscious mind works better with pictures than words, so show it exactly what you want to be your reality. This technique accelerates the achievement process dramatically (see principle 11 in *The Success Principles* by Jack Canfield and Janet Switzer). Remember the tag line for the old commercial? "A mind is a terrible thing to waste," so put it to work for you daily.

Q. How do I find the pictures that represent my goals?

Once you are finished with this chapter, go and start searching for colorful, detailed pictures, scenes, and the like that represent your completed goals. There are many free sites online that you can use to pull pictures and symbols (e.g., freefoto.com, sxc.hu, morguefile. com). Just enter "free pictures," "free images," "free photos," or "free graphics" in your search engine and you will get a lot of options. Pull pictures from magazines, flyers, advertisements, and similar media that represent specifically what you desire. Don't be afraid to make up a mock picture with pieces of other pictures so it matches just what you are looking for. These will be free or cost very little and are really effective, so they are well worth putting some time into.

Create a hard copy as well as an e-version, if possible, so you can use it as a screen saver and for other uses, like a PowerPoint slide show or your own e-video that you can put together for free at *www.animoto.com*. Have copies of your most important ones to post in several places, carry with you, put in your briefcase, etc., so you see them many times per day.

Q. Can I use a basic picture if I can't find a good one?

It is very important to make the vision as close to your completed goal as possible so that you give your mind clear direction. Try to match colors, tones, scenery, and backgrounds so that it seems like the true scene. Spend some time building your specific picture. You really want to connect with that image so your mind accepts it as true and gives you direction toward achieving it. On the other hand, get something completed now so that you can begin using it right away, and then update your pictures regularly. It doesn't have to be perfect, just something useful and reflective of what you desire.

Q. What methods do people use to apply this technique?

Vision boards, binders, screen savers, and slide shows are used most frequently to display the pictures that represent completed goals. Many successful people have used these for years and recognize their influence. There are simple ways now to make your visions your screen saver (search "vision board screen saver" online). At *www. jackcanfield.com*, you can find screen saver software that makes it look more professional (see "dream big vision board" under products).

Date it so you see how quickly you are progressing toward your goals. Estimated completion target dates keep you progressing forward. Don't make the deadlines so ambitious that you can't possibly meet them, but be aggressive enough to keep the fire lit and motivate you. If you travel somewhat regularly, create something you can take with you. A vision book is obviously easier in those cases, but you can at least carry a set of the pictures printed in a folder.

Q. How much time do I need to spend with each vision?

Don't just rip through all of the visions in a few seconds. Look at each one individually for at least 10 seconds to make a specific connection to each one. The amount of time is not as important as taking whatever time is needed to truly, vividly picture the completed scene with all of the details you can muster. Allow yourself to experience all of the emotions you will feel when that occurs. Do this without interruptions and distractions.

Activate as many senses as you can, as if you had completed each goal. Consider how it will look when you reach that goal, how it may smell, what it may sound or taste like. For example, if your goal is to be a professional baseball player, picture the sold-out crowd on a sunny summer evening. Imagine the feel of the bat in your hands, the smell of peanuts and popcorn, and the sight of the big screen with your name and stats displayed. Or perhaps your goal is to be a dentist. Imagine being in your office in your white lab coat, with sterilized utensils ready at hand, the sound of the drills and suctioning—ugh, I'm having a nightmare just thinking about that one! But whatever your goals are, personalize your vision with specific details. This will amplify the effect and accelerate your actions to complete your goals.

Take some extended time to really feel these emotions fully so you can recall them easily each time you go over your visions. Go slowly through the vision to really see each little detail. Each time you see the image, you need to really, deeply believe it is true and take the necessary actions with a never-give-up attitude to accomplish it.

Q. How often do I have to look at my visions?

Make certain you look at each picture multiple times daily (at least three times) and stop at each one to feel the emotions you would feel if it were a reality. If you read your goal and the corresponding affirmation (you will learn about these in more depth in the next chapter) then look at the related picture, you will be able to put all of the pieces together and it will make a bigger impact. Continue this for each of your other goals and affirmations to make the strongest impact.

Look at the picture and read your goal-statement and affirmation first thing in the morning to fill your conscious mind as well as your subconscious mind (SM) with your completed goals. Going through this process at least once at midday (or more as time allows) and then again before going to bed is a good routine to develop. Doing so just before bed will program your SM to continue to work on achieving your goals even while you sleep, further reinforcing the belief that you will achieve them.

Q. Where should I post these visions?

Post these pictures where you will naturally see them multiple times a day. Get used to reviewing them along with your goals and affirmations while you are doing routine chores that you don't really need to concentrate on, such as brushing your teeth, washing the dishes, eating lunch at your desk, and similar daily functions where your attention can be on your goals while accomplishing something else.

It is helpful to post them on your nightstand, on the bathroom mirror, on your dash in the car, on the cupboards in the kitchen, in front of the kitchen sink, on the refrigerator, on the coffee table, where you watch TV, and similar places.

Q. Do I need a picture for every goal?

If you only have time for your top four or five goals, that is a good start and you can always add later. Don't put pressure on yourself to be working on all areas just because they are listed. You know which ones are most important to you and your family right now, so start with them. You will build your confidence by taking one or two steps forward each day and will get a lot accomplished in just a month. Getting started now is the key to achieving success.

Once you make progress and have some additional time, I recommend you get clear pictures of your top one to three goals in each of the suggested goal areas. You can choose to skip an area or two right now so that you can focus on the most important ones and then add to the other areas as you move forward. This will help the process go more smoothly as you gradually work in the goals for each area of your life.

Q. How am I going to achieve these big visions?

You're going to have to trust me on this one. The first step is just getting your desires down on paper. You have to let go of the "how" when going through this exercise. Each of these techniques I am explaining will help you reach the "how" part of the equation. Training your mind to work with you and for you is a key to learning how to accomplish your goals. To accomplish any big goal, there's a series of tasks you need to complete to get there. Take some time and identify these tasks. Then, list the steps you'll need to take to accomplish each of those tasks. That is the "how" portion you are wondering about.

You will have both parts of your mind, conscious and subconscious, aligned with your desires to give you direction on what actions to take. Positive thoughts draw you to more positive thoughts. You'll start to pick up clues about how to achieve your desires. Follow these clues to achieve your dreams.

Q. How long do I have to achieve all of my visions?

You set the time frame for each of your goals, but you need to establish a reasonable timeline that you can achieve. Your mind must believe it can be done as outlined or you won't truly be committed. The timeline will be different for each of your goals. There are a number of tasks to complete for each, and they will take different amounts of effort and time. Some of these tasks can be subcontracted out to others that can complete the task for you, while for others you will need to be involved or do entirely yourself.

When you define the steps, you will get a complete picture of how long it will take to accomplish the step, so you will have a better picture of the time needed to complete the goal. At that point, you can put a deadline on each step. Some goals may be big enough that you will need to accomplish them in stages, so you would make stage one the goal right now along with its steps. When you complete that, you will update your list by replacing stage one with stage two and its steps. You can have pictures for each stage, so you can envision what each completed stage will look like.

For example, if your goal is to become a lawyer, you may mock-up a picture showing you walking across the stage at the university getting your undergraduate degree. Another picture may be a mock-up of you taking the LSAT and your scores that qualify you for entrance to the law school you chose. Another picture may be of a published article of yours as a law review writer or trying a case in competition on the mock trial team. You could then mock-up a picture of you graduating on the law school stage with a cum laude honors cord. You could continue this to your first job as an attorney, on to giving an oral argument on appeal, your ideal office with all of the furnishings, awards, partnership offer, etc. This would easily take 10 to 15 years to complete.

Q. How do visions relate to the other techniques?

All of the techniques I am laying out are complementary and further train your mind to work with you and for you to achieve your deepest desires. As you continue to use multiple techniques together, your mind will become a stronger ally to assist you in expediting the completion of your goals. The key is to start with at least a few goals and add these techniques so you begin to learn how to use them together. You will naturally get better with each of them as you practice. Don't skip this visions area; the mind really responds to them.

Q. How long before I can expect to see results?

Your SM has been developing your current habits for many months or years, so retraining it for new, better habits won't happen overnight. Many studies have shown that you can start to replace a bad habit with a better one by using techniques like those described in this book for a minimum of 30 consecutive days, at least three times per day. Don't skip days or you will need to do it longer or start over to get results.

Your mind will start to revert back to your bad habits if you don't feed it the new ones several times a day. There will initially be some conflict in your mind, but you will eventually override it with the new habits. After 30 days, you should really be connecting to your visions since you will have fed them to your mind and felt the related emotions nearly 100 times.

Q. Have others already been successful doing this?

I have heard many students of these techniques explain where they were before using these techniques and what they have achieved since using them. All of them are in awe of how their life has changed. They did not believe it was possible until they started using these techniques. It was also important to stick with them during challenging times. Read some of the teachers' stories in *The Secret* and other materials concerning the law of attraction. Listen to coaches of those techniques and you will be amazed at their stories.

Talk show host Ellen Degeneres recently talked about her ambitious goal of becoming the first female comedian on the Johnny Carson Show many years ago. That show was the most popular late night show at the time. She had not been a comedian long and was poor, barely making enough to survive. But every day she would picture herself in that chair next to Johnny Carson, and she would tell herself she was going to be the first female comedian as a guest on his show. Within just a few years, she became the first female comedian on his show and her career exploded with that publicity.

Jim Carey, the famous actor, used a $10 million check he wrote himself to strengthen his belief that he could truly accomplish his dream of becoming a famous actor. He took the action necessary to get the right contacts, try out, and eventually land the role in *Dumb and Dumber* that earned him his first $10 million payday. That check represented his deep desire and allowed him to picture it as reality.

Jack Canfield and Mark Victor Hansen, the *Chicken Soup* authors, could not get anyone to publish their first book. They went to many publishers, conventions, and book fairs, but kept getting turned down. Since they believed they had to have a publisher to reach their goal of being on the top of the *New York Times* Best Seller List, they printed the current list, pasted their book title and information on the #1 slot and posted copies of the image all over their office and living spaces. Soon they found a publisher and within several months, the book hit #1 on the best seller list and stayed there for many weeks.

Canfield and Hansen also had a five-a-day technique they used for getting promotion for their books. They each conditioned themselves to take five actions daily and posted pictures of themselves getting specific promotion from the sources they wanted. They did get lots of promotion from these sources, and their actions greatly expanded the reach and sales of their books. They used and taught the techniques in this book to keep themselves focused on their goals. Their *Chicken Soup* series has become the biggest selling series of all time.

Bruce Jenner, 1976 Olympic decathlon gold medalist and world record holder, lost in the 1972 Olympics. But, he took pictures of the winner of the gold medal on the platform and pasted his face in place of the winner. Over the next four years as he conditioned daily, he visualized those pictures of himself as the gold medal winner of the decathlon in the 1976 Olympics. He won the gold, broke the record in that Olympics event, and has had further success since that time. Many other professional and Olympic athletes have similar stories about their use of visions.

Q. Can I start with just my most important goal?

If one goal stands above all others and you are 100% committed to it, start with that one only. Post it all over as I have explained. Carry it with you. Keep it top of mind throughout the day. The more it stays in your mind, the more your mind will work with you.

Alex Mondossian, a teleseminar host, shared on one of his teleseminars that he was struggling financially years earlier, and he had an urgent family need that required him to make a lot more income, which gave him an intense desire to find a way. His goal was to convert his approximately $45,000-a-year income to his monthly income within three years. He had no idea how he was going to do it. He wrote it on his bathroom mirror with dry erase markers and posted his goal everywhere, so that it was on his mind all the time. He got direction to ultimately get into the teleseminar business. He has now made a lot of money interviewing experts on teleseminars and webinars. His teleseminars are usually free, which attracts a lot of listeners, but he records them and then sells the information packaged in several ways. He splits the proceeds with the expert and has multiple income streams from these products. Using visions and other techniques described in this book, he met his goal in less than two years and has become financially secure, dramatically expanding his new business.

Another student explained in a teleseminar that she was strapped for money and badly needed to get out of a housing situation that was causing too much stress. She had found a house that would solve her problem, but she needed $20,000 to get it and had no idea how she could get the money. She used visions heavily. She received a fake $20,000 bill in the mail as part of an advertising promotion. She enlarged it and put copies of these big bills all over her apartment, hanging them above her bed, in her car, purse, on the refrigerator, etc. Her friends thought she had lost it, but she stuck with it. Within a few months, she received an inheritance from an aunt she had been close to years before, received some money from a small lawsuit settlement, sold a play script she had written years before, and won money in a drawing. All of this money totaled more than $20,000 and she got her house. She completely believed she would get the money, used these techniques, and accomplished her goal.

WhaT WOuLD JEFF Do?
(Fun action steps to try this stuff out)

1. Start finding pictures that represent your completed goals and create an e-version (with a scanner) so you can use it electronically. I realize we have not gone through that chapter yet, but you know what most of them are now.

2. Put your set of pictures in a grouping of some kind (binder, slide show, vision board) that you can refer to daily. Something mobile is best.

3. Go through your pictures at least three times daily, very slowly, stopping to draw in as many emotions and senses as possible to truly experience the feelings associated with completing that goal.

4. Post your pictures in your most traveled areas so you will see them many times throughout the day.

5. Focus your mind on truly believing these goals will occur and you will attract positive thoughts to assist you in making them come true.

Once you've finished these steps, write me to let me know what happened and what you learned at *stories@lifescheatsheets.com*.

Now, think like Nike and Just Do It!

UPLiFTiNG MeSSaGeS To MoVe You ForWarD (AFFiRMaTiONS)

Q. What are affirmations and how do they help?

Affirmations are positive statements that support the achievement of your goals and help you to grow and improve in other areas of your life. They help train your mind to take daily action to obtain what you desire. Affirmations also help convince your mind that you can accomplish whatever it is you desire, regardless of how daunting or far fetched it may currently sound to you. They work with your goals, visions, and other techniques to expedite the completion of your strongest desires. On top of this, affirmations regularly build your confidence and self-esteem, which further improve as you complete steps toward accomplishing your goals. The more you use them, the more you believe your big dreams and take steps to attain them.

The structure of your affirmations needs to follow these guidelines:
- Word them in the positive
- State what you want, not what you don't want
- Write them in the present tense so you can see them already accomplished
- Keep them short and specific

- Start with words like "I am..." so you own them and are telling your mind to take action now
- Use action and feeling words to elicit emotional responses
- Don't use comparisons to others
- Stretch yourself, but make them believable
- Cover the areas of your life to create balance
- Add "or something better" to the end of appropriate statements to allow them to expand beyond your thoughts
- Make them personal to you, not others

Don't get upset if you can't make them specifically fit all of these guidelines. Do your best and get started with some now. You can always modify them to more closely match these guidelines. Also, realize that you will have growth-type affirmations and goal-specific affirmations. Growth-type affirmations relate to areas such as self-esteem, confidence, and happiness where you will lay out the steps you will take to improve.

A FEW EXAMPLES OF AFFIRMATIONS TO GET YOU STARTED:

- I am excited watching my eBay auctions grab high bids on the new products I negotiated a wholesale deal on, or something better.
- I feel so pleased that my Maltese won best of show at the state dog show, or something better.
- I am very thankful and relieved that my latest health checkup is positive (as compared to "I don't have cancer").
- I am so happy that I found a new, higher-paying job with great benefits within a 15-minute commute of my house, or something better.
- I am so proud of myself for being assertive and successfully negotiating a large discount on the purchase of my new SUV, or something better.

- I am completely relaxed on the deck of my new, 4,000-square-foot home on Virginia Beach, watching the waves roll, or something better.
- I am amazed that I made more than $1 million dollars in my real estate business this year, or something better.

These examples give you a feel for how you can make your affirmations relate to goals that are important to you, which will build your confidence and enhance your attitude daily.

I strongly suggest that you dream beyond what you are comfortable with at this point in your life. Stretch the limits of what you think is possible, especially if you are an older adult who is starting these for the first time. You will be surprised at how much you can accomplish if you just strive for it. The first step is writing down your personal goals. Using affirmations will then help you reach those goals.

Once you have written your affirmations, read them out loud for greater emphasis, when possible, so you can hear yourself actually saying the words rather than just thinking them. Consider recording them on a digital recorder, CD, or tape so you can also listen to them.

Q. How frequently do I need to read my affirmations?

Read or listen to your affirmations at least three times daily. Use the same schedule as your goals and visions: first thing in the morning, at least once midday, and as the last thing you read or listen to before going to bed. The more you see or hear them, the more they will be top-of-mind, which in turn will reinforce your new mentality and make the path to your goals more smooth. You need to do this for over 30 consecutive days (without skipping) to start to see some results. This is enough time for your mind to start overriding the conflict between what it sees as real (current scenario) and what you feed it as real (your completed goal).

As you read or listen to the daily affirmations, vividly picture them as true and imagine how you will feel when you accomplish your goals. Try to keep the numbers of statements you are working on reasonably small so you can focus on the most important ones to start. When you have made progress on them, combine them with additional affirmations that you want to focus on.

Q. But how am I going to achieve these goals?

It's normal to not have the "how" part of the equation figured out and to have some anxiety attached to this uncertainty. So take a few deep breaths and let them out slowly, realizing you are normal. Your affirmations and the other techniques will all start assisting your mind to find ways and actions to get you closer to your goals. Actions you take will sprout other actions, and you will get direction from your subconscious mind (SM) on what to do next.

I am betting you have completed a project, term paper, or some other undertaking that you weren't sure how to complete when you started. But, you just started it and figured it out along the way. Using these techniques to achieve your goals is similar. Just believing that they will happen is the first step. Your beliefs will get stronger as you start to take steps toward your goals. Trust yourself and your mind to find a way to get what you really want. Positive thought and attitude will attract more positivity to you.

Q. What if I really don't believe they are possible?

If the typical affirmation structure doesn't work well, you can refer to *Beyond Positive Thinking* by Dr. Robert Anthony and the intention statements that take affirmations a step further. Let me explain. In some cases, affirmations may invoke negative self-talk in response to the affirmation (if you truly can't believe it). If you find that is happening, convert your affirmation to an intention statement that your mind will more easily accept as true. Once you believe the intention statement, you can try eliminating the intention language and use the original affirmation.

For example, your affirmation could be "I am getting straight As during this spring semester [insert year] at state college." If you have not gotten As in the past and don't believe you can get them, your negative voice may dismiss the statement by not accepting it as possible. You may find yourself responding to the affirmation with thoughts like, "You've never done it before and have no chance of doing it now" or "You're dreaming; that will never happen."

But, if you use an intention statement like, "I intend to work harder than ever before and I am so excited about getting straight As during spring semester [year] at state college," your mind tends to accept it because it can more easily see it happening. This format will eliminate the negative self-talk. This change may be needed for you to truly accept and believe some of your affirmations. You need to eliminate disbelief so your mind works for you, so pay attention to how your mind responds as you speak, read, and hear your affirmations.

Q. Why should I write these as if I've achieved them?

Recall that your SM does not have reasoning power. It believes what you feed it repetitively, and it works for you to make certain it is true. Acting as if your goals are already achieved, and wording your affirmations accordingly, will program your SM to work to make them a reality. Picture each completed goal as you read the affirmation to help strengthen the belief. Believe, and the actions needed to complete your goals will follow automatically.

Remember, many people constantly feed themselves negative messages such as that they are fat, ugly, no good, losers, bad, can't do things, etc., even when they are not true. But, because they continue to mentally repeat such thoughts, their SM begins to believe they're true. The person then acts as if they were true, regardless of the real truth, so they ultimately believe these false statements. It works the same way with positive statements, so use this to your advantage.

Q. Why would I write affirmations in the present tense?

The present tense is another trigger to help convince your mind that the affirmations are already true. Once you have gone through the process enough, your mind will start overriding your current beliefs with new, positive beliefs, and your SM will be working for you to accomplish this.

Q. How specific do I need to be in writing my affirmations?

Affirmations need to be specific about what you truly desire so everything is laser-focused on the specific goal. The more specific you are, the better your mind can work toward fulfilling that desire. If it is something that can be measured or given a value, state it in those terms. Eliminate any possible confusion. Confusion and lack of clarity causes friction in the mind, which slows the process. It may help to close your eyes and clearly picture your completed goal and then open your eyes and describe it in words. This description can be used as your affirmation. You can edit it to match the guidelines above once you get it down on paper.

Q. Why do I need to write them as positive statements?

The mind does not recognize negative qualifiers like not, won't, and don't. Try this. Tell yourself, "*Don't* think about beagles." What are you thinking about? Your mind only hears, "Think about beagles" and leaves out the "don't." Now, don't think about ducks. What image just came to mind? A cat? Nope. Admit it. You were picturing a duck. Likewise, if you say, "I'm not fat", your mind hears "I'm fat" and filters out the "not." Realize this limitation and write your affirmations in the positive. Write statements that influence you to do something, not ones that suggest that you won't do something. This will focus you on what you want, what you are going to do, and what you will have.

Q. Can I compare my accomplishments to others?

These desires are about you and not about you as compared to others, so don't use comparisons in your affirmations. For example, don't write, "I am proud that I placed higher than John in the city league tennis tournament this year." Instead say, "I am proud that I placed in the top three in the city league tennis tournament this year." That is your objective goal regardless of where John places. What if John broke his foot and couldn't play, moved from the area, had the best match of his life, his opponent forfeited, etc.? Write about you, individually, what you want to accomplish, and forget others. Others are outside of your control and should not affect what you do for yourself.

Q. What should I do once I complete a goal?

You are responsible for making the affirmations accurately reflect your current goals and desires. Change is inevitable in life, so you will need to modify your goals, visions, and the related affirmations when circumstances change. If it doesn't apply anymore, delete it. If a new one surfaces, add it. These are all fluid and will change as your life changes. Keep them reflective of your current desires. You are the only one that will be aware of your deepest desires from day to day.

Q. How can I get the most benefit from affirmations?

To make these statements more powerful, say them out loud while looking at yourself in the mirror. Listen intently to each of the statements as you go through them and pay attention to the details related to each statement, so you can visualize them also. Reading them without really experiencing the desire will dramatically reduce their effectiveness, so make a conscious effort to connect with each statement. Try to evoke as many emotions as you can.

Q. Should I also post my affirmations?

Just like your goals list and vision pictures, post your affirmations where you will frequently see them each day, preferably with the others so you can mentally walk through all of them in sequence. Posting them on bathroom mirrors, refrigerators, desks, car dashes, and the like makes them easy to access and read multiple times daily. Make certain they are simple and easy to read so you don't see this as a chore but as a way to truly improve your life.

Q. How do affirmations build confidence and self-esteem?

When you complete tasks, you will be proud of yourself. You may also receive compliments and support from others who see you progress, which will further increase your self-esteem and confidence. As you complete more tasks and build momentum, you will continue to build your self-esteem and confidence. You will see that you can accomplish whatever you set your mind to and may decide to go after more of your goals. You will begin to dream bigger because you have progressed beyond the mental limits you started with.

You can also create growth-type affirmations that specifically help you boost your self-esteem and confidence. Draft positive statements that reflect the beliefs you want to have about yourself. Some examples include:

- I look hot, and I am so confident in my fitted white blouse, short black skirt, and black strapless heels
- I am proud of myself for being able to easily introduce myself to, and carry on conversations with, new people
- I am great at, and enjoy, public speaking
- I am excited about promoting my new book to large audiences around the country
- I am thrilled to be fit from my daily exercise and healthy from eating right
- I look great at my ideal weight of 110 pounds and I am attractive to guys

Q. Why should I even try using affirmations?

This is another technique that doesn't take much time or effort, but has the ability to help you control your mind, which controls your future. There is no monetary cost, and it is easy to get started. Just start using them now and see how it affects you. If you get past the first 30 days and don't see any change, you can stop. But if you give it full-blown effort and believe it will work, the effect can only be positive. Isn't it worthwhile to at least give it a try when it has the potential to help you reach beyond your current limiting thoughts to accomplish your goals? What do you have to lose? If you want to learn more, read Jack Canfield's *Key to Living the Law of Attraction Guide* as well as *The Success Principles* for additional direction about many of these techniques. I have learned a lot from him and like his work in this area.

WhaT WoULD JEFF Do?
(Fun action steps to try this stuff out)

1.   Write your top 10 growth-type or goal-specific affirmations following the guide in this chapter. You can modify the goal-specific ones once we finish the goal chapter soon.

2.   Read them (aloud if possible) at least three times daily and look at the corresponding pictures you have pulled that show the completed goal that matches your affirmation. Take time with each one individually to truly experience the feelings you will feel as it's completed.

3.   Convert any affirmation to an intention statement if you really can't believe it's possible right now. Listen to your mind when reading the affirmation and hear how your mind responds to it to detect this issue.

4.   Use these 30 consecutive days and see if you feel more confident that you can accomplish your goals. You may want to "up the ante" and increase your goals when you hit this stage.

Once you've finished these steps, write me to let me know what happened and what you learned at *stories@lifescheatsheets.com*.

Now, think like Nike and Just Do It!

"You can't soar with the eagles if you hang with the turkeys."

"Education is an investment, not an expense."

"Do what you can where you are with what you have."

Devour Growth Materials Daily (Read/Listen To Positive Messages)

Q. How can I improve my attitude daily?

Take 20 to 30 minutes daily to read, listen to, or watch something positive, motivational or growth-oriented. This will help build your independence, confidence, and self-esteem. Do any suggested exercises in them to gain the maximum benefit.

Use these materials to influence your demeanor and remain positive. You will learn to take on the day rather than merely "surviving" it. Learn to charge ahead and get things done rather than "sliding in the back door late" and doing everything at the last minute.

I'm certain you've heard that with a positive attitude and enough determination and persistence, you can accomplish *anything* (that is possible) that you set your mind to. I have proven this personally and witnessed it many times so I know it is correct.

American Idol just completed another season and Crystal Bowersox, from just outside my town (Toledo, Ohio), showed extreme determination and courage going all the way to the final two. Even though she clearly performed better and should have won, her runner-up status is getting her enormous opportunities and she will be able to accomplish some huge goals. Coming from a small town, she continued to believe she could accomplish her big goals, took steps to do so, and is now well on her way toward exceeding her goals.

But please don't focus on something that is not possible. For example, I have conceded that it is not possible for me to be a professional volleyball or basketball player at my age and size even though I am good at these sports and may want to do so. To believe I could accomplish that goal would eventually bring my attitude down because I would be defeated.

Your attitude is responsible for how your day goes. I know that you will accomplish much more, be happier, and nicer to be around with a positive attitude. In contrast, with a negative, defeated attitude, everything will be viewed in a bad light. Each task will be dreaded and will take you longer; therefore, you will get less done. You can learn to build and maintain a more positive attitude that will let you shrug off annoyances that others seem to dwell on. With a good attitude, you will look forward to the day, get up in the morning, and start accomplishing tasks. You will attract more positive people because you project that aura around you.

Q. How do I know what materials are best for me?

Look at the areas you want to improve in your life as well as your goals. For example, especially when they are about to enter unfamiliar territory, most people can benefit from boosting their confidence and self-esteem. Start with materials targeting these areas. I would sample materials by different authors and companies to see which ones you connect with best. Use the library as well as online resources before you invest much money in them. Once you find something that suits your needs, consider purchasing the material so you can go through it multiple times. Don't buy too many materials at any one time because ultimately many of them may just sit on the shelf. I am guilty of this one.

As I pointed out earlier at the end of Chapter 2, several mentors have repeated the old adage that you will be the same 10 years from now, except for the information you take in (and take action on) and the people you are in contact with. I agree with this concept now.

Both have a big impact on your future direction. Rather than the relentless negativity in the daily news, why not feed yourself positive messages that will help you to grow daily?

Q. Is there a recommended time to read positive materials?

Feed your mind as early as possible so that you start the day on a positive note. If you start the day with a full head of steam, pumped up by positive, uplifting materials, you will get more accomplished and feel better about yourself. You will look at the day with excitement rather than dread.

Q. Why should I reduce the amount of news I take in?

Don't start your day by feeding your mind a lot of news that typically highlights stories about victims, bankruptcies, foreclosures, unemployment, war, tragedies, crime, and other negative subjects that the media sensationalizes. Our society tunes in to stories about pain and suffering much more than positive stories, which is why news stations, newspapers, radio stations, and other media pump out those stories multiple times a day and as quickly as they can get the gory details out.

Media sources know this type of story attracts more viewers, readers, and listeners. This, in turn, gets media companies higher ratings and more advertisers, which translates into more income for the companies and higher pay for their workers. Limit your exposure to those types of stories by reading only the headlines to stay up on current events, but ignoring the details. Instead, latch onto those that build people up. Look for news stories that recognize people for reaching key goals, being a hero, paying it forward, and other accomplishments. Just reducing the negative news that you take in will help your demeanor and improve your outlook.

Q. Have you ever seen news with only positive stories?

I have never seen or heard of a predominantly positive newspaper or TV station. Wouldn't it be great to have a place to share positive stories? Something that would make people feel good and inspire them to do good for themselves and others? The world could use daily inspirational news rather than more of the gloom and doom reporting that we have had far too much of lately. One of my goals is to start a site online that does just this. Visit *www.greatnewsforachange. com* and contribute stories to it. Negative thoughts spawn more negative thoughts and vice versa, so why not go with the positive?

Q. What if I don't get much from reading (except what I have gained from this amazing book!)?

As you sample materials, pay attention to which type of medium you retain the most information from. Jot this down as you sample more materials. It's wise to understand how you learn best and focus on that medium to the extent possible. You might respond better to visual (TV, DVDs), auditory (CDs, mp3s, iPod), in-person seminars, or written materials that you can highlight and tab. Regardless, figure this out and focus on the methods that work best for you. It is helpful to use the same content with different media and see which one helps you absorb the information most effectively.

Q. What medium should I use if I have a busy schedule?

If time constraints prevent you from using the medium that allows you to absorb material best, go with the one that allows you to get the information in the time you have. The key is to take in the information daily however you can get it. For example, use the time on your commute to and from work by listening to a cassette, CD, mp3, iPod, or handheld recorder even if you typically learn better from visual media. It's better than not getting the information at all due to your busy schedule.

Q. Is it easy to get these materials in my medium?

There are so many different resources today with print, video, audio, e-documents, online streaming information, e-courses, downloads, etc. You should be able to find one that works for you and is in your price range. With materials discounted at places like Amazon. com, it is easy to get most materials immediately or within a few days.

Many books have an e-book option as well as an audio version so you can download it as soon as you pay for it. With Amazon's Kindle, Sony's readers, and other electronic book readers, you can carry hundreds of books around with you on that small device. They continue to upgrade these devices and will probably make them more affordable soon.

Libraries are still a source for some of these materials. Depending on whether you live in the big city, a small town, or a rural area, your library's resources will vary. But whatever your library offers, it would be worth the time to rent it. It's free, so you have nothing to lose. If you only use the library and don't plan to purchase anything, become an avid note taker or copy pages there so you can refer back to the best points in the materials multiple times.

Q. Should I spend the time to repeat any of the materials?

A number of studies, including one by the University of Illinois, show how little is retained from seminars unless you put the information to use right away. Results of the study conclude that:

- Within 48 hours after the seminar, you will remember 50% of what you heard
- After 1 week, you will recall 20% of what you heard
- After 1 month, you will recall 2% of what you heard
- After 6 months, you don't even recall going to the seminar

Reviewing the materials multiple times is wise because it allows your mind to retain more of the best material and it will become more implanted in your memory as important information. For your best materials, I would get them in several media and take them in as much as you can. Maybe you will have some time to listen in the car, read while you wait, listen during your workout, and watch them on TV, instead of watching a *Law and Order* rerun for the tenth time (yes, I'm guilty), etc. If it helps you progress, it is worth it.

Q. What if I'm just too busy to do this now?

Is it really important to accomplish your goals? Is it really important to achieve your dreams and satisfy your deepest desires? No matter how busy you are, you can set aside time to build these positive habits into your schedule if you really want to move forward. Look at the time wasters and less important activities in your schedule and replace them with these techniques. Your personal growth is at stake.

Implementing this strategy will allow you to complete tasks daily toward reaching your big goals. Eliminate some TV time, listen while you drive, and read while you wait or eat. I carry materials with me everywhere I might have some extra time. I keep them in my car all the time and take them to the gym to read while I am on the elliptical machine. Ask your family to leave you alone for an hour a day while you devote some time to yourself.

The point is that we all have the same 24 hours and it's up to you to decide the best way to spend them. Ask yourself if the other activities that are keeping you so busy are getting you further toward your goals. If not, you may be letting distractions or current tasks derail you from what's really important. Don't wake up 10 years from now and regret that you put this off.

Q. Will this really help motivate me to achieve my goals?

(No, I've been lying in extreme detail for several chapters to sell some books.) I wouldn't take all of this time and energy to lay out these techniques if I had not seen great results with a lot of people. Build these habits into your daily schedule for the next month and try them out, strongly believing they will work. Once you have done this daily for 30-plus days, look back and see how much you have learned and grown.

Strengthening your attitude each day will reduce the negative chatter in your mind and help focus your energy on finishing tasks that move you closer to completing your goals. At the end of the week, month, and quarter, you will be amazed at how much you have accomplished. Daily steps will get you there.

WhaT WoULD JEFF Do?
(Fun action steps to try this stuff out)

1. Take at least 15-20 minutes each day to take in (read, listen, watch) positive, growth-oriented material without interruptions. Expand this amount of time as you see the material help you feel better, do better, and respond better.

2. Reduce the amount of negative news, naysayers, and drama in your life. Monitor your demeanor and attitude once you have done this for more than 30 consecutive days and see how it has improved.

3. Sample materials in different ways (listen, read, watch, in-person) and see which way you learn best. Focus on your best method.

4. Sample different media (CD, DVD, mp3, e-books) and see which ones are easiest for you to learn from. Focus on the ones that suit you best.

5. Review your favorite materials that most help you many times over several days to retain as much as possible. Revisit them monthly.

Once you've finished these steps, write me to let me know what happened and what you learned at *stories@lifescheatsheets.com*.

Now, think like Nike and Just Do It!

*"Believe in yourself and the rest of your life
will be the best of your life."*

"Positive thinking turns obstacles into opportunities."

"This too shall pass."

GiVE YOUR BODY SOME QUiET TiME (MEDiTaTiON/YOGa)

Q. Why do my mind and body need quiet time?

Being able to reach a quiet, peaceful, relaxed state of mind is very helpful to your success and is essential for a healthy mind and body. People have had physical ailments completely disappear after incorporating a daily routine that includes quiet time to make an inner connection. Your body responds negatively to too much stress without breaks, and long-term problems may develop if you do not relieve that stress.

You can get direction from deep within when you take the time to really listen to your inner voice and block out the external world. Many people never take the time get in tune with their inner self; this precludes them from being as happy and content as they truly could be. Many times they don't follow their true passion because they don't listen and follow the direction from within. Fortunately, it's never too late to learn, grow, and get on the path toward your true calling.

I found I was guilty of this and have taken action to correct it. I had faced several years of annoying difficulties and had adopted a negative demeanor that was irritable, snappy, and on edge. It felt like I was close to becoming one of those people in the movies who snap and go off (go postal) on a bunch of people for minor reasons. I found that setting aside quiet time to listen to my inner self removed some of my stress and gave me a new direction. At times, it has been difficult to listen to myself without focusing on what I believe other people think about me. But through the techniques described in this book, I've come to more easily accept that this is my life, and I care less about what others think of me. You can have the same results in your life.

Detaching yourself from the busyness around you and quieting the noise in your head may be difficult until you have regularly practiced techniques that allow you to reach a calm and relaxed state. This was tough for me. As you look around, it's easy to find people who are constantly running to functions, attending to work needs and household chores, etc., without setting any time aside for themselves. Those who set aside a short time each day for quiet time to get in tune with their inner self are better able to manage their daily responsibilities and are happier people.

Q. How do I focus on my inner self?

The best method for tuning in to your inner self is a simple meditation technique. There are many types of meditation, so you may need to experiment if one doesn't seem to work for you. It is very important to set up your environment appropriately. You need to eliminate distractions and empty your mind of the daily clutter, responsibilities, and to-do lists so that nothing is distracting you.

We live in a busy, noisy, distracting world, so it is important to find a quiet place to practice many of these techniques. Turn off all of your e-mail, text messaging, voice mail, phones, TVs, and similar distractions. You need to slow down and tune out all other thoughts, wiping the slate clean so nothing is in the way of making this connection. This will allow you to listen to and get direction from your subconscious level.

Once you reach this calm, relaxed state, pay attention to the signs and directions that are coming to you from within. What you are passionate about will come to the forefront of your mind once you tap into your inner self and listen to its direction. I have to admit that it is difficult to do this at times, but when you are successful you will lose track of everything else around you and find inner peace. I have found that the longer you practice meditation daily, without skipping, the better you get at it.

Q. Do I need a particular setting for this to work?

In setting up your environment, you may wish to burn a candle (you can also take advantage of the benefits of aromatherapy by choosing a particular scent). Some use a small fountain to create the relaxing sound of a running stream. I recommend having the lights turned low to help relax your eyes. Play peaceful meditation or yoga music that is only instrumental and can block outside noises to help you reach a focused state of relaxation. Turn off all devices that could distract you or move them out of this space so you will not have interruptions. Your goal is to create a serene environment.

Most instructors recommend that you sit up straight with your legs crossed (a few allow you to lay flat on your back). Place your forearms on your legs and your palms up with the fingertip of your middle finger touching the tip of your thumb to form a circle with each hand. Some put a light above where they sit and picture this bright, white light coming down their spinal column, filling them with light, eliminating everything else around them, using this medium to connect to their inner voice for direction. Others will picture an empty room, a blank wall, the sky, or the ocean, any place where the mind can't be distracted. These are all techniques to empty your mind so you can focus on your breathing and mantra (explained below) to reach a deep, peaceful state.

Atmosphere is important with meditation because it makes it that much easier to reach a deep meditative state. You don't necessarily need everything I mentioned, but make certain you have a quiet area, low light, and all possible distractions eliminated.

Q. When is the best time for meditation?

Jumping immediately out of bed when the alarm goes off can be a jarring way to start the day. Many have found that meditation in the morning prepares them for the day much better because they start out calmly. Others find it is best to meditate just before bed (if you're not like me and can stay awake) to relieve the stress of the day and enter sleep in a calm and relaxed way.

Look at your schedule to help you determine the best time for meditation. Communicate to your roommate or family that you need this short span of quiet time without interruptions and they are not to enter your space once you have started. It is very important to this process to eliminate distractions. Emptying your mind already takes effort, and distractions will only make the process more difficult. You will probably have to start over if you have a distraction that stops the process. If you have multiple distractions and background noise, it can ultimately defeat the purpose of trying this technique.

Q. How do I learn to meditate?
Is there a simple process I can start with?

You can learn meditation in a class environment, but many learn meditation independently, in their own environment. There is a fundamental foundation to most of the techniques. Some of them have minor variances, and once you learn the basics you can tailor it to your preferences. You may want to use a relaxation CD before this if you are having problems focusing and screening out the daily noise. Some CDs are available with relaxing music, while others are narrated to take you through tensing of your muscles followed by a relaxing action with each muscle area throughout your entire body. These muscle techniques can release tension within a few minutes.

Once you are in a relaxed environment and in a comfortable position, control and focus on your breathing with your eyes closed. Breathing is an important component of meditation. Make certain you are breathing from your stomach and not your chest area. Put your hand on your stomach and confirm it is moving in and out as you breathe. Slowly breathe in through your nose and out through your mouth (some use their nose only, which has worked for me). Count slowly to three or four as you breathe in, then count slowly to four or five when you breathe out to focus your mind on the counting, which eliminates other distracters. You count just a little higher on your breath out to exhale slightly more air than you take in to clean out your lungs of leftover air. Without trying to breath deeper, you may naturally increase the number you count to as you breathe in and out. Your heart rate will slow down as well.

When you have gotten to a point where you have reached a calm, consistent breathing pattern, stop counting and substitute a mantra (word or short phrase) that you say to yourself slowly, either out loud or internally. You've probably heard of "ohm" as the typical mantra. I use "calm" which gives the same sound and helps to slow my mind down (remember I'm a little hyper so it can be tough to slow down and relax). Some have a little prayer or another word they can add the ohm sound to. This sound has proven to have a calming effect. You also need to choose a word or short phrase (for example: "deflect," "so what," or "whatever") that signals to your mind to get back on track when you stray into the day's noise. Once you have returned, start your mantra again along with proper breathing. Don't get discouraged if, early on, you need to refocus and restart multiple times until you get better at focusing on relaxing and emptying your mind.

Here's an example of what may go on in your mind at the beginning. Breathe in (slowly) *1, 2, 3, 4… * breathe out *1, 2, 3, 4, 5…—I wonder how long I have to do this before it works…* Deflect and breathe in *1, 2, 3, 4…* breathe out *1, 2—crap, did I remember to set my alarm for tomorrow?* Deflect, breathe in *1, 2, 3, 4…* breathe out *1, 2, 3, 4, 5…* breathe in *1, 2, 3, 4…* breathe out *1, 2, 3, 4, 5… Hey, it's getting slower like he said it would…* Deflect and breathe in *1, 2, 3, 4…* breathe out *1, 2, 3, 4, 5… Ok, what's my mantra? I will use "calm."* Breathe in *callllmmmmmm* (instead of numbers), breathe out *callllmmmmmm*, breathe in *callllmmmmmm*, breathe out… *I'm gonna be ticked at Bob if he doesn't show up for golf tomorrow, I already called twice to remind him, oh yeah, I'm supposed to be meditating…* Deflect and breathe in, *callllmmmmmm*, breathe out, *callllllmmmmmm—But I should probably call him again tomorrow just to be sure—* deflect and breathe in *callllllmmmmmm*, breathe out *callllllmmmmmm*, breathe in *callllllmmmmmm*, breathe out, *callllllmmmmmm*, breathe in… *Wow, I'm still hungry. I already ate too much today. I swear; I need to work out more and start eating healthier. Oops…* deflect and breathe in *callllllmmmmmm*, breathe out *callllllmmmmmm*, breathe in *callllllmmmmmm…*

You will find all sorts of thoughts flooding your mind. What happened recently, your concerns and fears, your to-do lists, your regrets, feelings of happiness, excitement about upcoming plans or people you care about, etc. There are other times to focus on those thoughts. Meditation is for finding peace that has no outside pressures. There will be times when you can't take two breaths in a row without having to deflect from distractions. But daily practice over the next several weeks will minimize those thoughts and allow you to shut out the outside world and focus only on your mantra, allowing the peacefulness and relaxation to fill your body and mind. If you're lost like I was, looking for what's next in life, this practice can give you peace of mind and start giving you some of the direction you are looking for.

The toughest part is clearing your mind of everything you are doing and everything around you to eliminate the "noise of life" and empty your mind. Start with 20 minutes and force yourself to get through those 20 minutes, regardless of how much you stray. You can extend it to 30 minutes or more once you have a better handle on it. When you are able to reach this state regularly, listen to the direction that you get from your inner voice. This voice is different from the distractions that interrupt the process. Unlike your to-do list, your worries and fears, your inner voice ignores the naysayers and other obstacles that get in the way of you following your passion. It is a reassuring and confident voice that will guide you.

Q. What if I don't have any time for quiet time?

I don't know of anyone who can't find 20 minutes for their own health per day. If you believe you don't have this much time, then start a log of your day and record what you are doing in 10 minute increments throughout the entire day from the time you wake until you go to bed. With this log, you will be able to see how you spent your day, decide what tasks are truly needed, and which tasks you can eliminate. Most people are able to find some additional time once they truly look at how they are spending their time. See if you can delegate a function or two, if you need to find more time.

Ultimately, you may need to make a decision about your priorities and what's important to you. Is it more important for you to mess around on Facebook, play video games, or watch TV than to take care of your physical and mental health? Perhaps you are truly tied up with work and family responsibilities. In that case, you might have to sacrifice a little sleep to fit in meditation. However, you may find that 20 minutes of meditation leaves you more relaxed, and ironically gives you more energy afterwards, than 20 minutes of sleep.

Not being able to take a small amount of time daily will continue to put stress on you that will eventually come out in some negative fashion that you probably won't like. Everyone needs some time to focus, so this time should take priority over many other functions. Set aside this time and make sure there are no interruptions. Once you create this time and see what it can do to for you, you won't want to give it up.

Q. Can yoga help me reach my inner self?

Some yoga includes meditative components that can have the same results as meditation, while many other types do not. The yoga classes I have tried have very little meditative qualities, so I have stuck with doing meditation. I understand from instructors that hatha yoga is more meditative than others. Many yoga classes are more about stretches, positions, and balancing than meditation. Along with these awkward stretches, you may be distracted by a stray fart followed by a student who can't contain their laughter so they just lose it out loud as I did once, so consider this fair warning! Realize you may also have to travel to attend the class, so you may not do it every day as recommended. If you enjoy yoga, it can serve as a complementary feature rather than replacing meditation. If you can do it on your own each day and get both sets of benefits, that is the best option.

I have not been around monks and others who are very good at this, but the local yoga instructors and veteran students I have been around are noticeably different to me. Look for a good instructor. Take a try-out class with a few instructors to see if any connect with you. Many of the instructors I've talked with seem so connected to who they are and what they want. They seem more unaffected by the day's challenges and they take things in stride. They are not wound as tightly as most business people I am around. I'm certain they have deadlines like everyone else, but their demeanor is much calmer. They convinced me that you can get rid of the clutter in life and focus on the most important stuff.

Q. Is meditation an option for people who are energetic?

I am slightly hyperactive and have been since I was a child. I used to (and still do) rattle the pew in church by shaking my legs until someone gave me the stern, stop-it look and I would consciously stop for awhile, only to start again. If you tend to be very active, you will need to put forth more effort to be successful. I was getting frustrated until I made it a daily routine at the same time in the same environment for the same amount of time for a number of weeks.

I heard Ellen Degeneres on her show explaining that she was trying to learn meditation or yoga ever since it had been recommended to her. She then verbalized the thoughts that went through her mind as she tried it. It was very much like my experience and went something like this:

*Calmmmm…*this sure is a comfortable chair…
*Calmmmm…*wow I can't believe how big that bird was this morning…
*Calmmmm…*did I turn off the stove this morning…
*Calmmmm…*wonder who's on my show tomorrow…
*Calmmmm…*think I'm going to get sued over my last comment
        yesterday…
*Calmmmm…*what should I wear to the movies tonight…

Calmmmm…is Portia going to drive or should we take a cab…
Calmmmm…is a thong as uncomfortable as it looks…
Calmmmm…what do I want for lunch today?… Calmmmm…

Ellen is very distractible and energetic too. It is tough for some of us to get focused and shut down the chatter in our mind even for a short time. For this reason, the other parts of the process need to be in place to try to help offset this.

Q. What if I can't reach a quiet, relaxed state?

Very few people start out being able to reach this deep state right away, but if you keep at it you will improve. Don't punish yourself for not being able to quiet your mind. It takes practice at first, but then it becomes a habit. Penalizing yourself is not helpful. Support your effort by blowing off the distraction and quickly returning to your calm state of mind with appropriate breathing. Our minds are very busy in today's world, so force it to be clutter-free with practice.

Q. How long do I need to do this to start benefiting?

This technique, like the others, requires more than 30 consecutive days of continuous use to start showing the benefits. You will find that you have good days and bad days, in large part based on what you are involved with during the day. If something is already on my mind and bothering me, it is tough to empty my mind of that subject. It is also helpful to experiment with different times during the day to see what is best for you.

Q. This seems out there; what if people make fun of me?

Truth be known, I used to make fun of it a little myself, but now I'm a believer. I have experienced a couple of decades of life since then and now think more for myself and less about what I perceive others think about me. I have met more interesting people, become more open to different ideas, and seen the negative effects of stress. I have also learned that you shouldn't be afraid to be a little different and try something new. Acting outside of your comfort zone may be a risk but it is great for your personal growth. Taking risks may cause you to make some minor mistakes, but will allow you to learn to embrace them.

I have been around many uptight business people in corporate settings who go off on little things because they are under constant pressure with no relief. They tend to pass judgment on people who have not taken their path, yet their stress levels stay high and most are not happy. They live within defined boundaries and their thinking becomes very limited and stifled. Those are the people who seem silly now; not those who take control of their life by setting their own goals and applying these techniques to reach them. The people I have seen that are good at meditation and yoga are much more comfortable being themselves, regardless of whether some limited thinker passes judgment (which is better than gas) on them.

WhaT WouLD JEFF Do?
(Fun action steps to try this stuff out)

1. Carve out at least 20 minutes of quiet time each day. Try some of the simple meditation steps I outline and eliminate the noise in your life for that period of time. Continue this to reach your inner self and follow its direction.

2. Continue to practice this meditative technique to block out all distractions, getting more "in tune" with yourself daily.

3. Set up your environment as best as possible and sample different times of the day to determine what time is best, then schedule meditation just like any other appointment.

4. Practice your breathing until it comes naturally. Find a mantra that assists you in reaching this quiet state.

5. Track your time if you believe you don't have 20 minutes daily to devote to yourself and your health. Find the time by eliminating something that is less important or can be delegated.

6. Sample a yoga class or yoga DVD and see if that is a better method for you to reach this quiet state. Do what works best for you.

Once you've finished these steps, write me to let me know what happened and what you learned at *stories@lifescheatsheets.com*.

Now, think like Nike and Just Do It!

"100% of the shots you do not take don't go in."

"Life gives you time and space; you decide how to fill it."

"Learn as if you were going to live forever.
Live as if you were going to die tomorrow."

iDeal Daily Routine for, Success

I'm ending the mind control section with a quick summary of the techniques and a guide on how to pull them all together and utilize them as a group to grow daily.

Q. How does this routine help me accomplish more?

Recall that the conscious and subconscious minds (SM) are different. The SM doesn't have the power of reason, so it doesn't question what it is fed. It believes what you tell it to be true and goes about gathering information that supports it being true. Therefore, if you feed it positive, uplifting messages daily that assist you in pursuing your desires, your SM will work for you regularly. You will start completing tasks that move you closer to your goals and improve your overall demeanor. Eliminating much of the negative information that you feed it right now will allow you to expedite tasks to eventually complete your goals.

These techniques will set up your mind to succeed in whatever you do each day. They will help start you out on the right foot with a positive attitude from the start of the day. They don't cost much, if anything, and they don't take a lot of time. So you have nothing to lose and everything to gain from incorporating these activities into your daily routine. Don't worry if you forget or occasionally miss a step once you have been doing them for a few months. Just pick it back up and move forward.

Q. What daily routine do you recommend?

I recommend you start by reading your goals, saying your affirmations, and doing your visualizations each day since they work together to help you achieve your goals. Finding quiet time each day for meditation, feeding yourself positive information, releasing mental clutter, and completing entries in your gratitude and success journals should all be added as quickly as you can. Maybe you can add some of these as a weekly or every other day activity to start. These activities may be second in priority, but they are still important for creating the right mental demeanor.

Converting negative thoughts to positive right when you think them and taking action steps are two daily activities that you need to do regularly, but you will not do them in one setting like the others. You need to work them in as positive habits that kick in naturally as needed.

Start by reducing the amount of negative news you take in and replacing that information with positive, growth materials. Utilizing the releasing and forgiving techniques I outlined in Chapter 3 will further this transition.

Q. How do these techniques help me overcome challenges?

As you train your mind to think positively daily, you will become more confident and receive more positive comments from others who will notice the difference in you. Your self-esteem will grow, and with this stronger, more confident mind, you will respond to issues directly without procrastinating and letting them overwhelm you.

Please realize you will still run into challenges. View them as new opportunities to grow and learn, and remain focused on the goal so that you will overcome them. You will adopt a "try another way" mentality to overcome any difficulties.

Q. Should I wait to start these until I learn more about them?

I have to confess I am guilty of a little too much analysis at times before I get started on something new. I've found that it's wise to get rolling with these techniques right away and start practicing them. Build them into your daily routine. You can always add to them, revise them, and eliminate those that are not effective for you at a particular point in your life; but the routine will already be in place. Keep them in mind, though, as you may later find that a technique you previously eliminated can push you toward a new goal. The key is to get started and stay with it for more than 30 days to begin seeing some of the benefits.

Q. Will my life be great if I use these techniques?

You will still face obstacles, and the reality is that some of them may ultimately be insurmountable, so you will have to revise your plan. An injury may prevent you from going pro. A credit crisis may prevent you from buying a home as soon as you would like. Your family circumstances may interfere with your dream of traveling the world. Nevertheless, with a positive attitude, confidence, and the peace of mind that you develop with these techniques, you will be equipped to handle life's setbacks. You will more easily adapt by revising your goals to enrich your life. You will persevere and achieve what is most important to you, even if your priorities change.

This is an exciting time if you have not previously used these techniques. You will start learning a lot of new, helpful information that will help you grow as a person. Moreover, when you are achieving your goals and feeling on top of the world, these techniques will strengthen your resolve, help you in taking calculated risks, and remind you to take time to appreciate all that you have.

Nurture the belief that you can overcome anything life presents to you and that you can achieve just about anything you set your mind to, regardless of what happens around you. When you are faced with a difficult situation, greater confidence will stimulate you to dig in and solve the problem rather than run (fight rather than flight). A helpful affirmation for this is, "I feel great because I can handle anything."

Take responsibility for your actions and recognize that you are in control of your life. You are not merely controlled by outside influences. Remember E + R = O. Life is a series of [E]vents, and for each one, you must choose what your [R]eaction will be, which determines the [O]utcome. So choose a constructive reaction and you control the outcome. Your self-image and demeanor determine how you are treated by others, how you present yourself, and whether your interactions are positive or not, so continually develop these areas throughout life. With this assertive, confident attitude, you will accomplish much more than you thought possible.

Q. Where can I learn more about these techniques?

This book only provides the basics about these techniques so that you can start using them right away as your foundation. You can take these to an advanced level. Many self-help teachers have their own programs and can share information on their specific techniques. Visit your local bookstores, search online, see if community organizations offer classes on these topics, keep an eye out for materials at garage sales or auctions, and of course, check your library for free resources.

These are not new concepts. Mind control has just become more well-known with the popular movie and book called *The Secret* by Rhonda Byrne. These techniques are closely tied to the law of attraction, which is the dominant concept in the movie. Rhonda has pulled a number of self-help specialists together to teach these concepts. A quick online search will link you to these professionals.

If you would like more black-and-white examples of how this can work for you, other experts including Jack Canfield, Mark Victor Hansen, Bob Proctor, John Assaraf, Michael Beckwith, John Gray, Marci Shimoff, and Joe Vitale offer numerous success stories of students who have experienced unique and powerful changes in their lives as a result of using these techniques. Most of these students were not rich or famous before using the techniques, but had excelled far beyond their goals after applying them in their life. I was skeptical initially, but after hearing from so many people I had to at least give it a try.

A Lesson I Learned from "The Street"

If you are a people person who needs some interaction daily and you work independently or from a home office, you will probably need to use these techniques even more. You will find that you really need to motivate yourself when you don't have supervisors or co-workers to encourage you each day. I struggled with this for a number of years after law school. For 18 years I had run good-sized companies where I could regularly bounce ideas off others, get their opinions if I was stuck, get some positive reinforcement and compliments on specific tasks or projects, and generally share with others.

If you have your own business, no one is going to check on you, no one is going to care whether you get anything done, and you don't have to report to anyone or explain your actions. Motivational materials can help you overcome feelings of isolation, lack of support, and mild depression that accompany this situation. You can also join groups, sports, associations, etc., to get the interaction you are lacking.

WhaT WOuLD JEFF Do?
(Fun action steps to try this stuff out)

1. Start your daily routine today, using your affirmations, pictures, and goals at a minimum (you can modify your goals once you complete the next chapter). Take your time with each one to really experience it fully.

2. Implement one of the methods I outline for converting and eliminating negative thoughts to fill your mind with more positive thoughts each day.

3. Adopt the "try another way" mentality to overcome speed bumps and road blocks along the way to accomplishing your goals.

4. Remember the E + R = O formula and take responsibility for your actions and reactions.

5. Listen to some of the teachers of *The Secret* and see if their materials help you with specific areas where you want to grow further.

Include your family or roommates in all of these exercises because you've learned something that can help them. Once you've finished these steps, write me to let me know what happened and what you learned at *stories@lifescheatsheets.com.*

Now, think like Nike and Just Do It!

P.	Programming Your Mind
A.	Accelerate Success with Crucial Skills
L.	Life Planning 101

Blueprint to Success System

Section 2:
Accelerate Success
with Crucial Skills

In Chapters 9–15 I outline several crucial sets of skills that allow you to move forward quickly, accomplish more, and get what you want. You probably won't learn this stuff in school, but it can dramatically improve your life so it's very important to soak up this information now.

Converting Your Wishes into Reality: Dream-Big Goal Planning

Q. How do I set dream-big goals?

I recommend that you go through an exercise where you make a list of your 101 life goals. Eliminate any distractions, close your eyes, and let yourself imagine what you want to achieve in your life without any limiting thoughts. The bigger you think, the better. Stretch your comfort zone "to the max." Ignore thoughts like:

- How in the world am I going to do this?
- I have no clue how this could even happen.
- There is no way I can do this, but I would like to.
- People are going to think I am nuts to try this.
- This is way beyond what I can do.

The "how" part will come later as you continue to build habits and focus on your goals, so just trust me for now. There is no penalty for not reaching a particular goal. You will never know if you can do it until you decide you want to do it and move forward toward accomplishing it. I urge you to go through the exercise and put it in writing. Don't stop until you get all 101 goals on paper. Try to complete the list in one sitting, but it is OK to come back and add more to reach 101 if you can't finish the first time. Challenge yourself to finish by looking far beyond where you are now and picturing what you want to be, do, have, finish, achieve, etc.

A number of years ago, I went to a seminar at the University of Toledo where Mark Victor Hansen (co-author of the *Chicken Soup* series, *www.markvictorhansen.com*) was speaking about *The Power of Focus,* a book that he co-authored. He used this 101-goal exercise to get people to think big, way beyond their comfort zone. His whole program stressed the importance of setting goals, focusing on them, and building good habits to ensure you will reach them.

Make certain the goals that you write are truly your goals and not things that you believe someone else would like you to accomplish. You have to own these goals as your own and be passionate about accomplishing them.

What I have grown to understand over the last 25 years is that people can accomplish anything they truly set their mind to and take action to achieve. When you hear what many wealthy and famous people have overcome to get to where they are today, you can't believe the determination and drive they had to have to go from where they were to where they are. Read the background story of some famous people you like and you will find that many of them had to really believe in themselves and conquer huge obstacles to reach their current status.

Q. What are examples of big goals accomplished?

As mentioned earlier, Jack Canfield and Mark Victor Hansen's first *Chicken Soup* book was turned down by 144 publishers before one decided to take the chance and publish their book. They used goal setting and the other techniques explained in this book to convince themselves that they were going to find a publisher. They approached every contact they had, attended conventions, and displayed at book fairs, but kept getting turned down. Now their *Chicken Soup* series has sold more than 140 million books and their bigger goal for the series is to sell one billion (with a B) books by the end of 2020.

Did you know pro basketball superstar Michael Jordan got cut from the varsity basketball team in high school, but came in early and stayed after practice every night to continue to improve his game? He set aggressive goals, focused on them daily, worked very hard, and improved dramatically. He went on to become one of pro basketball's best players of all time and set records that will stand for many years.

Similarly, pro basketball superstar LeBron James set very high goals, coming from a rough part of Cleveland, Ohio, a couple of hours from me in Toledo. He practiced very hard, focusing on getting better daily. He succeeded so well in high school basketball that he skipped college and advanced directly to the pro draft. He had confidence in himself and a deep desire to play pro. He has excelled beyond belief at the professional level coming directly from high school, which is unheard of in that sport.

Briefly mentioned earlier, Jim Carey, star of *The Mask, Ace Ventura, Pet Detective, Liar, Liar,* and many other hit movies, was an unknown comedian when he decided to write himself a check for $10 million dated Thanksgiving, 1995 (about eight years in the future). He wrote in the memo blank on the check "acting services rendered." He carried that check in his wallet for years, looked at it daily, and pictured himself getting a real check for that amount for a hit movie. Ultimately, he got a break and signed a contract just before Thanksgiving, 1995, that paid him $10 million to star in *Dumb and Dumber.* Since then he has received multiple checks for twice as much money for additional hit movies. He had a goal, reminded himself of moving toward that goal every time he got out his wallet, and struck gold in the movies.

Q. How does limitation thinking affect my goals?

Most people's beliefs about their limitations are unfounded. They are the result of constant negative self-talk growing out of the false beliefs they have built into their subconscious mind (SM) from hearing negative or false statements in the past. Researchers have shown the average person has 30,000 to 40,000 negative thoughts per day. When parents say you can't, you won't be able to, you will never, and the like, the SM accepts those statements and forms a belief that they're true. Unlike the conscious mind, the SM has no reasoning ability, so it takes in information and believes it is true, regardless of its content. It then works non-stop to make that information true. You may have heard "what you think is what you become." That is true. Whether you think you can or think you can't, you're right. By implementing the techniques described in this book for at least 30 consecutive days, you can program your SM to help you reach your goals by changing your false beliefs and removing limitations.

One of the most common areas of limitation thinking is with money. Most people have a goal to make more money and build wealth. But most people earn low to middle incomes and have been raised in that environment, so they typically have limiting beliefs about money. Think back to comments your parents may have made about money and wealthy people as you were growing up, and write them down. Some common examples are:

- There's not enough money to go around
- Money is the root of all evil
- People with money are greedy and unethical
- You are selfish if you make a lot of money
- You don't deserve to have luxuries like that
- Those things are only for the rich
- Rich people lie, cheat, and steal
- Very few people can be rich and you're not one of them
- Money doesn't grow on trees
- Rich people take advantage of others
- You can't make any more than your parents do

Now write true statements that contradict your specific limiting beliefs and commit to making these new beliefs your reality. Really believe these statements as you say them aloud. Samples of typical contradicting statements are:

- There is plenty of money for everyone
- Money allows me to enjoy life and help others
- Rich people are generous and upstanding people

- I work smart and make lots of money because of it
- I have money to buy anything I want
- I have all of the money and material things I ever wanted
- Rich people are honest and earn their income
- Anyone who wants to can be rich
- Plenty of money flows to me effortlessly
- I am wealthy and liked by others
- I happily make as much money as I want

Include positive money statements like these in the affirmations you wrote in Chapter 5. Make certain your statements support you making lots of money. Not just some money to get by, but a boatload of money. There's no reason you can't be filthy stinking rich and be a good, generous, honest person. Repeating these statements multiple times daily will work to replace those limiting ones you have carried around for years and allow you to see yourself building wealth as reality.

Q. Why do I need to write SMART goals?

A well-tested technique for setting your goals is to set SMART goals. This stands for Specific, Measurable, Attainable, Realistic, and Timely. When setting goals with this method, you are more likely to work toward them because you will be able to clearly understand and visualize the completed goal. Make certain all of your goals pass the SMART test once you have written them and you will be well on your way toward achieving great things.

A [S]pecific goal has a much greater chance of being accomplished. To set a specific goal you need to answer as many of the six "W" questions as apply: Who?, What?, Where?, When?, Which?, and Why?. For example, "I want to lose weight" is a general goal. "I want to lose 20 pounds by [fill in date]" is more specific. After you set your goal, list as many reasons why you want to attain that goal. For this example, your list might include:

- So I can fit in my black, size eight holiday dress
- So I will feel more alive and happy
- So I won't be as sleepy in the early afternoon

- So I can work out for an hour without getting winded
- So I can swim laps in the pool without feeling self-conscious
- So I can increase my confidence and accomplish more
- So I can start the new year trim and feeling great
- So my spouse will see me as sexy again
- So I can look great in my size eight jeans again
- So my back will ache less by the end of the day
- So I can start running two miles daily again
- So I will have more energy to play with my kids, etc.

Really challenge yourself with your why-list and be specific with each one. The more reasons you can list why you want to achieve your goal, the stronger support you will have for reaching that goal, so make it a convincing list. You will have ups and downs when working on your goals. You want as much motivation behind you as you can muster while you are taking action to achieve your goals, so come up with as many whys as you can. The "whys" build your case for completing the goal. If you want to quit, go read your why-list for that goal. This should motivate you to get back on the horse and move forward.

Establish concrete criteria for [M]easuring progress toward the attainment of each goal. When you measure your progress, you are more likely to stay on track, reach your target dates, and experience the exhilaration of achievement, which spurs you on to reach your goal. To determine if your goal is measurable, ask questions such as: How much? How many? How will I know when it is accomplished?

You can [A]ttain most any goal when you plan your steps wisely and establish a time frame that allows you to carry out those steps. Once you've identified the goals that are most important to you, you will begin to figure out ways to make them come true. You develop the attitudes, abilities, skills, and financial capacity to reach them. You begin seeing previously overlooked opportunities, bringing yourself closer to the achievement of your goals. Goals that may have seemed far away and out of reach eventually start to seem attainable, not because you lower your expectations, but because you have to grow as a person in order to reach your goals. When you list your goals, you build your self-image. You see yourself as worthy of these goals, and develop the traits that allow you to reach them.

To be [R]ealistic, a goal must represent an objective that you are both *willing* and *able* to work toward. A goal can be both high and realistic. You are the only one who can decide just how high your goal should be. Be sure that every goal represents substantial progress. A high goal is frequently easier to reach than a low one because a low goal exerts low motivational force. Some of the hardest tasks you've ever accomplished may actually seem easy, simply because you were very motivated to complete them. Your goal is probably realistic if you truly *believe* that it can be accomplished. Additional ways to know if your goal is realistic is to ask yourself what conditions would have to exist to accomplish this goal then see if those conditions are possible.

A goal should be grounded within a specific [T]ime frame. With no time frame, there's no sense of urgency. If you want to lose 20 pounds, when do you want to lose it by? "Someday" won't work because it is not specific. If you tie a specific month, day, and year to it, then you've set your unconscious mind into motion to begin working on the goal. If you don't complete the goal by your initial date, review where you are with the goal and reset the time frame to one that you can work with. This will keep you moving forward toward that specific goal. Don't punish yourself, just recognize what you have gotten done, what you have to do yet, and establish a path for completing it.

The 'T' can also stand for [T]angible, which allows you to experience it with one of the senses (taste, touch, smell, sight, or hearing). When your goal is tangible you have a better chance of making it specific and measurable and thus attainable.

Q. Is there a goal-setting process you recommend?

In addition to writing SMART goals, it is helpful to follow a process so you complete your goals. I agree with another author, Ronald Miller, about the process for goal setting. In his book *It Works,* he outlines the process in more detail and explains how to program your mind to work daily toward accomplishing your goals. We principally agree on the following process for goal setting and successful achievement:

1. Begin with an intense desire and a 100%, absolute belief in your goal
2. Write it down and post it to see it daily
3. List reasons why you want to accomplish your goal and the associated benefits
4. Determine where you are starting from and set an assertive deadline
5. List the obstacles to achieving the goal that you will overcome
6. Identify any other information, goods, and people's help you will need
7. Draft your plan and the tasks needed to accomplish it
8. Visualize the goal accomplished in as much detail as possible, using all of your senses
9. Decide to never give up

As you can see there is some overlap with mind programming because those techniques also involve your goals. If this seems like a lot of steps, realize you don't need to spend lots of time on each step, but it is helpful to work through each of them quickly so that you really commit to each goal and have a good handle on what it will take to complete it. If you find you can skip a step or two and still complete it, have at it. Taking this action puts you on a path to accomplish your desires.

Since this chapter is longer than most, if you need an infor-mation overload break for awhile, or a plain old potty break, this is a good place to do it. Then, you will be refreshed for the second half of this section. [No need to thank me.]

Q. Why do I need multiple sets of goals?

Once you understand how to write your goals, you will also need to understand that some will be short-term (less than one year), some will be mid-term (one to five years), and others will be longer-term (over five years). If you label them this way, you will know which ones to prioritize and start working on now. This allows you to focus on the most pressing ones and put the longer-term goals in perspective.

Your goals will continue to change as you change, so continue to revise your goal list as needed. Review your deadlines each month or quarter to determine whether you are still on track or if you need to revise them. Don't be concerned about revisions. They will change several times as you learn more and see how long tasks are taking. Update your list each year. This is a normal process for goals. Once you reach a goal, see if it is the type of goal that you can revise to reach higher and further. Think bigger than you did when you originally set it. If you can reach further, set the higher goal and replace the completed one. You may add or subtract goals as your priorities and interests change, and as you experience more of life. Stay on track and monitor your progress.

Once you have succeeded in reaching a goal, stop to recognize yourself for reaching it. Look back at the path you took to reach it and celebrate your accomplishment. This step is very helpful for building your confidence and showing yourself that you can expand your abilities and reach high. It is also helpful to write down your thoughts and experiences along the way then go back and read the journal when you accomplish a goal. This step gives you more courage to go further.

Q. Why do I need to put balance in my life?

In addition to different timelines with your goals, you should try to maintain balance in your life by setting goals in several different areas that make your life full and complete. Typical areas to set goals in include (in no particular order):

- Finances
- Professional and Career
- Relationships and Social Interactions
- Family and Friends
- Spiritual and Inner Self

- Relaxation, Fun and Hobbies
- Giving Back (helping others)
- Health and Fitness
- Intellectual and Personal Growth

Adapt the areas to make sense in your life. Take some time away every three months (quarterly) to review how you are doing, update your goals, confirm that you have balance and are not heavily skewed toward one area, and revise your course as needed to stay on track. With balance, one area might not be going well, but the others are typically OK. You won't focus so heavily on the one negative area because it is offset by all of the other positive areas. This is a similar concept to diversifying investments where some will be up, some will be down, and others neutral.

One area to be careful with is your profession. Don't allow yourself to be controlled by a limited-income job demanding all of your waking time. I've done this, and you lose touch with others. It skews the balance in your life if you put too much emphasis on one area. If that area has problems, if the company goes out of business, or you lose your job, it throws your whole life off. You react much worse, and I know of people who committed suicide after losing a job. Life is much bigger than a job, so keep that balance in mind as you commit more time to your career. With many more businesses closing, downsizing, and going bankrupt, it is becoming much more obvious that everyone's job is potentially temporary, and the days of working for one or two companies for your whole working life are over. This also makes it very important to become financially independent as quickly as possible through your own businesses and investments. This is another reason I highly recommend reading my follow up *financial habits* book.

An additional technique to make goal setting more specific is to give each goal a level of importance, or "weight," from most important to least important. With this weight system, you can allocate your time according to your weights within each area and focus on attaining certain goals more quickly than others.

Q. Why do I need to write and read my goals so often?

One of the keys to goal accomplishment is to write your SMART goals on paper because the process triggers positive actions in your mind that assist you in accomplishing your goals. They must be written in the present tense with plenty of detail so you have a crystal clear picture of it being accomplished. As I said before, you should read them aloud morning, mid-day, and at night (three times) with enthusiasm. If you write your most current goals on index cards and carry them with you, you have a better chance of reading them regularly. Picture each one completed and feel the emotions tied to it.

Studies show that between 2 to 5% of all people actually write their goals down and less than 1% of these people review them daily. Not surprisingly, the people who write goals down report progress, and those who review them regularly report achieving more goals than any other group by a significant margin. The process commits you to your goals much more than just letting them randomly enter your mind. This process implants them in your subconscious mind and causes that portion of your mind to work on them day and night.

In *Freedom from Fear Forever* (a follow-up to *Freedom from Fear;* website *www.MattesonAvenue.com*) author Mark Matteson has a dashboard decree technique where he has you post your most important goal (that will make the biggest impact on your life) on your dashboard so you will see it multiple times per day when you are in the car. This technique will let your mind continue to burn that goal into your subconscious mind. You will use time you are already spending while driving to and from work, the grocery store, and dry cleaners to better your life. You could adapt it to include a few of your most important goals also. His books are very inspirational and all about living your life to the fullest. Don't sit on the sidelines; take control of your life.

Mark Victor Hansen (mentioned earlier) recommends writing your most important goal (he calls it your Big, Hairy, Audacious

Goal (BHAG)), on a special business card you carry with you, saying it aloud at least three times daily. Picture it as if it were accomplished, and recognize all of the details in the picture with as many senses as you can. Whichever of these techniques work for you, do them. You will probably need to try several and continue to weed out ones you don't follow, keeping those that you do put into practice.

Q. How can I keep my list of goals current?

Once you accomplish a goal, don't just stop there. See what else you want to accomplish beyond that goal and start taking action to reach the next level. In the summer of 2008, I was at the Jamie Farr LPGA women's golf tournament which is held in Toledo each year. Paula Creamer is a pretty, young pro, then 21 years old, who wears a lot of pink that matches our local Owens Corning (OC) Pink Panther mascot. She is a local favorite since OC typically sponsors part of the tournament.

In the first round, she shot an 11 under par 60 (par is the typical number of strokes for each hole if you are very proficient and have become a professional at golf) for the course record and was one stroke off the lowest score in LPGA history in a pro tournament. I was near her when she finished, and she was swarmed by cameras, microphones, autograph seekers, and personal bodyguards (who were needed) to keep people away. As soon as she was done with all of them, the bodyguards escorted her to the driving range, where she started hitting practice balls to gear up for the next day's round. It was inspiring to see her determination, focus, and maturity at such a young age. She could have gone out partying after accomplishing her goal of shooting a record round, but she stayed focused on her bigger goal of winning that tournament, and she ultimately did.

The point is that you can always think bigger. Once you've accomplished one goal, think of how you can expand on that, move to another goal you have not worked on, or add a new goal that has come to you upon finishing this one. Always move forward and grow. Life will be exhilarating.

Q. What mind programming will help me achieve my goals?

Once you understand the programming techniques covered in previous chapters, you will realize the vast power you have within yourself. You will not need to depend on others to accomplish what you desire. Those techniques specifically tied to your goals include affirmations, meditation, and visualizations. All of the other techniques improve your demeanor and help you to accomplish more which, in turn, helps you complete many of your goals.

Q. Why do I need to take action now?

If you only write your goals down and stick them in a drawer, without implementing any of these other techniques, you obviously will not be much further than you were before writing them down. Action is the key to everything. Taking clear, focused action daily will help you to complete your goals. You'll find there are lots of "talkers" in life, but very few "doers." Associate with those who take action and accomplish what they set out to do.

Procrastination is another goal killer for many people. If you have a tendency to procrastinate, break tasks into mini-tasks and include multiple mini-tasks on your "to do" list daily. By the end of the week, month, then year, you will see you have completed many tasks and will be building the habit of taking action, overwriting your inclination to procrastinate. Read some articles and books on overcoming procrastination if you still struggle. You will also find that no one is going to take action to reach your goals for you, so you are going to have to do it yourself. You care most about reaching your goals, so you need to put the most effort into reaching them.

Q. What if my goals seem overwhelming?

When you break your goals down into daily tasks, you will see that you can complete these smaller tasks without a huge effort. With only one a day, in a month, you will have 30 or more tasks completed that will bring you that much closer to completing your goals. But, make certain you break the goal into achievable tasks. You will find that your mind accepts these smaller tasks much easier than a big goal that it doesn't know how to accomplish. This keeps you from being stuck at the starting line and gets you moving forward.

Q. What traits are important for achieving my goals?

Consistent perseverance and persistence are two qualities that you'll need to complete your bigger goals. You need to have the mentality that quitting is not an option. You never know if your next action step will move you much further along. There will be steps that don't seem to move you further, but taking action toward the goal is all you need to do daily. Water boils at 212 degrees, but doesn't at 211 degrees. That one degree is all it takes to accomplish the goal. There will be many steps to most significant goals so just remember that the next step could really advance you toward accomplishing that goal. Using the other techniques mentioned earlier, and tying strong emotions to each goal will also help you continue to move forward.

Q. Why do I need to do what others are unwilling to do?

Something that usually separates people who accomplish a lot in their life from those who don't is their willingness to do what others are unwilling to do. Michael Phelps, famous Olympic medalist in swimming, had a coach who always pushed him beyond what others were doing. Michael would also push himself and practice more than others, never taking his focus off winning the Olympic events and being the best swimmer in the world. Michael Jordan, the most famous pro basketball player of all time, was always the first at practice and the last to leave. Tiger Woods was practicing when he was three years old and continued to practice his entire childhood, getting better and better, and now he has set most of the PGA golf records and is ranked #1 in the world. You may feel it was easy for these athletes, as if they were simply born with a supernatural ability, but each one clearly worked harder than almost everyone else to get to where they are today.

Many of the tasks needed to move toward your goals will be difficult to accomplish and will take you out of your comfort zone. You need to move forward regardless and work through the uncertainty, taking one step at a time. Belief in yourself and your goals will help you move forward. On my desk, I have a rock from *www.successories. com* (a great store) with the inscription, "Real leaders are ordinary people with extraordinary determination." I firmly believe that and have followed it in my life.

Q. Can this really change my life?

If you follow these techniques and ingrain your goals into your subconscious mind you will get into a habit of taking action that will move you toward accomplishing them. You will create much more depth in your life, you will see more, do more, and accomplish much more than you ever thought possible. You will continue to grow throughout your whole life and live a more full life. You will replace bad habits with good ones and continue to use these new habits to grow further. People will notice a difference in you and your demeanor once you incorporate these techniques in your daily life. You will wonder how you ever got things done without them.

Q. Why is it important to learn these techniques early in life?

It is best to implement these techniques as early in your life as you can. The longer you wait the more fear builds up inside your head and stunts your growth. Having gone through several bad experiences a number of years ago, I became much more conservative and negative, believing that I had to protect what I had rather than expand. Fear had built up because of this string of bad experiences despite exceptional effort that I had put toward my goals. I used these techniques to combat my fear and create better habits.

If you start learning and using these techniques early in life, you will spend less time developing poor habits that you later have to overcome. You will limit the negative self-talk that impedes your goals and impairs your self-confidence and have more years ahead of you to achieve more goals. It's never too late to use this information, but the sooner you start, the better you'll be able to make use of your opportunities. Why spend years making mistakes, beating yourself up and digging yourself out of a hole when you can start improving the quality of your life now?

Q. How do I deal with others who are naysayers?

I have been focusing on personal development for a number of years now. I have noticed that many people who have not learned or practiced these techniques are skeptical and negative much of the time. It is said that you are a product of the five to ten people you are around the most. In my own life, I have come to realize how important it is to surround myself with positive influences.

If you start recognizing that your family and friends are not supporting you, that they are naysayers and skeptics who create fear rather than lending support, you need to consider spending less time or sharing less of your ideas with them. I have purposely limited my interaction and ignored input from people close to me who were negative about every new idea and endeavor that I researched or tried that didn't fit their way of thinking. I have shared less of my thoughts with those individuals because they are conservative and cannot share my expansive mentality. If you run into this situation, you have to continue to believe in your goals and move forward, regardless of their support.

Fear of failure is one of the top fears of most people. This tends to grow as you take on more responsibilities and have a family to support. Uncertainty breeds more fear and it grows when others around you are naysayers about your ideas and actions. Some will not want you to grow because that will make you more accomplished than they are. Or they may feel threatened by your new-found confidence, not wanting to admit that they are too fearful to go for their goals. It is a vicious cycle you have to remove yourself from, or you will continue to follow the path of fear.

A job and steady paycheck can actually build this fear because you may structure your lifestyle to become dependent on that company and your income from it. With all of the bankruptcies, downsizing, and businesses eliminating jobs, the workforce has become more and more fearful. They realize their dependence on their income is in jeopardy, which increases their fear of loss.

I fought this way of thinking for years as I faced difficulties in my extensive occupation search after law school, outlined in Chapter 11. I had to negate this job dependency mentality many times before looking at other income avenues that would not leave me so dependent. Ultimately, you need to establish multiple streams of income (explained in Chapter 16 and further in the follow-up *financial habits* book). Maybe open a side business or be self-employed entirely, maybe get a sales or incentive-based job that has strong income potential and a flexible schedule, make your investments in different, diversified vehicles, etc. These are all ways you can break out of the one-job, one-income model that may be the only possibility programmed in your mind.

Q. How do I overcome my fear of failure?

FEAR is "False Experience Appearing Real." More than 90% of the time, your fears and worries don't occur at all, and in the 10% of the time they do occur, they are not as bad as your imagination makes them out to be. Look at your fear and try to recognize what is the worst that realistically could happen if you took the risk you are considering. Usually this allows you to recognize that the worst is not that bad and you can deal with it.

One way to combat fear is to plan to do things that involve calculated risks each day, then do those things right away in the morning. If you do them early in the day, you won't build them up in your mind and put more pressure on yourself. What you do later in the day will seem easier. These don't have to be huge risks. In fact, you should start with smaller risks to tone yourself for bigger risks as you go forward. Examples of these:

- Asking a girl for a date
- Calling a company to find out about a job
- Inquiring about a property that you heard was for sale by owner

- Taking the lead on a work project
- Cooking with a new recipe
- Calling on a new apartment for rent, etc.

The key is to step outside of your comfort zone daily, and preferably multiple times daily, so you expand your mind and your life. You will experience more and become more knowledgeable about many different things, and your fear level will be reduced. If you do the same things the same way you will get the same results. Are those the results you desire, or do you want more?

Resist becoming too cautious about trying something just because it might not work. Failing is really just learning what doesn't work, and you will make a more informed decision next time. Thomas Edison was unsuccessful more than 10,000 times while trying to invent the light bulb. (Loser? NO!) When asked how he could go on failing so much, he said, "I never failed, I just learned 10,000 ways it didn't work so I knew what not to try next." (Go Tommy, Go Tommy) There are no guarantees in most of your life. The more you try, the more successful you can become. If you resist taking risks, you will be assured to accomplish very little.

Q. Why should I believe in this and give it a try?

These life skills are missing from our schools' curriculum, but they clearly shouldn't be. These skills can take a life that is mediocre and make it awesome. You will be able to accomplish and experience so much more if you just follow the techniques in this book and the *financial habits* follow-up book. Unfortunately, calculus, history, chemistry, and the other required subjects have continued to override other real life skills that could, by far, assist young adults more than most of these subjects. Since it is missed in school, most adults don't learn or implement these skills. This is one reason we have so many people who are not happy with life and why we are in an economic crisis. We need an overhaul of our curriculum to incorporate these subjects because they help us to overcome the challenges that, in one form or another, every one of us will face.

A Lesson I Learned from "The Street"

I went through a stage when I was overly cautious and my perfection-ist traits limited me. It was tough to move beyond my fear of not making the "right" decision, of losing, of not reaching my goal, and failing. I had actually taken more risk earlier in life and succeeded very early. As I look back, I see I had succeeded many times in a row without any big setbacks so I had ignored the possibility of not succeeding. I ultimately backed off on several investments and became very hesitant after I tried a few things that didn't work out. I ran into liars, big talkers, and shady sales people. I consulted on risky projects and business turnarounds where an owner or President controlled key areas that caused projects to fall apart after I had invested a lot of my time, so I didn't get the return on any money and all of the time I had invested. You will find that life is rarely black-and-white. You need to read between the lines, pick up non-verbal cues, and follow your instinct as well as clearly investigate (due diligence) whatever you are considering.

Living through too many of these discouraging experiences, and lack-ing significant, positive experiences to offset them, caused me to become more skeptical. I have learned that you have to fight this tendency, get back on the horse, and believe that the next project will work out. You can't let the projects that go south dictate your future. Those are a part of your past that you can't change, but you can use them as learning experi-ences for a better future. The techniques in this book will not only help you achieve your goals, they will help you get back on track when you are not successful in getting the results you want. Sometimes, timing isn't right. But if you keep your eye on your goals, you will continue working toward them or they may even point you to something better on the horizon.

These techniques don't take much time to learn. Just compare them to daily volleyball or basketball practice and you will see they take minimal time. In fact, compare it to the time that you spend talking to or texting your friends, playing around online, and just "hanging out." The biggest difference is that these techniques will take your life so much further than those activities. They will keep you positive and optimistic.

Even if you don't reach all of your goals on your initial timeline, you will accomplish much more than you would have without these habits in place. When it works you will be impressed with yourself, which will motivate you to accomplish even more. I know this from my actual experiences in my 20s and 30s. This will be a life-changing experience that you will never want to stop. You will be surprised at how much you expand your goals, once you start accomplishing some that you didn't think you could. Go, step out of your comfort zone, and enjoy life to its fullest.

Please share:
I'd love to hear what you have accomplished, so take a moment to send me an e-mail at stories@lifescheatsheets.com and tell me what your couple biggest goals were, how you accomplished them, and what you overcame to do so. Add this phrase in your e-mail: "I consent to have Jeff Wilson and his companies share my story in his materials." I want to share them and need your permission to show others what you have done and how these techniques really work. Don't worry; I'll protect you and won't list your personal information.

WhaT WoULD JEFF Do?
(Fun action steps to try this stuff out)

1. Set time aside to complete your 101 goal list. It will change regularly, but if you get it down now, you will have started the journey toward accomplishing your goals.

2. Complete the exercise about limiting money beliefs, write your new, contradicting statements, and include the most compelling ones in your daily affirmations. Work to change your mind in this area.

3. Write down your top 10 S.M.A.R.T. goals today. If you have more, write those down too. Feel free to follow the sample process or use your own method, but make certain they pass the S.M.A.R.T. test.

4. Now put your goals into the different categories of your life. Use the list I provided or create your own. This will let you determine if you have balance in your life or if you need to make some changes. Feel free to add and subtract goals as applicable to your life and keep your list updated so you are focused.

5. Now you have all of the pieces you need to focus on daily (goals, affirmations, visions). Read through these and truly experience them multiple times each day. This process will embed them in your mind and help you accomplish them.

6. Once you've completed a goal, stop and celebrate, congratulating yourself on your accomplishment. Journey back in your mind and review the steps you had to take to accomplish it. If you journaled your experience, re-read that journal to build your confidence. Now think bigger and replace the goal with a new, bigger goal that will take more action to accomplish.

7. Analyze the people you spend the most time with and if they are negative or naysayers, change something about that situation so you are less influenced by them. Maybe learn how to change the subject or tune them out if they start down the negative path.

8. Implement the calculated risks process into your regular day and get outside of your comfort zone a few times a day. You will grow each time you do.

See if your family and friends have specific goals. If not, help them with this area because you've learned something that can now help them. Once you've finished these steps, write me to let me know what happened and what you learned at *stories@ lifescheatsheets.com.*

Now, think like Nike and Just Do It!

"People don't plan to fail, they fail to plan."

"Courage is not the absence of fear; it is the mastery of it."

"Burying your talents is a grave mistake."

Build Your Intrinsic Value With Marketing and Sales Savvy

Q. Why does everyone need these basic skills?

Marketing and sales skills are a must if you have your own business or work in a smaller business where everyone interacts with customers. Cash flow is king in any business and these skills get that cash flowing in. Whether you are your own boss or work for someone else, your ability to generate more income for your employer through marketing and sales efforts will make the business more successful, making you a more valuable employee. You will also improve communication skills as you focus on effectively interacting with your target audience. You can also apply these skills to market yourself to prospective employers through job applications and interviews.

But these skills are also very helpful in other aspects of life, even beyond the employment context. You can use them for selling items for school or sports fundraisers and garage sales, and selling bigger ticket items like homes and cars. A basic understanding of marketing and sales techniques will also make you a more savvy buyer and help you improve your negotiation skills. Developing these skills will help you generate more income and acquire more stuff. Who *wouldn't* want to learn how to do that? The one who dies with the most stuff wins, right? (Hint: it's a cheap bumper sticker saying.)

Q. How are these skills ultimately a key to my income?

As an owner or employee, building customer relationships is key. After all, sales to customers generate the income that allows the company to pay its operating expenses, its employees, and then its owners (in that order). If a business spends minimally or too much on ineffective marketing or has poor sales staff, it will not be successful in getting customers, it will not have sufficient cash flow to pay its bills and employees, and it probably won't remain in business.

Maintaining quality staff that effectively generates sales for the company is one of the initial keys to short-term survival as well as the long-term stability and growth of a business. All of the functions that follow the initial sale to a new customer must be carried out well or the customer will be lost. To be successful, the business must incorporate a customer service component into their sales process to make certain the customer is pleased with the goods and quickly resolve any problems that arise. Many different positions assist with this customer service role, so again, it is important for everyone to learn these basic skills.

Many surveys conclude that marketing to a new customer costs the company eight to ten times more than it costs to stay in touch with and maintain a current customer. Some companies just don't seem to understand this principle (e.g., cell phone companies that only give new customer incentives). It is important to build rapport over time and maintain long-term customers, while continuing to build and diversify the company's customer base. It may take quite a while to gain a new customer, but because a customer can be lost quickly, everyone needs to be in tune with marketing and sales functions.

Those things affect the company, so why should *I* care? If the company that you own or work for generates more income from effective marketing and sales efforts, it is more likely to stay in business, which means you get to keep your job and income. And if the company is financially successful, this may result in higher pay, better benefits, or perks for you. The company may be able to expand, creating oppor-tunities for you to advance to a better role. It may be possible for the company to afford to invest in better technology that will make your job easier. The company may be in a better position to contribute financially to a charity or cause that you support. More income may lead to happier management and more satisfied employees, making the workplace a more positive environment for you. The company may grow and expand to new geographic markets where you would like to relocate. By contributing to the success of the company, you may personally reap the benefits. These are skills that will help you become successful in other areas of your life, too.

Q. Aren't other people hired to handle these areas?

This old mindset is wrong, especially today when buyers have many choices, so businesses need to be ultra-competitive. Marketing and sales are the skill sets necessary for building a business and income, so if everyone has these skills, there is a much greater chance that the business will succeed. Large businesses can get away with having specific departments handle specific functions. But you will be more valuable to both large and small businesses if you have these skills.

Another reason to develop these skills is the fact that all busi-nesses must be lean. Everyone in the business must be focused on contributing to the bottom-line profit. Every employee and owner has the potential to influence customers positively or negatively and needs to act appropriately. Please understand I am not saying an engineer doesn't need engineering training. I am saying they should also have some marketing and sales skills.

Q. How can all employees apply these skills?

Treat every interaction as a potential marketing opportunity. Present your employer as an entity people would like to do business with by telling people what you do in a way that promotes the com-pany. For example, don't just tell people you're a cashier. Tell them you are a cashier for a company that offers great deals on office sup-plies. Don't just say you're a waitress. Tell them you're a waitress for an Italian restaurant with the best lasagna in town and great lunch specials. When asked, tell your friends, family, classmates, and even complete strangers what your company does.

Maybe you work for a nursing home and your aerobics instructor's father recently had a stroke and is need of rehabilitation. She won't know that you might be in a position to help them with a referral, potentially helping your company, unless you take the opportunity to talk about what you do in a favorable way. Be enthusiastic and be especially mindful of how you act while you are "in uniform" or otherwise reflecting your employer's image. If someone interacts with a rude slob wearing an ABC nametag or uniform, they aren't going to have a very good impression of ABC. Improving the public image of your employer is beneficial for you.

Just having a pleasant attitude and dealing with people in a positive way while performing your job can positively impact marketing and sales. I saw an example of a person in a non-traditional sales role assisting at my wife's law firm. They had a cute, blonde female receptionist (Sandy) who could carry on a conversation with most people; she was upbeat, spunky, and helped lighten the mood with visitors who were waiting. She also did a good job representing the firm as the first person people would talk with on the phone or in person.

She enhanced that firm's image, which is part of marketing, and helped visitors get started on the right foot by being pleasant and helpful. Her actions would put the visitor in a more positive mood, which could assist with resolving a dispute (one way to "close a sale" in a law firm). Recognize that many law firm visitors are parties to a lawsuit, so it can be a tense setting. Even in that unique environment, marketing skills helped this receptionist contribute value to the firm. Several visitors asked about her after she left and considered it a loss when she was no longer there to greet them with her pleasant demeanor.

My niece Stephanie has managed a couple of restaurants and is now a Culinary Institute of America trained chef and hostess at a high-end restaurant in New York City. I am certain that when she greets patrons with her curly blonde hair, cute outfits, and bubbly, up-beat demeanor, it puts them in a better mood, increases their spending at the restaurant, helps get the wait staff good tips and encourages the customers to return. She was recently honored with one of the highest awards for restaurant employees in the entire state of New York (out of several thousand applicants) so it's clear she has a big influence on marketing and sales even though it is not her primary role.

Talk with a crappy receptionist or have the janitorial service steal something or leave a dirty restroom without restocking the supplies, and you'll recognize how every employee can kill the company's image and sales as quickly as a poor salesperson can. Customers can be fickle and leave for the strangest reasons, so it's important for you to help bolster sales and maintain customer satisfaction, regardless of your title or position.

All employee-managers and owners need these skills and should always be using them with each of their contacts and conversations, regardless of their role in the business. I have seen people in traditional roles, like me, switch to marketing or sales because of the recognized importance of these components to the company and their abilities in the area.

Q. How can I use these skills to my advantage?

You can help your employer identify potential new customers. Look at whether certain groups might benefit from the goods or services that you offer. Can you market to a local school? Have you seen an ad in the paper for a trade show that might provide an opportunity for your company? Is there a local athletic team that the company can sponsor and offer t-shirts to get better name recognition? Does it make sense to propose a survey of existing customers to see how the company can improve its customer service and sales? You can also look for ways to cut costs for the company. Are you aware of an upcoming sale on items that your company uses? Do you know a classmate who can get the company a deal on insurance? What other ideas can you come up with to generate income, reduce expenses, and improve the company? Offer those ideas to show you are a team player interested in helping the company succeed.

Depending upon your role, you could start tracking and documenting in a report to your owner-supervisor information about referrals, new customers, initial sales, back-end sales (sale after the initial sale), up sales (getting the customer to buy more than originally intended), and continuing sales that you have influenced. This report could lead to a transfer or promotion, a raise, or a bonus. And it doesn't need to be just a one-time benefit if you can persuade your employer to reward you with incentive pay for your continued efforts to generate new business. Taking the initiative to prepare this report would also allow you to position yourself as someone with unique skills (your personal brand). You would be perceived as having a higher value than others and you may have an edge if the company is faced with a downsizing situation or has a new role to fill.

Q. How can I apply these skills outside my business?

Fund raisers for non-profits, churches, and schools need these skills desperately. Negotiating discount purchases, trying to convince others to follow your plan, leading volunteers, resolving conflicts, and communicating with others are all situations where you can use these skills.

Analyzing who you want to reach and how to reach them in the most economical way can be used in many settings. Internet marketing is very helpful today because it is much less expensive and can help you stay in touch with lots of people regularly. The point is to learn the basics right now and continue to build on them over time because you will be surprised at how frequently you can use the skills in daily situations.

Q. What is the difference between marketing and sales?

Marketing is typically aimed at the entire target market whereas sales is normally more focused and aimed specifically at targeted buyers to make contact and build rapport. Marketing examines the target market for the goods. It involves gathering a lot of information on that target market like psychographics, demographics, buying patterns, buying triggers, determining buyer needs and wants, how they buy, their problems (that need solved), and the like. A marketing campaign then uses different media to influence buyers' perceptions. The goal is to reach as many potential buyers as possible for the least cost. Marketing implements the campaign to get potential customers to contact sales representatives or provide their information so a salesperson can follow up with them.

Salespeople take the hand-off from marketing and focus on specific buyers to determine their particular needs, wants, and their specific problems. They show buyers how the company's goods benefit them and solve their problems, alleviate their problem or fill a need. They point out the competitive advantages of their goods as compared to their competitors' products. Many times there are long-term benefits that can be highlighted for a better Return on Investment (ROI) in addition to guarantees and warranties. Salespeople regularly build rapport and trust to extend the relationship into a longer-term, repeat sales relationship.

Another broad, but succinct way to look at the two is that marketing makes the target market aware of the goods and piques their interest to the point where the potential buyer is willing to provide information or make contact with the company. Sales then takes the lead, shows the customer how they can benefit from the goods, and closes the sale, getting them to purchase and pay for the goods. Marketing therefore precedes the sale, even if it's just in effective packaging that catches a potential buyer's eye that ultimately leads to a sale.

Q. Do you always need both marketing and sales?

This question will draw competing opinions and the answer depends on how closely you distinguish the two functions. The types and amount of marketing as well as the level of sales needed vary with each product. Some need heavy marketing and minimal sales and vice versa. Many commodity-type products need minimal sales because the prior marketing has already sold them; the buyer just needs an avenue to get it. With the increase in online sales, many products can be sold without a salesperson. The marketing information available is all that is needed to convince the buyer to make a purchase.

If the basic benefits and features of a good are known, companies need to differentiate themselves from the competitors in other ways to be perceived as the leader in that good. Marketing and sales techniques can help differentiate one from the other, regardless of whether the goods are the same. Adding different guarantees and warranties, other features, accessories, a better return policy, a trial period, and similar benefits can prove to be the deciding factor in buying a highly competitive, similar good.

Q. What is an effective marketing campaign?

A marketing campaign is a strategic plan to identify and attract potential customers by communicating key messages to your target audience at the right time and in the most effective way. It usually consists of multiple stages and various techniques focused on influencing your target market and drawing them to your company and its goods.

Some online methods include:

- Websites that can track visitors and sales
- E-mails that offer potential customers something to "opt-in" to, like receiving a free e-newsletter
- Using programs that respond automatically to those who sign up (autoresponders)
- "E-zines" or electronic magazines specifically designed to be accessed online that talk about topics that are related to your goods and appeal to your target market
- Web specials offering discounts for online purchases, etc.

These methods can connect you with your target audience more closely and with less expense, which will increase your campaign's effectiveness. You can split-test these methods, trying one type of wording, design, or color against another and see which gets a better response. There are many electronic tracking programs that accumulate how many e-mails are received, then opened, then read and responded to, etc. Tracking the effectiveness of each part of the campaign tells you whether to make mid-course changes or continue as planned.

I learned a great deal about marketing, and specifically direct-mail marketing, from Jon Goldman, a.k.a. "The Lumpy Mail Man" (*www.lumpymail.com* and *www.brandlauncher.com*). Jon ran successful direct mail campaigns for many Fortune 500 companies, increasing their response rate many times over. Jon's company examines the customer's need analytically, designs a campaign to fill that need, then tracks variables related to the campaign. Once they have the tracked results of the initial campaign, they see what has and has not worked and revise the materials to more closely grab the target's attention. This gets more customers to open and read the materials, and take the desired action the campaign was designed to elicit.

Jon recognized via a study by the Sales and Marketing Executives International that most people don't buy on their first contact, so they have campaigns that make contact with the target market in different ways several times (five to seven times was a typical series). This dramatically increased their client's successful contact rate and sales conversion rate. The study showed that 81% of those who were contacted bought after the fifth time (usually on the fifth, sixth, or seventh contact) and more buyers bought on the fifth contact than any other contact. Yet most businesses only made one or two contacts the typical way and stopped. The study showed that 48% stopped after the first contact, 25% after the second contact, and another 17% after the third or fourth contact. Only 10% continued with a fifth or greater contact, so 90% of the competition has already quit if you made five contacts.

This means that most businesses get minimal to no return on their marketing investment. Jon's company makes contacts in many unusual ways that really grab attention and get people to respond. Their creativity makes the mailer stand out and get a huge response. Even though their per mailer cost is more, they send out fewer mailers, target more specifically, and get a significantly higher return on invest-ment for the client. Some examples of their postal mailers include:

- Full-size watermelon with a note taped to it and a regular stamp
- Custom message in a bottle (like what you'd throw into the sea if you were trapped on a deserted island)
- Boomerang with a custom message on it
- Laptop PC locked in a metal briefcase that opens, turns on, and starts a video automatically when you open the briefcase
- Special message in a tube
- Flat pen with a message on it
- Fortune cookie with a custom fortune inside
- Puzzle with a piece missing they had to call for
- Mini-garbage can with a crumpled up note in it
- Special shaped magnets and clocks with a custom message
- Parts of an item that requires a call to get the other parts, etc.

Q. What are good techniques for making a sale?

Finding out the potential customers' goals and what they may have tried in the past will assist you in determining how your goods will fill their need. A buyer's goals may include:

- Paying a low price
- Acquiring a brand name item
- Buying cutting edge technology
- Being practical
- Impressing their friends
- Meeting a deadline
- Satisfying a compulsion or meeting a true need
- Switching from a competitor they are unhappy with, etc.

While your goals or your company's goals may include:

- Increasing sales or profit
- Getting rid of unwanted inventory
- Reducing returns
- Reducing customer service calls
- Diversification by offering complementary goods
- Adding repair services

- Increasing the number of products in the marketplace
- Increased referrals and word-of-mouth sales, etc.

Be curious, listen, and learn more about the customer, and then offer solutions that are consistent with both of the parties' objectives. Remember you have two ears and one mouth; use them in proportion so that you listen more than you talk. Ask questions and let the answers "school" you. If you know the potential buyer needs to get a new computer before classes start the following week, emphasize the fact that you can fill their order with a customized system within a matter of days. If you know that the potential buyer is looking for a new apartment that is close to where he or she works, stress the fact that the apartment you are subletting is close to the expressway and will make it easy for him or her to get to work easily. Explain all of the benefits, but be aware of the customer's particular needs that you can satisfy.

Consider how infomercials make sales and utilize some of these techniques. For instance, bundle options to increase the number of items that you sell while having the buyer see they are getting a deal. "But wait, there's more!" If it's possible to add something to sweeten the deal, offer a further incentive if they "act right now!" We've all heard that before.

If you create a sense of urgency, they are more likely to buy now. If you only have a limited quantity of the product available, stress that to the potential buyer. If the price is likely to increase in the near future, be sure to let them know so they are less inclined to sleep on it and possibly change their mind. You don't have to be obnoxious, and you should definitely be honest. If you tell them the price will go up next week, and they call back next week and it's the same price, you will lose credibility and show that you cannot be trusted. But if it is truthful, you are actually helping the buyer by letting them know why they should buy now.

Closing the sale and obtaining payment are also key parts of your sales skill set. Zig Ziglar has lots of materials out on these areas and has trained many people over several decades. I read a regular e-zine by Jeffrey Gitomer *(www.salescaffeine.com)* that has great sales and customer service advice weekly. Roger Fisher and William Ury have an older book out named *Getting to Yes* that offers great advice about negotiating and putting deals together. Spencer Johnson has a good, short sales book out named *The One Minute Sales Person*. I always learn from Jay Conrad Levinson's *Guerrilla* books. He has a full series out with several on marketing and sales. Dan Kennedy, Bill Glazer, and Joe Vitale all have good materials out on these areas. Scott Ginsberg, a.k.a. "The Nametag Guy," has several books and a loaded website on being approachable, increasing contacts, building relationships, increasing business, etc.

Tracking sales, following up with potential customers, resolving problems with current orders, and keeping current customers satisfied may all be part of your role, depending upon the size of the company and its structure. There are countless materials out on all of the subjects mentioned in this chapter so pick up a few and get more educated to increase your value as an employee or owner. You are part of a team and your efforts can benefit the company—and yourself.

Q. Do I need to act like a stereotypical salesperson?

Don't become the stereotypical used car salesman. This is where you can differentiate yourself as you become your own brand. Be yourself and build a relationship with customers to maintain them long-term. Trying to be someone else is tough to do over time, and the customer will probably see through this at some point. You want to be genuine and build their trust. There are so many poor sales people out there that a genuine person they can depend on, even when your role is not specifically sales, will be welcome.

If you put on an act, you may annoy them and seem like the rest of the herd, rather than someone unique who they will want to return to. If you are yourself and build rapport, then you don't have to act a role. This will build a long-term relationship and create repeat customers, who are valuable to every business.

Q. How can I apply these skills to my own business?

These skills are more critical if you are running your own business. Since getting income to flow as early as possible is the key to getting a business off the ground, an owner or manager of a new business must be involved in these areas. Inadequate marketing and sales kill most new businesses in the first year or two since cash flow is king. Showing good cash flow gets you credit. No cash flow, no credit, no business. It's that simple. Alternatively, doing well with these skills in another business can prompt you to open your own business.

You will have a limited budget for marketing and need to utilize it well. Track all customer contacts you get (leads) from each marketing method to see what methods are getting you the best return on investment (ROI). Initially, try several methods with a small cash outlay on each to test what has the highest ROI then put more of your budget in those methods that get you the most responses. Word-of-mouth marketing (you and others spread the word verbally) is the cheapest and has the best ROI. Personal referrals are invaluable. Always remember to ask current customers to refer others and offer them something of value (discount, coupon, gift certificate) if they do refer someone new who makes a purchase. Personally recognize all referrers with an e-mail, phone call, handwritten note, or some other way to thank them once a referred sale closes.

When you are the owner and have this responsibility, you quickly understand why it's important to do these things, even if you delegate many of the functions to employees in marketing and sales. If you rely on others to have this relationship with your clients, and they don't do a good job or leave, you quickly learn how fickle some clients can be as your income takes a dive and you are scrambling to keep your company afloat. Be involved with your customers now.

WHƏT WOULD JEFF DO?
(Fun action steps to try this stuff out)

1. If your primary role is not in marketing or sales, come up with a few ways you can build your skills in these areas and put them to use in your business today.

2. Ask your boss or the person overseeing these two areas about some ways you can help them build the bottom line. Offer some suggestions that you learned in this chapter that are tailored to your situation. Get involved now and expand on your skills.

3. Consciously be pleasant at your business. Just being friendly and helpful can brighten someone's mood and make the day better for all.

4. Tell others about your company and find ways to generate new business. Once implemented, track the different areas, customers, and so forth that you have affected and put it in a report to your supervisor or manager. You will get recognized for your efforts.

5. If you are involved in marketing or sales, do more homework on these areas. Read and listen to more material that is targeted to your field or industry. Consider whether an approach in a different industry can be applied to yours.

Once you've finished these steps, write me to let me know what happened and what you learned at *stories@lifescheatsheets.com*.

Now, think like Nike and Just Do It!

GO GET WHAT YOU WANT (OCCUPATION JOB SEARCH)

If you are looking for a new role or occupation, is important to actually schedule at least a portion of your day to search for the role you want. I use the words occupation and role rather than job because I believe job implies you work for someone else doing some specific function for them and that may not be what suits you as you search for a match for your interests and talents. Make it your role to search for employment, and take multiple steps each day to progress. The people who are most successful in their searches are typically those who stick with it daily and persevere each time they receive a "no." Think of "no" as "next," and move right on to the next possibility. You need to fight letting "no" get you down or taking it personally. It is not personal; it just may not be a good match at that time. Train yourself to let "no" roll right off you and move forward immediately.

Q. What if I'm a "non-traditional" candidate?

If you are unique and don't fit the typical mold, like me, it may be tough to find a match because most employers limit their thinking to what they've done in the past, even when it hasn't worked well. It is hard for many people to think outside of their mental walls and expand beyond their comfort zone to see how your unique skills or

A Lesson I Learned from "The Street"

I added this chapter at the request of many young adults I surveyed when coming up with the title for this book. I had already finished a later chapter on connections where I talk about a massive occupation search I undertook after law school starting in 2001. I received more than 1,500 rejection letters in my first targeted mailing with the executive marketing company I partnered with. My search was prolonged, and it was especially frustrating because I already had 20 years of solid work experience; I am an overachiever used to setting and achieving my goals. As a result, I fought "job search" depression for a few years and understand its ugliness all too well. Just be aware that the more "nos" you get and the longer your search goes on, the harder you will need to fight this depression, especially if you have an overachiever personality like me.

experience could benefit them more than the "normal" candidate. Additionally, you will be intimidating to some people if you have the confidence to take risks and demonstrate the potential to shine. They may feel threatened by these qualities and think that you could be promoted above them or that you are a high-quality candidate that won't stay long because you will get other opportunities.

Because of my background, I had this happen countless times to the point where I rarely ever submitted my complete résumé. I "dumbed down" my résumé to get interviews, which is sad, but true. Even though you may be a young adult, if you have several stellar accomplishments already, you may find the need to be more conservative on your résumé to more closely fit the position you are applying for and not get screened out for being overqualified. You can still sprinkle in some strong distinguishing qualities that make you perceived as more valuable than the other candidates. While you need to be honest and want to present yourself as the most qualified applicant, you should at least be aware of this potential and consider toning down a glowing resume to show you are suitable for the role you are seeking.

"A Lesson I Learned from "The Street""

As I did, you may run into many people in supervisory or ownership roles who are not qualified for or ill-equipped to handle them, but they stay in those roles for a myriad of poor, illogical reasons.

For example, when I increased my efforts toward becoming in-house counsel (a company's fulltime employee-attorney) late in my search, I found a faulty, long-term precedent that no one questioned. I had worked short spans in law firms, as in-house counsel, and had nearly 20 years of experience running and owning companies. I was eliminated as a finalist by companies for in-house roles because I didn't have a couple of years of experience in a law firm even though none of their company attorneys had any prior company experience. So other law firm attorneys were hired to provide legal counsel to a company, yet they had no prior work experience in a company? What? Because company management and supervisory in-house counsel didn't have company and law firm experience, like I had, they didn't realize the functional differences between a law firm attorney and an in-house attorney.

A lot of companies make these kinds of mistakes, so be aware that you might run into some strange situations and some upside-down thinking. But you'll have to ignore this sort of thing to achieve your objective or, as I did, start looking at other options.

Q. Can I run my own business without prior experience?

It is tough to start a business from scratch without any experience and some saved money. But if you have an entrepreneurial drive and business instincts, you can be successful in starting a business while you're in school or when you first graduate. I and a few other students I knew ran a business while in school to get that experience early.

Some of the businesses I know of that are run by college students include: painters (College Painters), screen printers for promotional items, internet hosting, web site design and maintenance, computer sales and repair, book buyers and resellers, birthday-anniversary-baby sign rentals, and health/makeup sales (Mary Kay, Arbonne). I had a rental housing business that I started in high school and kept for 20 years. Some houses were entirely paid off by renters, and then I sold some of them for twice what I paid.

Two of the all-time greatest examples of our time are Bill Gates (Microsoft) and Michael Dell (Dell Computers). They both dropped out of college to grow the companies that they started while in college. Neither ever finished college, but both have become billionaires, and Bill Gates has been the world's most wealthy person for many years. They both had an idea, started on a shoestring and a prayer, and took their companies to unbelievable heights, so don't rule this option out if you have a good idea and a business plan that is supported financially.

If you have not sampled some jobs in your interest areas while in school, it may be best to sample some before starting your own so you have a better idea of what you really want to focus on. Once you get some experience, it's easier to market your skills and go out on your own. While doing this, learn to live lean and build some savings so you have money to live on and start up the business. Many people start a business as a sideline while at a typical job and build it up before quitting their regular job. Alternatively, you can invest in multiple areas and let those investments build while keeping the job, especially if you are on performance pay (not a set amount, but paid based on sales, profits, production, etc., where your pay is not limited) and doing well.

NOTE: **For the remainder of this chapter, I am going to lay out the key elements of an effective, assertive job search. This will apply to the majority of young adults who will begin their career working for someone else's company. But I would recommend that you look for a position that offers a performance pay plan or convert to one in your current role. Or start a side business of your own, in conjunction with your job, so you'll have more control over your income and avoid financial limitations. If you desire, your side business can grow to become your primary business and main source of income once you get it off the ground. You should start** making use of additional investment strategies at the same time, like those listed in the last section of this book on Life Planning and in my *financial habits* follow-up book.

Q. How do I assess my skills and interests?

Start by defining your ideal role, and be as specific about the role as you can. For any role, there are variables: some pay more than others, some require you to work weekends, while others have a straightforward schedule, etc. Then, look for jobs that come as close as possible to this ideal. You can be more precise about what you're looking for by weighting the variables or ranking them so you have defined which ones are the most important to you, then try to find jobs that match those first. This is a list of the variables I have used:

Title	Corporate level	Consistent or inconsistent pay
Pace of work	Span of control	Independent or team style
Functions	Corporate culture	Ownership, options, or none
Pay level	Support systems	Profit and loss responsibility
Responsibilities	Geographic area	Emerging industry or established
Accountability	Physical environment	Closely or loosely supervised
Company size	Management style	Manufacturing or service
Industry	Inside or outside	Business cycle phase
Travel demands	Contractor or employee	Interaction with other people

Using this list as a model, define your ideal job. Give this some serious thought in a quiet environment and really decide what you want. There are many books and materials on this area. Take several of the career defining/matching-type assessments you find in these books and online. JIST Works, Inc. (*www.jist.com*) has many of them. Once you have taken several of these assessments, you will find many of them tend to be similar to one another. They help you identify your true interests, passions, natural skills, and things you like to do and would do without pay. Finding a way to make a living from them will come later.

You should also consider taking "The Passion Test" by Janet and Chris Attwood (*www.thepassiontest.com*). David Riklan at *www.selfgrowth. com* has a lot of resources on passion, self-esteem, confidence, etc., that really get you thinking about who you are and want to be. *What Color is Your Parachute* by Richard Nelson Bolles is a long-time favorite of many for defining a good match to your interests and how to find it. He updates it annually so look for the latest version.

Q. With our economic climate, how can I stand out?

With the tight economy and the millions of jobs that have been eliminated in just the last couple of years, you need to be seen as different from the pack (in a good way) to have a higher perceived value than others with the same or similar experience. Unskilled jobs have been cut drastically, so there are many people looking for fewer of those jobs. Landing one will require some luck—being in the right place at the right time, having something in common with the interviewer, or perhaps knowing someone who can refer you to a personal friend or business contact inside the particular company. If you are looking for this type of role, you will really need to find a way to be unique and have your own personal brand. Otherwise, you will just be included in the big group of applicants with no reason to get pulled out of the bunch. Regardless, I would not plan on staying for long in that type of position because I believe there will continue to be fewer of those roles as we go forward.

William Arruda of Reach Branding Club (*www.reachcc.com*) has many materials on building your unique, personal brand, specifically as it relates to a job search. Your brand is a unique trait or set of unique characteristics that define you and your specific skills and abilities. It becomes how people see you so when they have a need that matches your unique brand they think of you right away. It's like when I want a facial tissue, I ask for a Kleenex, not a facial tissue because Kleenex fills the role of a facial tissue for me. They have branded the company to be the chosen facial tissue in my mind through their marketing efforts over the years. Once you have defined your brand you will no longer be one of the group, but you will be known by your unique qualities and value that people associate with you.

William and his partner Kirsten Dixson have a book out called *Career Distinction* on the subject. They hold teleseminars, publish a newsletter, offer coaching, and have a site with a lot of information. To brand yourself over time, you need your message to be consistent, clear, and concise so that when people hear or see it they immediately associate it with you. This keeps you at the forefront of their minds when they have a need so they will contact you first.

You want a potential employer to see you as unique so you shine above the other candidates. If you have a personal brand that makes you unique and perceived as more valuable to the employer, your chance of getting that job increases dramatically. Obviously, if you brand yourself as a great Italian chef, you are not going to be seen as valuable for an accounting job so you need to look for roles that match your brand. But, when you do match the role, that personal brand with some accolades to back it up will move you to the front of the group.

Q. How do I prepare a résumé?

With word processing and computers, these are a snap. I used to have to use an IBM Selectric typewriter when I started (OK, you can knock off the old jokes anytime). Résumé styles change over time so search online, in the bookstore, or the library for the latest style. The format for a younger, entry-level person is straightforward (see a sample in the Appendix).

Start with a header (good looking font, bold print that gives your *personal* information similar to letterhead) and then an objective (optional-defines what you are looking for), followed by your key skills (optional-I would include these; this is a list of your key qualities that make you exceptional to that employer), then experience and education. If one of these last two is stronger than the other, use that one first, but if one area is more relevant to the job you're seeking, put that one first. End with volunteer, other activities, and groups you belong to. You never know how you are going to make a connection with the interviewer.

My wife attended Miami University (in Oxford, Ohio) for undergraduate work for a few semesters and an interviewer had gone there too, so that played a large part in her getting her first law job.

References are typically not included at the end of a résumé anymore, unless a particular person would be recognizable by the reader and it would help your cause.

When starting out at an entry level position, load up your résumé so that it fills one page. Don't overlook specifics that might make a connection with the interviewer. Match the résumé style to the role and type of company you are applying to. For example, accounting firms, law firms, and similar conservative companies prefer very bland, professional résumés, while marketing, graphic arts, and advertising companies look for résumés with flair and pizzazz that grab attention and show your creativity.

Be careful with special letterhead, colored envelopes, unusually-shaped materials, UPS/FedEx deliveries, delivering your materials with gifts, and other outside-the-box thinking. I know of some instances where that creativity has worked, but I know of more situations where it turned off the receiver and removed the candidate from consideration. I personally would look at the candidate as a potential asset, but many other conservative business people are not open to a unique pitch.

Make certain you run spell check multiple times, read the résumé on multiple days (with a break in between), and have others critique and edit it for you. Misspelled words and bad grammar make a poor and lasting first impression. If your résumé is sent and read electronically with Word, the program will underline these errors, which makes them look worse. You need it to be flawless so the door stays open.

Carry a few copies with you at all times. You never know when you will run into a good opportunity. Someone may introduce you to a good prospect or you may start a conversation with someone who can assist in your search. I made up resume business cards that gave my resume highlights on one side and personal information on the other. You can get very inexpensive (under $10), professional-looking cards and other print materials sent right to your door at *www.vistaprint.com,* and many other sites.

Q. Should I prepare a sample cover letter?

Definitely prepare a cover letter sample before you need one. Look at several resources to see the latest style, but it should rarely fill a full page. There are standard three- to four-paragraph models that should work well for you. Start with why you are writing. For example:

- I have done research on your company
- I have read about your company and I am interested
- I see that your company won an award
- I spoke with employee X and he suggested…
- My mother works at your company and suggested…

Note in the letter that you have an interest in meeting to discuss opportunities with the company. Make a specific connection right away. Show that you have done your homework to learn about the company and have a specific interest in working there, not just a general interest in a job.

Follow this initial paragraph with a set of bullet points or a paragraph or two outlining your unique skills that meet their needs and how those skills would benefit the company. Work from a job description, ad, or information from someone you know who works there. Speak directly to their needs as listed and show that your skills fill those needs. If they have had a problem that you read about or saw on their web site, outline a way you can help. If you see you can increase their income or reduce their expenses, outline very concisely those ideas to pique their interest. Focus on how you can help them, not on how the job will meet *your* needs.

Close with a few sentences reiterating how it appears that your background fits their needs and request a meeting at their earliest convenience. If they have a specific company culture or cause you support, note how your values are similar. If you have any other way to make specific connections to them, make them here. Explain that you will follow up by phone on a specific day and time and make certain you do. Put it on your schedule as an appointment and make that call.

On this call, leave a short, professional voice mail message if you don't reach the person directly. If you don't hear from them, wait two to three days and call again. Do it again in two to three days if they don't respond. And if you still have no return call, see if you can reach them through the receptionist or their assistant and schedule a call. You need to be professional, but persistent. You could also try an e-mail or short follow-up letter if you still are not reaching them. Have a professional outgoing message on your answering machine to receive a message from them. Be careful and don't have a corny one that turns them off. Even if you go through all of these steps and don't reach them, let it drop for two to four weeks, and follow up with a call and continue this process for several months if you like the company. Needs change daily so they may have a need in a month that they didn't have when you originally made contact.

If you are like me and have developed several skill sets so you can apply for multiple types of positions, you should prepare cover letter samples for each of these. When you see one come up, you can customize the sample to the role and get your materials in quickly. When the role requires a slightly different template, or is a previous one you've applied for before, just "save as" the prior one and customize the new one. I ultimately had more than 250 different cover letter types saved after my massive job search.

Q. What is an "elevator speech"?

An elevator speech is no speech at all. The phrase comes from the amount of time you'd have during an elevator ride to tell someone about yourself. It is 15 to 30 seconds maximum. I suggest you have a shorter and a longer version so you can pique some interest if you only have 10 to 15 seconds or can deliver the longer 30-second version. Obviously it is helpful to have the ability to succinctly inform someone about what you do and how you may be able to help them.

Only highlight your unique skills, experience, and education—then shut up. You never know when you will meet someone who could have a great lead for you. You want to be able to easily and comfortably recite a quick summary to grab enough attention to get her contact information so you can follow up.

Practice this heavily before needing it so it flows easily and confidently. You don't want to fly through it too fast, and you should smile while reciting it. Do this in the mirror several times to get it down and make sure it comes to you easily without having to think about it. Focus on skills, experience, and education that can benefit most companies. You can always tailor it if you happen to meet someone in a specific company that you are familiar with.

Try out several of them with minor differences and see which ones flow best and are filled with references to transferable, cross-trained skills and key experience that most companies need. Read several examples of elevator speeches through job search services online to craft yours. Continue to make it better as you come up with new thoughts to enhance it. If one doesn't seem to be working, revise it and try some new material.

Q. How do I network to expand my job search?

Always be on the prowl for additional contacts that may lead to the role you are interested in. Pay attention to all of the details you pick up in conversation and bring them up in a follow-up letter or in-person meeting. Maybe they say something about their kids, pets, or work issues that you can mention in the letter to make a connection with them. This shows the receiver that you were paying attention and that the details are important to you. Everyone wants to feel important and using someone's name, as well as specific details about them, will help you connect with them.

Be assertive, but not aggressive, in networking at church, school, sports events, etc. Don't overlook or blow off any person or group you have a connection with or where you can form one easily. Select some target companies that you are interested in and talk with folks you know to find an inside contact, using this person's name to make the connection.

You can also get involved in networking groups, like Business Network International (BNI). But you may want to pick a less structured group so you don't have to attend all the time, provide X number of leads, and complete other requirements. When networking at any function, don't put someone on the spot by asking them for a job unless it is clearly appropriate for the conversation. Normally, you would never directly ask unless you already knew them or had built some rapport over time. If people are uncomfortable, they will typically shy away and not help, so don't put them in an uncomfortable position. Many people can't handle this direct approach.

I joined a lot of networking groups, and attended all sorts of events, lunches, etc. for upper level roles I was looking for, and it did not help much. I found that virtually everyone I was with was at a lower level than the role I was looking for and they didn't have upper-level contacts. It seemed like they believed I would be in the way if they wanted to move up. Ultimately, I kissed a lot of gluteus maximus with minimal return on my investment (ROI). I found that if there is no perceived competition or intimidation from you by the receiver, there is a much better chance that they will help you in some way.

Q. Should I apply for roles on online job sites?

With all of the online job search sites that have popped up, searching for a job might seem easier. But, what I found is that you have to look at this as a numbers game. There are so many people using these resources that most of the submissions don't even get reviewed because the interviewer is overwhelmed. A few of these companies I had applied to said they had hundreds and, sometimes, thousands of responses for one position.

There are automated services that use electronic spiders (software that searches many job and company sites to find keywords that match your search) to find and electronically forward your résumé and a standard cover letter to any job that it finds on any site that matches your set of predefined variables. The more spiders you have submitting your materials, the better your chances of getting a response. But I found that online resources offer the lowest success rate, so you need to spend very little time on any one of these sites and not count on these exclusively.

I would be certain to prepare e-documents (résumé, cover letter you can adapt, transcripts, and references) that can be e-mailed or uploaded to sites quickly as needed; but invest very little time since the ROI is so low with these sites. Many of the sites require you to build a profile which can take 30 to 40 minutes if you have an extensive background. Be quick with these and move on. If you believe a position seems like a great match for you, customize your response and see if there is a way to follow up or call them directly so that you stand out from the heap of online applications they receive.

Q. Should I use social networking sites in my search?

With the growing popularity of sites like Facebook, LinkedIn, MySpace, and Twitter, you can let a lot of people and groups in multiple countries know that you are searching and what you are searching for. I would not make it too obvious and constantly ask for help, but mention what you are doing every few days in the course of your job search, working in phrases about interviews, where you are looking, what companies you are targeting, etc. Mentioning things like this in small posts will keep people aware of your search, and someone might suggest a lead or at least some helpful information. Intersperse other, unrelated updates also so you don't sound like a broken record.

Keeping those you dialogue with on these sites informed of what you are doing can definitely spread your network further and enhance your search. I have been on teleseminars and read multiple e-books and mini-manuals on how to use these to grow your online groups and make more contacts. I attended a social media teleseminar series with Leila McKinley (*www.leilamckinley.com*), who has a strong background in this area and a offers lots of good suggestions. These teleseminars and webinars are a great way to stay current in this area. Since the world of social networking is changing daily, you should be on the cutting edge and know how to use this resource to advance your search, rather than just playing around on MySpace!

There is not much printed material on using social networking sites to further your job search yet, but with so many jobs being eliminated, it has become a topic that others are starting to write about. Most of these sites have a good online help system to help you learn more about them and learn ways to extend your reach with their site's tools. Get connected and join some bulletin boards and forums about your specific needs. They usually have current information to help further your efforts.

Q. What should I do if I get a lead from one of my sources?

Start by thanking your source for keeping you in mind and forwarding the information. Also, keep them informed of what happens with the lead. Give them some idea of how things went to let them see that you didn't drop the ball. Many times I even offered a finder's fee to anyone in my network who provided me the contact for a role I ultimately accepted, which enticed a few contacts.

Research the company, the person to contact, interviewers, as well as your potential supervisor. Look for ways you can use your skills and background to help or enhance something in the company or department. Use their web site, library materials, other online sources, financials (balance sheet, income statement, statement of cash flows), auditor reports (findings, explanations in end-of-year audits), public filings (SEC, stock issuances, stock purchases and sales, key officer changes, acquisitions, sales, etc.), media articles, Google and Yahoo searches, etc., to conduct your research. Learn about the company, its owners, officers, and its track record.

Call or write the contact directly. If you write the person, follow up with a phone call when you say you will and schedule a meeting with the appropriate person. If this is an inside lead that has not been posted and you don't want others to know about it, or if you believe you may have too much competition when the word gets out about the opening, call to inquire right away. See if you can send them your résumé and cover letter by e-mail, fax, postal mail, or UPS/FedEx, and get them in their hands quickly. Be prepared with your elevator speech so they can quickly see that you qualify and are serious about the role.

Be timely with these actions and follow up right when you said you would. Make the follow-up appointments right away so they don't consider others in the meantime or forget your qualities by getting sidetracked with other responsibilities. Don't ramble on with voice mail messages. Get right to the point and set short deadlines. The quicker you can move through the process, the better your chances are of securing the role.

Q. What should I do to prepare for interviews?

Assuming you have already researched the company and any relevant individuals, as I talked about above, you should have some good questions for the interviewers. Try to uncover weak or problem areas that you may be able to help with. Make sure you get the correct spelling of each interviewer's name to use later. Ask for a job description to know how your strengths will be beneficial to the role.

Find online one of the lists of the top 100 most common interview questions. You don't have to go through all 100, but the more you practice, the better prepared you will be. Answer each one as you would during a conversation. Try to come up with the best answer for each question. If you don't like how you answered, go back and ask it again, then revise your answer and rehearse the one you think is best. It's helpful to give yourself only a couple of minutes to answer a question so you don't ramble. Get used to giving the best information concisely. They will ask if they want you to elaborate further. Otherwise, don't go on in heavy detail. Also, make certain you do actually answer their question in your response.

If you have enough experience to come up with examples, answer in the problem-analysis/action-response (PAR) pattern, including the outcome in the response. It makes a much stronger impression on the interviewer if you can give concrete, specific examples of your experience that relate to their needed skill sets and their specific issues in the questions.

For example, let's say the question is: Have you supervised coworkers before, and if so, what is one of the toughest situations you have had to handle? Using the PAR structure I would respond by explaining that I had a coworker/friend who was one of our company accountants. He had a noticeable personality and demeanor change and started having some "quiet-talking" phone calls. He then fell behind on his work. (Problem)

I had concerns, so I had another accountant help catch up on this work, which included accounting for all of the checks written from and deposits into the main bank account. I also started paying more attention to his mood swings and extra calls. One day, he quit without notice or explanation. This threw up another red flag so we finished up his project and then reviewed his work. (Analysis-Action)

We found that he had been paying himself twice each pay period by having two different authorized signers sign the checks and had taken for personal use a gas credit card that he had been using for a couple of months. We also found that he and his wife had separated. We had a special dishonesty section on our commercial insurance policy that required me to formally press criminal charges to get the insurance company to reimburse us for losses. The coworker was arrested and had a short jail stay. Ultimately he pled guilty to a lesser charge, but had a low level felony on his record. (Response/Outcome)

You should also be prepared to address the weak areas in your background where you don't have the education or experience they may want. Practice answering questions about these areas. Make certain you put a spin on your answers to make them positive by having a plan to get some extra education on a subject, a related experience that can cut your learning curve, or another angle that converts a weakness to a plan to eliminate a potential issue. Practice answering tough questions to reduce your stress and make interviews go much smoother. There are no "re-dos" in interviews, so make your first answer a good one.

Finally, be sure to prepare some appropriate questions to ask during the interview. They will certainly ask if you have questions, and you don't want to be caught off guard or appear as if you don't care enough to ask about the role, the interviewer, or the company. Some questions may be specific—about the company's plans for expansion or the nature of the position—but some will be appropriate for a variety of settings, assuming they were not already addressed in the interview. For instance, what does the interviewer like best about her job? What is the most important qualification or trait for the position? How would she describe the company culture or working environment?

Avoid basic questions about things you should already know from researching public information about the company, such as information posted on their website. Remember, you want to demonstrate that you have an interest in the company and have done your homework. Don't ask how long the company has been in business if their website says when it was founded. Also, as a rule of thumb, do not ask questions about compensation or benefits in the interview. Let the interviewer offer the information or wait until you receive an offer to talk money.

Q. How should I handle the actual interview?

Make certain you are dressed appropriately, well-groomed, wearing minimal jewelry and other unique or distracting items (e.g., piercings, tattoos, large or dangling earrings). Try to aim for a normal, mature look if that is appropriate for the role. Get directions from your contact ahead of time. Arrive there 10 to 15 minutes early so you will not be late and can review your résumé and materials about the company and role. You can highlight the key points you would like to stress so you can focus on them. Take copies of your cover letter and résumé for others who may step into the interview. You should already know who you will be interviewing with from your prior research and contact person within the company.

Be nice to everyone you interact with. You never know who influences whom, who is married or dating whom, who is family of the owners, or who can be your ally inside. I have had conversations with the receptionist many times and listened to other conversations while I was waiting, hearing additional information about the company I utilized. So don't ignore, be rude, or tick off anyone. Pucker up and take one for the team.

Maintain eye contact, but don't stare a hole into the interviewer. Be friendly and enthusiastic. Listen closely to everything they share. Remember that you are interviewing the company at the same time so this should be a two-way conversation to help you decide if this is truly a good role and company for you before you commit.

In the interview, let them do as much talking as they like and listen closely. Once you have uncovered issues, start working your skills into your answers, showing how you can help them with these problems. Don't assume they will make the connection. Make it for them. You will also want to get answers to any questions that you have about the company and role.

Before you leave, make certain you understand where they are in the process, what your next step is, and who you can follow up with. Feel free to jot down quick notes during the interview without losing eye contact for long, so you have key information recorded correctly.

When you are finished and leave, stop wherever it's appropriate, but as soon as you can, and write notes down about everything you can remember that went on in the interview. Jot down things they said in whatever detail you can remember. Note any areas they need help with and strengths and weaknesses that they may perceive in you. Just pour your short-term memory on paper so you can use these phrases as you write a thank you note and prepare for any additional interactions with them.

Q. Should I follow up after interviews?

Sometimes there will be specific requests from the interviewer to get back to them. When this happens, get whatever they need to them as quickly as possible with a personal, handwritten note. Invite them to contact you if they need anything else after reviewing what you have provided.

If you do have to get them additional information, include your handwritten or laser printed thank you note. If you are close enough, personally hand deliver the materials directly to the interviewer to make an additional contact that will get you back in her mind. If you are hot (or handsome), definitely do this so you will jump to the forefront of their mind (might as well use it if you have it).

In your thank you note, reiterate how you seem to be a good fit for the role. Respond to any specific issues that came up in the interview that you didn't already respond to well. Follow up by phone, unless they clearly specify another method, in the shortest timeframe they suggest to see if they need anything else or are ready to schedule a second interview.

Try to move the process along with language that assumes you are still included in the process without being too pushy. Word your statements in the positive and give them a couple of choices, assuming you have not already received a no. For example, "I have free time on Wednesday afternoon and also on Thursday morning if you would like to schedule a second interview now." Compare that to "would you like to schedule a second interview?" This makes it easy to answer no and just move on. Don't give them an easy out.

Q. What is my goal in doing all of these things?

The best case scenario is that you get multiple good offers and are truly interested in all of them because each of them would be a good fit. If this happens, you need to compare and contrast each of them side by side, feature by feature. I also suggest you do a pros and cons analysis. If you want to make it more precise, rank or weight each of them on a scale of one to five. Usually, the lower the number, the more important that variable is to you and conversely the higher the number the less important it is to you. Really analyze each offer in monetary terms as well as tangible (money in your pocket or retirement account, leased car, sky box tickets) and intangible (time off, work environment, co-workers, growth experience) factors.

With multiple offers, you have some built-in leverage where you are usually able to negotiate some additional income or benefits, playing one offer against the other. I would be very hesitant with today's very tough job market about trying to bluff your way through negotiations, letting them believe you have another offer without actually having it. They just might call your bluff and you will be without a role at all and back to the starting line.

Q. What should I do once I receive an offer?

If you have multiple offers and it's appropriate, I would very cautiously counteroffer (ask for something additional or different than they offered) your most preferred one with support for your counteroffer. Be creative and come up with some support, regardless of how weak you may believe it is. Be very humble and thank them for the offer because you don't want to tick them off and lose the option. Don't go in with hard ball negotiation tactics in mind. It could really backfire and cost you the opportunity.

You can also try to negotiate in additional perks that may not cost them more money but get you more time off like extra holiday time at Christmas, or a four-day work schedule with longer days but with Friday or Monday off in addition to the weekend, etc. You could also attempt to get other paid benefits that are not standard like paid time over 40 hours per week (even if you are a salaried worker), performance bonuses per quarter, paid parking, and so on. I would put a value on the commute length and cost. Is your commute during rush hour so it will be frustrating? You should also find out:

- What are the actual work hours?
- Can you work from home and telecommute some days?
- Is your schedule flexible?
- Are there advancement opportunities over the long-term?

- Can you get stock options or an ownership potential?
- Is the company stable?
- Is the market stable (e.g., automotive vs. healthcare and green technologies)?
- Are the goods they provide needed over the long-term or are they likely to be replaced, etc.?

Once you are done negotiating the best deal with each, sign with the best match and set your start date. Don't wait long to get started. Shine when you get there and don't burn bridges. Suck it up for awhile until you build your own following and gain respect. Don't buck the system early. Be flexible and learn who the players are. Don't be too talkative while getting to know the people you work with because you may stick your foot in your mouth without knowing it. Be friendly and get a feel for the culture while learning your new role quickly. Once you get settled in and are comfortable, start looking for ways you can increase your income to meet your goals. Start building your investments so you are not forced to work for someone else forever. Have some fun while you're at it, and enjoy the journey, always keeping your ultimate goals in mind.

What Would Jeff Do?
(Fun action steps to try this stuff out)

1. Sample some jobs that you may be interested in so you can weed out those you are not interested in.

2. Think of a business you might want to start, put a plan together, and assess whether this is the right time to do so. You will not truly understand the experience of starting and running your own business until you have done so. Reading about it only gets you so far.

3. Define your ideal role using the grid of variables I laid out. Take some assessments and see if they reveal a common theme then match types of roles to your theme. This will determine a direction you can investigate further.

4. Once you have defined a reasonable match, get an internship or shadow someone in that role to test it out and see if you really like it. If you do, identify ways to differentiate yourself from others that do the same job and start forming your personal brand.

5. Prepare your resume, reference list, and a few cover letter templates for specific types of roles. Make certain these are electronic documents that you can send by e-mail quickly. Now prepare and practice your elevator speech until it flows out of your mouth effortlessly.

6. Schedule your networking efforts and reach several different audiences so many people know you are looking and what you are looking for. Stay in contact with them regularly to build some rapport so you may come to their mind if they hear of a good contact or lead.

7. Sprinkle into regular posts on your social networking sites that you are looking and what for. Don't come on real strong or you risk turning people away. Make these search posts on a regular basis so you stay on your followers' minds.

8. When you get a lead from someone, thank them personally and update them as you move through the process. Pursue the lead right away, get them your documents quickly, and ask to set up a time to meet face-to-face if possible. Research the company and become a well-informed candidate.

9. Before an interview, practice the sample interview questions and come up with some specific questions you can ask about the business. Prepare everything in advance. Once in the interview, follow the guides I have laid out then follow up promptly without becoming a pest.

10. If you get multiple offers, analyze them completely and see if you can get a better deal by using them as subtle leverage. Never get cocky or abrasive. Be humble and thank them for the opportunity. Once you choose one, fit in and learn the lay of the land without stepping on toes.

Once you've finished these steps, write me to let me know what happened and what you learned at *stories@lifescheatsheets.com*.

Now, think like Nike and Just Do It!

Hone Your Ability To Negotiate and Barter Everything

Q. Why should I negotiate everything?

Negotiating is a learned skill that can really enhance your life. It is one of my most valuable skills. I have been hired to negotiate for others because people have seen the success I have had in my negotiations. Kids start early, negotiating with their parents on:

- Getting a new toy or new clothes
- Not eating their supper
- Getting an allowance or a raise in allowance
- Choosing what they wear to school
- Staying out later than curfew
- Dating a certain boy or girl, etc.

They don't formally call it a negotiation, but that is what is taking place. Usually there is some give and take, using leverage and concessions to ultimately end up at some agreement. Each side may not like the terms, but the negotiation ultimately ends in an agreement at some point. The more you pay attention to others, and read about and practice negotiating, the better you will get.

In *Gain the Edge* (*www.negotiationinstitute.com*, *www.GaintheEdge. com*) Martin Latz lays out his strategic negotiation process. He and I recognize that the best negotiators are those who use a calculated strategy rather than on-the-spot instinct, commonly known as "wingin' it." I have used a process very similar to his for years so we are in agreement on these five components of the process which are:

1. Research everything about the negotiation to gain whatever information you can before talking with the other party(s).
2. Maximize your leverage (where your case is stronger than the opposition) and determine your Best Alternatives to a Negotiated Agreement (BATNA's; these are your best options or back-up plans if your negotiation ends without an agreement), arranging them in a hierarchy from best to worst.
3. Use objective standards from other sources, not your own, to support your points (find charts, studies, statistics and so on to support your points).
4. Design your offer-concession strategy, including several offers (in order from the best you could get to the worst you would accept), counteroffers and concessions (things you would give up in the negotiation to get something you valued higher).
5. Control the agenda as well as the environment to get the "home field" advantage.

This process is solid and will lead you to the best outcome. Realize that this process is for more formal, relatively important negotiations, so you wouldn't necessarily take the time to follow each step for simple negotiations like convincing your parents or roommate what fast food place they should pick up your supper from. But, practicing this process on anything will build it in your subconscious mind which will get you in the habit of regularly using it.

Getting to Yes by Roger Fisher and William Ury is an older book with strong principles on this topic. Writings by Zig Ziglar such as *Secrets of Closing the Sale* are strong on sales and negotiation as well as maintaining motivation despite rejection.

Always have your BATNA's in mind before entering any negotiation so you don't have to bluff and then regret it later. Having a
plan before entering into a negotiation gives you more confidence
that usually leads to a better outcome. Also, have fun with it and
don't put pressure on yourself since most of the time the monetary
value of what you are negotiating for is relatively minimal in the big
picture. Every time I get someone to reduce a price, include more
items in purchase, add features at no cost, or include a warranty
with the product or service, I get a little sense of satisfaction. I feel I
have won, knowing that my efforts have gained me more value just
by asking and negotiating a little.

Since I am a challenge-junkie, I use negotiating situations as little
challenges just to see what I can achieve. Many people wouldn't even
think of trying or would talk themselves out of it if they did think
of it. If you don't ask, you'll never know. You will potentially spend
more than you needed to or end up leaving cash on the table if you
are not assertive and fail to ask for what you want. You talk yourself
out of it with excuses like:

- They will get mad if you ask. (So? You didn't do anything wrong.)
- It will be awkward or embarrassing. (Not once you get used
  to it.)
- No one should ask that. (Why? It's just prior programming—
  get over it.)
- It's not polite to want so much. (How do you know it's too
  much?)
- I'll never get that. (Wimp! Defeatist!—not a good attitude.)
- There's no way they will say yes, etc. (Don't need to repeat
  myself.)

Most of your thoughts will stem from prior programming that
you must overcome and change if you are going to make progress.

Jack Canfield and Mark Victor Hansen's *The Aladdin Factor* is all
about asking for what you want in life. The whole concept is that you
only have something to gain by asking, you haven't lost anything.
For example, if you apply to Harvard and get rejected, you were not

currently attending so you haven't lost anything. If you ask for a lower price on a car and your request is rejected, you can still buy it for the current negotiated price, so you haven't lost anything. If you ask a girl on a date and she turns you down, you weren't going out with her to begin with, so you haven't lost anything by asking.

Asking for what you want (with this concept in mind) will give you the confidence to go ahead and take risks. If you talk yourself out of it with "what ifs," you'll never know if you could have gotten what you wanted. Why not start finding out rather than wondering what if? You typically get only one chance to ask before moving on, so think like Nike and "Just Do It" now.

For the remainder of this section, I am going to be more focused on negotiating on items for purchase (expense items) rather than gaining more income, but these principles also apply to income items as well. Use these principles to ask for raises, bonuses, promotions, price increases, new fees, and so on. For example, let's say you are the CFO at a car dealership and you don't get paid what you are worth in salary and bonuses. Research comparable positions and pay, then take that information to the CEO/owner to request a pay increase, supporting it with a list of all of the projects you have completed, money you have saved them, return on investment, and similar performance measures that you have exceeded. If they still can't increase your pay, ask for a car that you can use while employed there and have it included in your compensation at no cost to you. Don't limit your thinking when it comes to ways you can gain more value than you are currently getting. Doing your homework, then strategically asking for what you want with appropriate support, will get you further ahead.

Q. What is bartering and how would I use it?

Bartering is exchanging one good or service for another and many times does not include any cash payment by either party. This is a great technique when you have something of value to offer others and want to get something of value from them without exchanging cash. Most of the time it can be done without incurring any taxes.

For example, my sister does small business accounting from her home office so that she can multi-task and take care of her family while "at work." Let's say she gets three new small businesses to pay her $25 per hour. She believes she can get more value for her services with all of her years of experience, but can't get an increase in the out-of-pocket pay so she brainstorms to see what else she might get.

She talks with Client one who is a dry cleaner and negotiates unlimited, free dry cleaning that she normally would have paid for, saving $25/week or $100/month. Client two is a local family restaurant, and she gets them to include up to five carry-out meals per week that she would normally have paid for in groceries and time, saving her a minimum of $75/week or $300/month. Client three is a local gym where her family works out, and she gets them to include her family membership for no cost. She saves $125/month. In this example she has in effect added income for her home business by eliminating $525/month in expenses. Her net profit increase is $6,300/year, and all it took was a little creativity and assertiveness in negotiating these additional services. She bartered her service for pay plus her client's services, and with creativity she may not have to pay taxes that she would have otherwise paid.

A more complex method of bartering may include multiple parties. For example, Sauder Woodworking near me in Archbold, Ohio, makes excellent Ready-to-Assemble (RTA) furniture. I really like many of their lines and the furniture lasts for years. Several years ago, I was talking with their CEO at the time, Maynard Sauder, when they had just started selling their furniture to an additional foreign country (Customer). The transaction generally went like this. To get paid:

1. Sauder needed to sell furniture through an International Broker (IB)
2. IB took control of the furniture temporarily
3. IB matched the furniture value to steel that Customer had to sell
4. Customer exchanged steel through the IB and got furniture
5. IB sold Broker's Buyer (BB) steel it wanted for US dollars
6. Sauder got US dollars for the furniture it wanted
7. Everyone sat around the fire singing "Kum Ba Yah"

Ultimately, all parties got what they wanted. The point is that you may be able to barter with a third party to get the first party's goods or services, but you need to assess values and coordinate the whole transaction. This is obviously more complex, but possible.

In this type of exchange, you or the other parties may need to provide "boot" (some cash) in addition to the exchanged items. If one has a clear value difference from the other, it may be worth it. For example, if your item is valued at $100 and what you are receiving is valued at $75, you would ask for a $25 payment in addition to their item. Whether sales tax is due and on what amount can be a gray area so you will need to check with your tax advisor for the states and/or countries involved to understand your tax options. If barter transactions recur many times or grow in dollar value, it may become more questionable as it relates to sales or use tax. Planning ahead for taxes and maintaining your documentation may avoid some tax problems.

These transactions are a great way to get what you want, possibly get rid of what you don't want that someone else can use, and not have any out-of-pocket costs. I have seen several online sale and barter sites gaining in popularity. Some have not had staying power and have gone out of business, but a quick search can return several options. Do a little due diligence before getting too involved with them so you are confident they will be there when you need them. eBay and Craigslist have been around for years and have a lot of satisfied users.

Q. How much could I save?

You may be wondering if it is actually worthwhile to learn these skills. Negotiating builds confidence, saves you money, gains you goods and services that you want at great values, and may get you more income, so how could it not be worth it? Like any sport, practice continues to make you better. The less you spend, the less you have to earn to meet your goals.

Many people don't realize that negotiation is a strategic skill rather than an instinct. As a result, they are not nearly as prepared or skilled at it. Fortunately, that makes it easier for those of us who do practice and prepare to succeed at getting what we want. At times I wasn't thinking big enough about what I might get, but I made a big request anyhow and got more than I wanted in the first place. I have talked myself into going for what I want by just asking for it, even when doing so seemed crazy, given the situation. I have used these skills to get several houses, cars, business purchases, longer-term agreements, groceries, electronics, furniture, jewelry, appliances, etc. As you might imagine, the savings are in the tens of thousands over a number of years.

A couple of years ago on the last week of the calendar year, I was negotiating for a vehicle. I had shopped around and was looking at several lightly-used vehicles. I came across a deal on a sharp-looking, new, loaded black SUV with a V-8 Hemi engine (gotta have a Hemi) that the dealership wanted to move by the end of the year. I used my techniques over a few days, getting down to the last sales day of the year, and when I was done I had that $42,000-plus sticker price discounted more than $15,000 (36%) to $27,000. You need to know what is driving the other party's motivation to sell and satisfy those needs.

As competition increases and technologies get better, prices go down and savings can go up if you use these techniques. I recently read that Circuit City (which went out of business) and Best Buy-type stores are starting to negotiate prices since we are in such a bad economy. Don't convince yourself that retail stores won't negotiate. Use this mental formula when haggling: [SW⁴]—Some Will, Some Won't, So What, Someone's Waiting.

If you get other services and goods included into package deals, your savings can be multiplied by saving on each of the items in the package. For example, during law school, my wife and I were able to get oil and filter changes included in a great incentive car lease after we locked in a price. While purchasing housing materials in a big-box store, I was able to get installation of flooring included at a substantial discount even though the materials were already at wholesale price. Another time, I got local padding/installation and home delivery included at a substantial discount while buying stock carpet wholesale, by the roll, direct from Dalton, Georgia manufacturers.

Let your imagination flow and craft some great deals most people wouldn't think about. The closer in the distribution chain you get to the manufacturer, the better your deal can be.

Q. Why should I consider negotiating, regardless of value?

Even if the item you would like seems inexpensive, practice your skills on these lower-priced items so that you will be prepared when you are working on higher-priced items like cars and properties. Make negotiating a habit so that it becomes automatic. You will regularly save money. My wife practices at flea/craft markets we go to. Most of the prices are low enough that you really can't hurt yourself by making a mistake, but you can learn from it.

Remember, every dollar not spent is a dollar that works toward your goals. If a five dollar bill was lying on the sidewalk in front of you, would you bend down and pick it up? Assuming you said yes, then save five dollars or more on your next purchase, and you will gain by not spending more money than you needed to. If your income stays the same and you save by spending less using these techniques, the resulting higher net income (income received less expenses paid) goes to work for you right away because you don't need to work harder or longer or get a raise to attain greater wealth.

Q. Why bother using coupons, sales, close-outs, etc.?

Even though I don't need to at this point in life, I still like to use coupons for regular purchases, get items free by mailing in a certificate, and find close-outs, blow-outs, good flea markets, wholesalers, warehouses, estate sales, high-end neighborhood garage sales, etc. I make it a little game to see what I can find at an unheard of price. It allows me to buy things I regularly use, and also buy a few things that I like, but won't normally pay the asking price for.

Over the last couple of years, I found spectacular deals at two nice neighborhood garage sales (I only go to a couple a year and choose higher-end neighborhood sales). I found a new, insulated, black leather baseball-style jacket that fit me great. It's a Detroit Red Wing signature coat that the homeowner, who was a salesman for a car parts manufacturer, was given when his company gave them to their best vendors that year, and he never wore it. It is at least a $400 coat that I got for $10. Yes, $10. The second item is a matching suit, coat and slacks, not hemmed, in a nice blue color with pinstripes from Macy's. It was never worn by the homeowner, who had outgrown it. It was a $300-plus suit that fit me well and I got it for $10. Yes, $10. As you can see, you can save some real bucks.

I also like to find distributors, inventory clearances, inventory liquidations, going-out-of-business sales, foreclosures, bankruptcies, and self-storage auctions, as well as online auctions. Pay attention to newspaper ads and get on their e-mail lists. These places will alert you when they have sales. During back-to-school season, office supply and discount drugstores offer both rebates and buy-one-get-one-free deals. Black Friday (day after Thanksgiving) has all kinds of deals if you can endure the crowds. For vehicles, as well as other goods, the end of the month and, even more so, the end of the year are great times to negotiate the best deals.

Conversely, convert your unwanted belongings to cash by selling them at an online auction or an in-person, local auction. View all of these transactions as little victories. Doing so will spur you on to bigger things. You can also talk with others at these venues and learn of other related venues that may allow you to pick up other deals.

Years ago, I would go to a multi-acre outdoor market in Shipshewana, Indiana (Amish country) and I would always negotiate with one of the largest vendors there for high-end, full-grain soft leather attaché bags. A number of these were Kenneth Cole (or sometimes one peg lower on the fashion scale) but sold for $200 to $300 at the leather shops in the mall. For a few years I had been negotiating deals on these with the vendor for $25 to $50. One day, the owner said to me, "Why don't you just wholesale with me since you are basically getting these near my cost." Through that interaction, I opened a side business where I bought several bags from him and sold them through shows and my personal network. I did the same thing with an Alpaca artwork wholesaler in Cherokee, North Carolina.

Q. Why do I need to understand markups and distribution?

You only need to understand the general process of how a product gets from a manufacturer to the retail store and ultimately to you as the retail customer. Some have more steps, and some have fewer, so I will lay out the basic, typical process and explain it as if we are talking about Sony as they manufacture one of their DVD writers:

- Sony buys components that go into the final product from component manufacturers (companies that make the plastic case, cardboard box, packaging, instruction book, etc.) that all have markup (3rd markup level) on each of the components that they sell to Sony.
- Component manufacturers have part manufacturers (2nd markup level—companies that supply the tray drawer, circuit boards, buttons, LED screen, etc.) that they buy parts from to assemble and manufacture the component.
- Part manufacturers usually have other smaller part/material manufacturers (screws, springs for tray door, gears for tray, resistors and solder for circuit boards, brackets, etc.) they buy from to assemble their parts (1st markup level). I am not going back in the process any further, but there are other markups before this stage with some products.
- Once Sony produces a complete product, it adds its markup (4th markup level) and sells to distributors (only companies that commit to buy very large quantities from Sony).
- Distributors add their markup (5th markup level) and sell to wholesalers (a few specific companies that will buy large quantities from distributors at low prices that they can disperse to retailers through their network).
- Wholesalers add their markup (6th markup level) and sell to retailers (places like Best Buy, Radio Shack, and other audio-type stores we normally buy DVD writers from).
- Retailers add their markup (7th markup level) and place them in their stores to sell to retail customers like you and me.

The amount of markup per level is not limited except by the competitors at their same level in the manufacturing and distribution process explained above. By the time a product gets to the retail store, it has been marked up several times. The fewer competitors at each level of the distribution chain, the higher the markups can be. It is common to see products like furniture, jewelry, leather goods and others marked up 400 to 500% over the manufacturer's price (4th level) to a retailer.

A number of years ago, I learned from a very well known cola distributor that a fountain cola drink in a typical restaurant had an actual material cost of five cents for the syrup and water, but they charged around $1.59 (now that's a markup). That is why they try to get everyone who comes to the restaurant to have a drink (other than water) and give free refills.

The point is to recognize that there is a huge markup on many goods by each of the handlers in the chain of manufacture and distribution to the retail customer. As you can see, the earlier you can get access to the product in the distribution chain, the better. It has much less cost added to it at the earlier stages so they can sell it much cheaper. How do you think I could buy those leather attachés at that price? Because of the cost of labor, U.S. products are often much more expensive than goods imported from Asia and other countries, despite the added cost to ship them by barge. Work to buy back in the chain as close to the manufacturer as you can and you can get substantial discounts. This is how many eBay platinum power sellers can sell for the prices they do and still profit.

Q. How do I build my case to avoid paying retail price?

You need to realize that retailers will lose money on goods just to get rid of them at times. They make money on moving inventory as quickly as possible. If an item doesn't move quickly enough, they will reduce the price to get rid of it, so it can be replaced with a more profitable item. End of season, out of style, last year's model, closeouts, excess quantities on hand, and post holiday goods all make for great deals. I have bought goods discounted 75 to 80% just by being patient and buying at the right time. Good targets are places that primarily want high traffic and sell a lot of goods (e.g.: Sam's, Kohl's, Wal-Mart, Kmart, Costco, Home Depot, Lowe's) rather than specific items like jewelry. Talk to the department or store manager if you want to make a particular offer that is unique.

Think of reasons it would be good for the vendor to get rid of the item. Examples might be:

- Build a loyal, new customer
- Increase sales
- Cutoff for monthly or quarterly reports is approaching
- There is too much inventory
- A new model has just been released
- Remaining inventory includes strange sizes or colors
- They need space for upcoming holiday goods
- They will pay personal property tax on it at year-end
- Bad time of the year for that item
- Declining popularity
- Demand has dropped
- Supply is high everywhere
- Good is not unique anymore and has become a commodity

Use these reasons as leverage when negotiating for price reductions, extra goods, amenities, features, warranties, service, and similar advantages. You can also use the "this is as much as I have in my budget; otherwise, I can't buy" approach and see what happens. Realize you shouldn't be wearing expensive clothes or jewelry when you use this angle. Remember to truly have your BATNA's (see negotiation rules at the beginning of the chapter) in place before negotiating so you know what to do if the deal doesn't go your way.

As it relates to your personal negotiating style, don't be combative, aggressive, or disrespectful. Be confident, calm, use a quiet enough voice so others don't overhear what you are trying to do, and build some rapport. Be upbeat and willing to help them move their inventory. Express some interest, but not at the terms they have listed (price, style, interest, warranty, etc.). Give the reasons that you are not willing to buy as they have proposed and make them an offer, letting them know you will buy now. Be sure to state your case in a way that shows how this will help them, not you. This needs to be a win-win type scenario in their mind. Word things as if you assume they are going to accept your offer and complete the transaction because it is a fair offer and will allow them to get rid of inventory.

If they say no, ask to talk with the manager-supervisor who has the authority to accept your offer. You may have some additional reasons you've saved for your manager talk, or hybrids of the reasons you've already used, to try to negotiate the purchase. Work through the terms right at the time and get their signed approval once they agree to the terms so you don't have to revisit it later. You don't want to give them the chance to change their mind and have to go through the whole process again. If the initial contact is not helpful and shuts you down, leave their area quietly. Go find the manager for that area or for the whole store if you really want to get what you are working toward. Approach this person in the same direct manner, wording things as if she will accept your offer based on the reasons you have provided.

Be polite but assertive. If they appear uncertain about approving your request, talk them into doing what you want by suggesting what they should do next. (Maybe you need to talk with your manager now. I will go with you if you want.) Walk them down the path you want to go, and they may become an advocate for you in reaching your objective. Don't talk in a passive or uncertain manner. Be confident that they want to sell you what you want. Reverse the logic if you are trying to sell something and utilize these tactics to convince them to buy.

I'll share a couple of examples from one store I'm not going to name (hint: largest retailer in the world) that my wife, family, and friends all told me was not even an option. A few days after Christmas a few years ago, we went to this store to see what they were clearing out after the holidays. We have an 18' vaulted ceiling in our great room. I had said it would be neat to have one of the big 12' Christmas trees in that room. They were normally $300 to more than $500, but we didn't want to spend that much for a few weeks of use, so we had decided against buying one. I happened to see six 12', pre-lit Christmas trees (with hinged metal branches) on clearance for 60% off their reduced price, or $120 off the previously discounted price of $300. We already had five trees in our house that I had gotten in different deals over the years, and I had decided we wouldn't spend more than $50 on any tree, even one that big.

I knew they did not want to store them for a year since they have limited storage space above the typical shelves to store extra stock. Also, very few homes could accommodate such a tree, and very few people shopping there would spend that much. On top of that, the tree weighed more than 100 pounds so very few people would be able to handle that much tree. So I said I was going to find the manager and plead my case. I also called some family and friends who might want one to see if I could work a bulk deal and provide additional incentive to the manager to sell multiple big trees now. Two friends wanted them if I could get a deal, so I pleaded my case to the manager who took it to the store manager and came back with a change order slip approving the sale of as many as I wanted for $50 each. My wife's mouth fell open, I thanked the supervisor, and the employees started loading trees for me. We tell people that story and they still don't believe us because they don't think it's possible with such a huge company. They talk themselves out of negotiating before even trying.

Interestingly enough, I did the same thing at the same store a few months later with a digital, mini-DVD camcorder and got it for the lowest price listed online from a refurbished vendor even though this one was new and just on clearance. I used the same process, printed a number of pages from the online site to build my case, presented it in a cordial, convincing manner, got the manager to sign off, and bought it. The clerk originally turned it down, so I asked if the manager was there and talked with her when she returned. The manager finally accepted my offer. My wife didn't question me as much this time; she just watched and took mental notes. She has been a litigator in a law firm for more than 12 years and regularly resolves issues with her cases using my techniques. She has seen me do this so many times that she continues to expand her abilities based on my success.

Practice will make you better and you will quickly see progress. Each time you do it, you get a little more confident. A lot of it is dependent upon mindset and presentation, as well as the guts to take action and accept no or a rude reaction, which I have gotten a few times.

Q. How can I have fun and not get stressed out?

You get the courage to move forward by convincing yourself that you only stand to gain from the experience and that you are doing nothing wrong. Be yourself. If you are stressing out about it, take a few long, deep breaths before you begin, letting each breath out slowly. This will relax you and calm you down. Don't try to be me or someone else you believe is really good at this. If you are worried that someone will think you're a jerk for asking, or if you fear looking "stupid," practice negotiating when you are on vacation or on business in another town. Tell yourself, "They don't know me anyway! Who cares if they think I'm stupid. I'm not. What does it matter if this person I will never see again thinks I'm a jerk?" This may alleviate much of your anxiety.

Jack Canfield, in a teleseminar, told of a bright student that he put through an exercise to break him of feeling stupid and being unsuccessful in this type of situation. He had the student walk into a 7/11, go to the counter, and ask the clerk where he could find a 7/11 close by. The clerk responded nicely saying, "You are in a 7/11. What can I get for you?" They could have made fun of him, ridiculed him, or thought he had lost it, but the key is that he did it anyhow. The experience helped to build his courage to ask for what he wanted regardless of the perceived outcome.

Being willing to walk away from the negotiation is another way to alleviate stress. Remember, in my Christmas tree example, I didn't have the tree to begin with and didn't need it. So my first BATNA was to accept a slightly higher price than my offer because it was still a deal and my second BATNA was to walk away and keep looking until I found the deal I wanted. Therefore, I was confident that I knew what I would do if they turned me down. I would have listened to a counteroffer, but it would have had to have been close to my offer for me to accept it. Also understand that I satisfied the retailer's need and we were satisfied with our purchase so it was a win-win. Having that confidence is very helpful, especially when working with a huge retailer. It makes it easier each time you practice the skill.

You could make it a friendly, competitive game with family and friends. Each member could include others in their deals, like I did with the Christmas tree. Maybe have a little trophy that passes around to the person who got the best deal most recently to keep the spirit of the game. This could get you deals you wouldn't normally know about as you build a network of people looking for deals.

Obviously, this approach is not one that sales clerks are used to, so you will need to politely persist and lead them where you need them to go. You will need to get to a manager many times, especially if you are getting shut down and you want to make it happen. It will not work all the time, but you won't know until you try it, and it works more often than not for me.

An example of a time it didn't work for me was at a Kenneth Cole (KC) outlet store in Orlando, Florida, a couple of years ago. I saw a soft leather attaché I liked and had not carried when I had my side business. It was on clearance, but still cost more than I really wanted to pay. I went to the manager and told him I wholesaled these very same bags in Ohio, but didn't carry this one. I said I bought bags like this for $25 (I was bluffing because I usually bought KC's for $40 to $50 and cheaper models for $25) and would like this one to add to my collection. Would he accept $25? He was very curt, said we don't reduce clearance bags any further, and walked away.

For a retail manager at a small outlet store, that was a poor way to handle it. He came across as demeaning and snooty, which doesn't match the role, but I brushed it off (after I called him names under my breath) and moved forward. I ultimately paid the $40 because I really liked the bag and knew I paid $50 at wholesale prices for some of my KC bags so it was worth it. But, I would not have known unless I tried. So the moral here is that I didn't lose anything by asking, and I could have saved an additional $15 had he accepted my offer. The only thing it really cost me was the few minutes it took to make my case. Your response to a negative interaction, like this one, needs to be "NEXT" and move on to the next deal (which I ultimately got on a killer Fossil watch a few stores down, yay me).

Realize that throughout your life you will encounter thousands of events and interactions, and your response to these interactions is what determines the outcome. Don't let others' actions determine your response or your demeanor. You control your feelings and emotions, so you control your responses. Remember the equation from an earlier chapter: Event + Response = Outcome. With the manager in the last example, I could have let him hear my thoughts (loudly) about his response and treatment of me as a customer, as I have seen others do. I could have threatened to talk to the District Manager to let her know, potentially causing him problems, but I decided he was not worth any more of my time, and I purchased the item without his assistance.

Q. How else can I network to find deals?

You could modify the game concept described above and form a network of people interested in working deals. You can assemble an informal group that meets to share the deals they have found, how they found them, and what they did to get the deals. You could also share items that other group members are looking for and have them be on the lookout to help everyone reach their goals. Since e-mail, blogs, forums, text messages, and cell phones are so popular and simple to use now, you could set up your group online, instead of meeting, and stay in touch with very little effort. You can teach your spouse or kids these skills and they can practice on the lower-value options while letting you negotiate more expensive deals once you are comfortable with the process.

Q. Should I not spend time on lower priced items?

As you gain more skills, experience, and responsibility, you will begin to value each hour of your day more highly. You will want to start comparing the amount of time you have devoted to some of these negotiations with the value you will receive, if it goes well. You will also want to assess probability of success beforehand, so you don't waste much time on long-shots. Some things will take too much time to be worth it, so give it your best try quickly and move on.

An example of something that was not worth it to me was signing up for a gas card that offered a discount of ten cents per gallon during the month you signed up. The discount did not continue past the first month. So if I bought 20 gallons of gas each week of that month, I would only save $2 per week for four weeks, or $8 for the month. The following month, the price reverted to regular price. There were no points or rebates if you used the card after that first month so there were minimal savings. That was not worth it to me because I would have another credit card to track that is only usable at one gas station chain, and I would only save a total of $8. I didn't take the time to complete the application.

Another example was at a nearby big-box superstore where they had writing pads on sale for five cents, regularly 99 cents. Since my wife and I write a lot, I wanted the limit of 20 of them, but missed the sale by one day. I asked the clerk if I could still get the sale, but was turned down. I ultimately asked for the manager, who knew me by sight, to see if she would honor the prior day sale price since I am there so frequently and just ran late getting home the night before. She did honor it, but as I was picking them out I found the five-cent sale sign from the day before mixed in some pads. So they would have had to give them to me for that price anyhow because they typically honor a sign they have out.

The point is that I spent $1 rather than $5 (they were still on sale for .25) yet I spent a decent chunk of time messing with it to get the deal. On the other hand, for someone just starting out, the experience of saving $4 and only spending $1 on 20 pads would be a positive experience that helps to build skills and confidence.

Q. How else can these skills benefit me?

When you are negotiating with different parties, give some thought to the nature of their business. You may spot needs in their business that you could fill and create a little side business that may lead to a bigger business opportunity. Depending upon your professional background and goals, this may get you a consulting assignment to assist the company in becoming more efficient or effective in some area. You can also get a great contact within the company to use for another job or company you work for or own. You might even be able to utilize the contact for a referral to another business that might need your assistance or fill your need for specific goods or services. You may also be doing some fundraising for your kid's school or another non-profit you work with and be able to utilize the contact to get a donation. The point is to not limit the potential benefits to each party from an interaction.

Overall, the skills needed to negotiate and barter can be invaluable for many reasons. They keep your mind active and creative. They teach you how to deal with many different kinds of interactions that can be stressful for many people. They enable you to be able to deal with many types of people and to be able to think on your feet. You will learn more about many different businesses that can assist you in future interactions.

If you think in terms of a win-win solution, you can eliminate any guilt that may creep up if you start to see yourself as a penny pincher or cheapskate. Thank people for calling you a cheapskate; it can be seen as a compliment if you use it properly and truly understand it. When my family or friends have teased me about this, knowing I have accumulated some wealth, I just smile and realize that what they don't know or won't do just lets me continue to get more deals. In that situation I win and they lose, but they just don't understand it. You must be willing to step outside of your comfort zone to learn and grow each day.

WHAT WOULD JEFF DO?
(Fun action steps to try this stuff out)

1. Ask for something each day from here forward that you would not have asked for before reading this book. Use the negotiation process to get the strategic pattern down so you can do it without thinking. Start with smaller items and move up in value as you get more confident and comfortable.

2. Think of something you can barter for each week for the next month and complete the exchange. Use the abbreviated negotiation process mentioned above before contacting the other party. During the second month, modify your approach and process with actions that worked best and eliminate those that didn't. Increase the value and frequency of your bartering each month moving forward.

3. Go to one higher-end neighborhood or estate sale each week this month and practice your negotiation skills to get at least one good deal. It will build your confidence.

4. Sell something online this week, making a profit, and continue this process for several weeks.

5. Look at something you are buying regularly or want to buy and research a way to buy from some party earlier in the chain so you can get a much better price. Once you do this, you will not want to buy retail again.

6. Think of family and friends you could share this with then work together to look for deals each of you would like. Be the group coordinator and stay in contact by e-mail or text message. More people looking will multiply your opportunities.

7. Do this enough to be called a penny pincher or cheapskate, then just smile and thank them. You just joined the deal makers, which is a great club to be in.

Show your family and friends these skills because you've learned something that can help them. Once you've finished these steps, write me to let me know what happened and what you learned at *stories@lifescheatsheets.com*.

Now, think like Nike and Just Do It!

Got Time? (Effective Time Management)

Q. **Why is time my most important commodity?**

As you continue through life, your time will become your most important asset because it will seem like you have less and less available. We all know that is not true because everyone still has 24 hours each day to use as she sees fit. When you take on more responsibilities (and believe me, you will), you will lose more and more of your free time. Therefore, you will have to make room for "your time." Once you take on college, work, spouse, kids, family, sports, etc., you may reach a point where you are overwhelmed and need to organize your life to make it more satisfying. You may feel that everyone else demands your time to the point that you don't have any left within your control. Efficient and effective time management will be critical.

Time is our most precious commodity because we can never get any more per day than anyone else. You have to decide how to best use it. You can get more material possessions, more money, and more friends, but you can never get more time. Not to be morbid, but you really never know when your body will give out due to trauma, disease, age, overuse, abuse, etc., so you really need to make the best of every hour of every day.

When I got out of law school, I interviewed with a $100-million, family-owned company near Detroit with a non-family member President. We were very similar and I was chosen as his successor if he were to "get hit by a bus." They were doing succession planning in case of his death because he was the lead management person and the active family members were not equipped to take over the company. I was "insurance" for them. They used the phrase "hit by a bus" many times and it has stuck with me. You may plan to live for many decades, but you just never know when your time will come.

This concept played out in a local tragedy recently when a mother and her 10-year-old son from Texas were visiting her family here. Her boy was riding his bike, veered into traffic, and was hit by a truck. He survived in the hospital for a number of days before he passed away. I'm certain his mother couldn't have believed he would die at such a young age and just wished she had more time with him. Since we have no say about when our time is up, we need to make the best use of the time we do have.

I still use the phrase *carpe diem* (seize the day), but I modify it to "seize the moment." You will find that each day offers many opportunities and you don't ever get them back. If you seize each moment, you will make the best of every situation and not regret afterwards that you should have done something different.

Q. When should I start time management?

I encourage you to read articles and books on time management techniques right now. Many years ago I used to teach time management to help colleagues utilize their time better. Time management, like the network-building skills described in the following chapter, is something that you need to start now and continue to build on. As a young adult, just out of high school, I recall not really thinking about this topic. Within a couple of years, when I started working full time, going to college at night and weekends, playing in volleyball, softball, and golf leagues, dating, and buying and maintaining rental real estate, I started reading time management books because I was severely stretched and was not getting much sleep. I remember wishing I had learned those skills sooner, before I found myself feeling overwhelmed. Fortunately, I made the time to read materials that could help me take control of my busy schedule and enjoy my life.

You will also manage your time better by learning to make decisions and move forward to implement them. Reduce the amount of time spent rethinking and questioning your decisions. I have some perfectionist traits from my mom. These can hold me back if I continue to try to make things perfect before moving forward and finishing the task. If you have these traits, get a handle on them now and accept less-than-perfect results. You need to realize that nothing is ever perfect, so recognize that good is fine and move on. Life is about moving forward rather than rehashing past events and wondering whether you made the right decisions. You will make good and not-so-good decisions, and you will learn from all of them. If you don't like the outcome of a decision, make a new decision to change the situation and don't waste time looking back, wishing you had made a different choice. You can't change the past so live in the now.

If you have extra time now or can give up some TV, texting, or other nonproductive time, use it to read and learn. I wish I had begun using personal development and motivational materials earlier in life because I believe I would have weathered bad times better and would have easily attracted even more good into my life. I am now giving my books to people for graduations because they can help people learn and apply these skills now rather than learning by trial and error over a period of many years. I have also given a book called *The Success Principles* by Jack Canfield and Janet Switzer, which is a compilation of some of the best life principles I have found.

Q. Will time management help me achieve balance?

You will find that it will become much more difficult to keep balance in your life as you take on more responsibilities. It will also be more difficult to allocate time to each of your most important goals. The better your time management skills, the more you will be able to fit in, and the better you can maintain balance. I found I was driven so much to succeed quickly in business that I lost balance in my life. It was sad, at times, because I lost track of friends and extended family. Even though I had made many friends in college and through various sports that I played, many of them were transient so they were not long-term friends.

Many people get consumed with their work to the point that it takes much of their waking hours and their life becomes severely out of balance. With many people losing their jobs and businesses closing, it is important to keep a balance so you still have a support network and other outside interests if you ever lose your job. The loss of your job can lead to depression and financial strain if you have not followed financial principles like those in this book and in my *financial habits* follow-up book.

Devote time and energy to achieving your career goals, and work hard in your occupation—then leave it at work. Make the time to review your financial plan and take action to further it. Take action to reduce your expenses and increase your income. But take time to stay connected with your friends, too. Set aside time and spend it with family. Take time to work out or engage in some kind of physical activity to maintain your health. Spend some time to develop your spiritual life. Carve out some time for yourself to relax, take a vacation, and engage in a hobby that you enjoy.

One area may need more of your time temporarily to meet a particular deadline, but revisit the others once you have met that deadline. You may occasionally need to spend more time to meet the demands of your job, a family medical emergency, a friend going through a hard time, a spiritual crisis, or a serious health condition. But don't put off the other areas of your life indefinitely. You don't want to wake up one day and realize that your failure to manage your time has left you with a decent career, but no family, few friends, poor health, no spiritual direction, no hobbies or outside interests, and no joy in your life.

Q. Why should I value my time and delegate?

Begin by tracking all your daily activities in detail. Track your time using 10 minute intervals. Then see whether you can skip those activities that have minimal value or you can delegate or pay others to do them for you. Note how much time you spend on e-mails and useless calls. Add up all of the time spent on each activity and put a plan in place to eliminate, delegate, or reduce the time that you spend doing things that are not income-producing and those that you are not skilled at or not interested in. Repeat this process every month for a number of months and you will see increased productivity.

As you become more educated and experienced over the years, the market will put more value on your skills and your time. If you are paid hourly, it is more obvious because your pay rate goes up. If you are paid on a salary basis, divide your salary, including your benefits, by the number of hours that you actually work to identify your hourly value. As you achieve more of your goals with effective time management, your value per hour will continue to grow and you can eliminate more "busy" activities from your schedule.

Consider subcontracting activities that are valued lower than your time. Look at things like mowing the lawn, shoveling snow, doing the dishes, grocery shopping, cleaning, paying bills, errands, etc. Personal shoppers, house cleaners, personal assistants, tutors, people who run errands, do yard work, provide pet care, and baby sit can do some of this work for you, and are probably available in your area. You may find that it ends up costing less to hire someone to do those tasks than it was costing you to do them.

You can then spend your time on higher-valued activities. You might spend more time working to generate more income. But some things have an intangible value, like attending your child's volleyball game, going to your spouse's Christmas party, or playing in a golf league. If those activities are important to your balanced life and you value them, make room for them. The point is not to eliminate all non-income producing activities, but to fill your life with a balanced selection of activities that are most valuable to you. Your priorities, and your budget, will change as you move through life, and you can adjust your time allocation accordingly.

Another way to determine the monetary value of your time is to see what the market pays someone who provides your service.

Divide the amount by the number of hours spent on those specific tasks. It's easiest to see the value on an hourly basis, but you may see another unit of measure that works best for your business. I realize you may not be earning as much as the market rate, but once you align yourself with your unique skills and reallocate your time, you will see your value increase.

It is also helpful to concentrate your work time on activities in which you are naturally skilled and interested and let others perform the functions that you are not best at or do not like. Everyone has unique skills, so find people who are good at doing the things you don't do best and hire them as subcontractors. You may find that you have been forcing yourself to do things that you now see can be hired out at a reasonable cost.

Commercial appraisers arrive at multiple values for land they are appraising. One value is based on what it *could* be used for (highest and best use), regardless of how it is currently being used. For example, if a self-storage facility is sitting on a high traffic corner in a growing city, an appraiser may conclude that the highest and best use of that land on that corner is a bank, a convenience store, or a fast food restaurant where it is worth $25 per square foot rather than self storage that is worth $1 per square foot. Use this analogy to determine if the work you're doing uses your skills for their "highest and best use." If not, change it so this is true.

Q. How can I focus my work time on my core skills?

One way to stay focused on using your time for your most valuable tasks is to post a question right in front of you at your work area so you see it many times a day. The question is, "Am I working on my highest income-producing functions right now?" If the answer is "no," then see if there is a way to expedite, delegate, or subcontract that function and realign yourself back to your core activities. If not, at least be aware and work quickly to complete that task so you can move on to more productive activities.

Most of your non-core activities are available outside or can be done better by another employee. The key is to focus your professional time on your core activities that utilize your unique skills. Don't let non-core activities and distracters steal much of your time. E-mails, meetings, and phone calls can be huge time wasters. Become efficient and minimize these types of activities.

If you own your own business, consider hiring a virtual assistant who is not in your office. In fact, she may not be in your state or country, but she can take over many office activities via technology. You can stay in touch electronically by phone, fax, and computers, and this person can work from a home office, taking care of her personal matters while fulfilling your need for an assistant. Many virtual assistants will work part time, if that is your need, and they can significantly reduce the time you spend on administrative matters.

As you start your career, a number of these activities may be part of your job. But once you have accumulated some time in your role at work, track these non-core activities and work with your supervisor to show him how the company would benefit from you doing more of your core skills and less of the non-core skills. Maybe you can trade off functions with someone better at your non-core skills. For example, let's say you are good with numbers and spreadsheet analysis, but not very good with typing and word processing. Perhaps a coworker is better at typing, writing, and word processing, but not good with numbers and spreadsheets. Some of your word processing functions could switch to her and her spreadsheet functions to you, which would more fully utilize both of your core skills sets and benefit all parties.

Q. Is being paid by the hour limiting my earnings?

Don't let yourself fall into the hourly-rate trap. Having a steady job that you love is great, regardless of how you are paid. Consider, however, that if you are paid on an hourly basis, you are trading hours for money and you will hit an earnings ceiling. You only have so many hours a day that you can devote to your profession. If you are able to get a position with an incentive, commission, or bonus system, you can then allocate your time to those functions that earn you the most income.

I found as a CMA (like a CPA) and as an attorney, that most of my colleagues are capped on what they can personally earn because everyone's time is limited. One common way to get beyond that limit is to leverage your practice by having staff perform many of the functions that you have in volume (like preparing lots of simple tax returns during tax season or reviewing rooms full of records for particular documents in a class action law suit) while you earn a portion of the income that they generate. You then perform functions that you are more skilled at and can bill out at a higher rate. Many professionals tend to be burned out by not delegating and become more negative about their work because of the high number of hours they continue to devote to their practice.

Q. What techniques should I use to be more efficient?

There are a lot of time management technique books in bookstores, libraries, and online so I have only listed a few techniques below to get you started.

- Look through your mail initially then toss it, delegate it, or deal with it right then. The goal is for you to touch your mail only once and have it dealt with. To recognize a problem with this one, each time (after the initial time) you touch a piece of mail, put a colored dot in the upper right corner and continue to reduce the number of dots on the right corner to none.
- Use a variety of desk organizers, wall organizers, document organizers and file cabinets to manage all of your physical papers, and organize your electronic files with a folder-subfolder hierarchy system. If you spend a little time getting and staying organized, you won't waste time each day looking for things.
- Use a calendar that functions efficiently for you. If you prefer, use a paper calendar rather than relying on an electronic calendar that you are not comfortable with. On the other

hand, having an electronic calendar, like Outlook, can help you be mobile.

- Use technology options everywhere you can. Most of them can make your work look more professional and can be much more efficient. Just make certain they are backed up regularly so you don't risk losing data.
- Respond to requests by e-mail if possible, then by phone or video teleconference if e-mail cannot work, and then by personal meeting as a last option to minimize the time spent on each issue. Have meetings just before lunch to keep them short, and consider standing rather than sitting to make them go even faster. Having food available tends to make meetings run longer.
- Use color coding for files, papers, reports, etc. to define priorities and other needs.
- Use marker boards to help you identify and prioritize important tasks for the day, week, and month and for motivational purposes to track and show progress on goals/projects.
- Use a prioritized to-do list with the top three to five tasks you need to do that day at the top. Get to those most important functions at the best time of the day for you. Some people are best in the morning, while others need a little time to get warmed up to be their best.
- Use formal project management software, like MindJet, for large projects and contact management software, like ACT, (outlined in detail in the next chapter) to maintain order and organization of your connections.
- Schedule no-interruption, quiet time every day, and multiple times per day if it's an option. Schedule all activities around these time periods. During these times, schedule activities that you need to have the most focus on. Don't accept a lot of needless interruptions, even outside of these times. Train others well to handle items so you can stay focused on your most important activities. Hold yourself and others accountable for your time, as well as their time.

- Schedule a short time period each day to learn an additional time management technique to increase your productivity.
- Stop the constant interruptions from e-mails and calls. Unless your job requires you to be *immediately* accessible all the time, change the setting on your e-mail to not alert you each time a new message arrives.
- Check your e-mail once every two to four hours if possible. Your productivity will increase if you can read and respond to messages in batches.
- Turn your phone on Do Not Disturb for portions of your day so your voice mail picks up, but make certain you do return the calls.

These are focused more on time management in the workplace, but you can also modify these ideas to apply to your personal life. There are countless other methods to help you make the most of every day. You will see improvement as you implement these techniques daily and see which ones best meet your needs.

Q. How can I utilize my time more efficiently?

Be creative. Brainstorm time-saving techniques with others. If you have multiple minds working on a solution, you will usually get many different options to try. Don't limit yourself with "normal" thinking or the way things have been done in the past. With others' input you can come up with new ideas for improving a process, eliminating redundancy, increasing your speed, reallocating resources, delegating tasks, eliminating waste, etc.

If you are in a supervisory/management role, set up tasks and projects for the staff in your department in a manner that limits your daily interaction. Also, have qualified and willing staff take over some of the tasks that you should have delegated but have been performing. Write down who is responsible for what, by when, who is to help, benchmarks for certain stages in the project, and similar project management criteria so you do not have to be involved daily. Make certain everyone has the plan and hold people accountable. I am not advocating that you avoid all interaction or never be available to assist. But there are ways to lead others without immersing yourself in the day-to-day activities once staff are adequately trained and informed. Let them know you need to focus your time more heavily on specific projects and need to reduce your daily involvement in tasks they are responsible for.

Mindjet Mind Manager software (*www.mindjet.com*) has been helpful to me in mapping out projects, goals, and plans. It also helps you to brainstorm ideas into tree diagrams. It lets you put your thoughts on paper in a graphic chart so you can see how an idea can take shape and become a reality. I find this software fun to use in mapping out a sequence of steps to follow to achieve a particular objective. It can be changed easily so it is very user friendly.

Stephanie Winston has several books on the subject including *Time Management for Dummies,* which I found helpful. Tim Ferriss also has a book called *The 4-Hour Workweek* that gives a lot of intriguing ideas about escaping the traditional rat race and living life to the fullest. In large part, it advocates outsourcing most of your life's activities to be free to do what you want to do.

Q. Will working at home save time?

Telecommuting is becoming more accepted and preferred in some professions. Obviously, there are some jobs that simply are not compatible with this arrangement. But many small businesses can fully function with employees and owners not sharing a common office. This reduces or eliminates a standard commute since most functions can be performed with phone, fax, e-mail, scanner, computer, and printer. Equipping a home office with these items will cost around $1,000 to 1,500. You can quickly recoup that money with vehicle savings, eliminating your time for the commute, eating fewer meals out, writing it off your on your tax return, and limiting your clothing needs.

Some businesses don't have a common office at all and use rented conference rooms, coffee houses, restaurants, etc. for meetings. It can be a huge savings on overhead, and for a startup company it can be the difference between staying in business or not.

If you work remotely with your office network computer system, make certain you have virus software that is up to date. You may use the Citrix system, popular remote user software, to interact with the office system. This type of access eliminates needless trips and saves on commute expenses.

If it is feasible for you to work from home, it is wise to pick a particular room for your home office that is quiet, away from heavy foot traffic, away from doors opening and closing, and that has its own door to separate you from the rest of the house.

Q. What can I complete online to save time?

If you want to continue your education, many courses are now offered online so you can take them from home. Teleseminars, webinars, conference calls, and video teleconference calls are all conveniently accessible from a home office.

A number of personal tasks can also be completed online to save time. Running from place to place for errands is really bad for your gas bill, so completing those tasks online can cut down wear and tear on your vehicle and reduce the amount of gas you use. Most businesses have online sites, so you can shop online and have items delivered right to your home. Banking and travel arrangements can also be completed online easily.

Please note that if you use one credit card specifically for online purchases, you only need to cancel the one card if you have a problem with the security of your account information. If you use PayPal, which is owned by eBay, or other similar services, you don't have to use a credit card, but you do have to give your checking account information. If you use one of these methods, don't keep large amounts of money in this account so that you're not as vulnerable to theft and fraud.

You will want to make certain you are working on a secure site whenever you are dealing with money, payments, receipts, and your personal information. Look for the padlock symbol in the upper area of your browser where the web site path is shown or other specific icons that show it is secure. Many secure sites have an "https" domain, rather than the typical "http" site, which shows that you are on a secure link.

Q. How else can I free up my time?

Another source of assistance when managing your time is your spouse/significant other and family. If you are a single person, or a single mom or dad, you may need to utilize your family and friends to help you fill in gaps in your schedule as you juggle a lot of responsibilities. If you are working toward your goals and you have shared them with your family and friends, they will naturally support you when you need assistance from time to time.

If you have children and they are old enough to understand basic concepts, assigning regular duties around the house is a great way to build their skills and sense of responsibility. The younger they are when you start teaching them these skills, the quicker they will learn to handle responsibilities.

If you have a roommate, splitting regular chores typically occurs. You can probably negotiate which ones you do so they fit your schedule if you are really stretched. Some of this is going to depend on your roommate's flexibility and willingness to help, but should be doable.

With dual-income families, spouses/significant others have to share the household responsibilities. I was single for many years, so I became self-sufficient before marrying. Even though I didn't like some of the activities, it was a great lesson and probably makes our marriage stronger, since I don't depend on my wife to do typical, daily tasks.

While you are trying to squeeze as much as you can into your schedule, don't neglect or forget to schedule time for your spouse/significant other, family, and friends. Things like date nights and weekends together are very important in sustaining a strong relationship. Enjoy your time along the way as you work toward your goals. We often take for granted that our spouses and family will be there for us, regardless of how often we are there for them. The prolonged strain from demanding jobs has significantly increased the divorce rate.

Your spouse is probably your best friend and the person you depend on the most, so make her a priority even if you have a very hectic schedule. The bond you have is very valuable and it is wise to include some one-on-one quiet time in your schedule to keep strong, open, and clear communication flowing. Time for your family should also be part of your regular schedule to avoid having that relationship break down. Make this a two-way street. OK, enough Dr. Phil.

Q. Do I get any fun and relaxation time?

Be sure to devote some time purely to fun and relaxation. This prevents stress from building up and keeps life from seeming like there is no reward for all of your hard work. You need time to relax, have fun, laugh, "let your hair down," and just be yourself. This helps balance good times with other activities you may dislike. It's the payoff for working hard, getting good grades, and taking care of your other responsibilities. You need to see this reward. At one point, I was guilty of working too much and have had to consciously stop myself and start enjoying life in between other projects.

You also regroup and refresh yourself when you take time off for a few days or a week. You then come back and can truly give it your best if you are not so burned out and tired of the same old thing. You can grow and learn about new places, see and do new things, meet new people, and learn about other cultures, all while refreshing yourself away from the same old grind. It's also healthy to give your body a break and free it of built-up stress.

Q. How can I fight procrastination?

One last area that can really waste a lot of your time is procrastination. Many people struggle with this to some degree, especially in areas that they are unfamiliar with, that are difficult, seem overwhelming, or involve an uncomfortable level of risk. Ultimately you have to take action and get that first task done which can give you the momentum to get the second task done and continue from there.

If you realize this from the start, you can get it over with quicker. Tackle those tasks that you are dreading first thing in the day rather than putting them off until the end of the day when suddenly you don't have enough time and they "have" to be put off again. If a project seems overwhelming, break it into small, sequential tasks and complete the first task then the second and so on. Seeing a big task as a series of small tasks makes it easier to start and keep making progress on until it's completed.

Many times, people put things off until they have to be done in a hurry. Doing things at the last minute usually ends with a job not done very well. Typically, last-minute decisions are not the best decisions and tasks are done inefficiently. A lot of wasted time is spent thinking about and dreading the tasks prior to taking action, which distracts you from the tasks you are better at and want to do. The point is that you need to consciously decide to get started, and it helps to complete the toughest tasks right away in the morning before starting those you are more interested in. If this is a stumbling block for you, research and read some books specifically on overcoming procrastination so it doesn't waste much of your valuable time.

WhaT WOULD JEFF Do?
(Fun action steps to try this stuff out)

1. Read some time management material weekly for the next month and look back at the end of the month to see what you have learned and put into practice. Use these techniques to achieve balance in your life.

2. Track your time as outlined for a full week. Look back at how you used your time and start to replace time wasters with actions that will move you toward accomplishing your goals. Start with replacing a half hour a day and increase it as you move forward.

3. Calculate the value of your time. Focus your efforts on the highest and best use of your time. Continue to take actions that will increase the value of your time.

4. Determine your best, natural skills that you put to use in your work. Analyze what other activities you are doing that are not core and come up with ways to focus more of your time on your best skills. This will increase your value to your company.

5. Draft a plan to get on an incentive pay system of some kind so you are not trapped by the hourly pay plan only. It may take some brainstorming and convincing others, but it will be worth it if you want to be paid for your efforts.

6. Ask someone each day who seems organized how they stay organized and efficient. You can learn other helpful techniques from those you know.

7. If telecommuting would help your situation, draft a proposal to see if that is an option for you to accomplish more.

8. Convert three to five tasks this month to an online method to save you time and effort.

9. Schedule time each week with your spouse/significant other so you don't leave them out of the equation.

10. Schedule some time for fun and relaxation to take a break and feel refreshed.

Ask others older than you how they stay organized and add their input to what you have learned. Share this information with others if you think it can help. Once you've finished these steps, write me to let me know what happened and what you learned at *stories@lifescheatsheets.com*.

Now, think like Nike and Just Do It!

IT IS WHO YOU KNOW (NETWORKING AND BUILDING RELATIONSHIPS)

Q. Why is my network so important?

The extensive, intangible value of a having a particular network has been the toughest lesson for me to accept during and after my first, formal all-out occupation search, when I finished law school (mentioned in previous chapters and explained at the end of this chapter). I wish this had been "preached" heavily to me late in high school or soon thereafter. What I got instead was the traditional advice that if you study hard, get good grades and degrees, work hard, and excel above others, you will continue to get the dream jobs you want and everything will be rosy. I now know that traditional path mentality is B.S. sometimes. The fact is, if you follow the traditional guide *and* build a carefully chosen network concurrently, your chances of achieving your goals will exponentially increase. That is the street smart lesson that I learned the hard way and you now know.

Q. How do I build my network continually?

For many of the reasons embedded in my story, you really need to build your network continually. Don't put it on your "to do" list, but make building it a habit, something you consciously keep in mind daily as you interact with people. Build a contact database and update it regularly as you interact. Remember key items about people that you can bring up in later interactions. It flatters them to know you kept them in mind and makes a stronger impact on them as well as a lasting connection. You never know when you may need a favor, and you may build a stronger, mutually beneficial relationship by using your skills or connections to help them.

Plan to go to an event weekly. Make certain you attend some events in person and not just online or by phone. Examples of events include Rotary, chamber of commerce, seminars, volunteer opportunities, Toastmasters, BNI, sports events, concerts, outings, etc. You should also maintain contact with network members through occasional e-mails, phone calls, text messages, handwritten notes on their birthdays, meeting at the coffee house, playing a sport together, etc. Social networks like Facebook and LinkedIn can help you maintain or renew important connections. For this reason, be mindful of your status updates because what you post could help or hurt you when you want to use some of those contacts for professional purposes.

The key is to be in network mode all the time because you never know when you will have a conversation that will give you a lead that will change your life. Pay attention and strike up conversations at the grocery store, video store, hair/nail salon, church, dry cleaners, sport events, kids' events, etc. Don't be pushy or put the other person on the spot, but just be curious and inquisitive about them. You'll find that people love to talk about themselves. Sometimes you can't get them to stop talking about themselves! Ask them questions about:

- What they do
- What challenges they have overcome
- Where they grew up
- Where they went to school
- Hobbies they have
- Charities they are passionate about
- Sports they play
- Movies or TV programs they like
- Their favorite books

- Who or what influenced the direction they took
- What successes they've had
- What their goals are, etc.

I came across a young guy in his 20s a few years ago who has continued to build his information and speaking business using his unique approachability concept. After attending a seminar on campus late in his undergraduate program at Miami University in Oxford, Ohio, he forgot to take off his name tag. Later he recognized that he was getting a lot of comments and connecting with many people just because of the name tag. At that point, he decided that he was going to wear a nametag all the time, 24 hours a day, 7 days a week, from then on.

He coined the term "approachability" and saw that this was a way to help people become more connected and more friendly. He could make people smile and help them enjoy life more by being approachable. He wrote a book on his concept while working as a furniture mover after college when he couldn't find the job he wanted. He had a conversation with a stranger one night on the bus going home after work that changed his life. He didn't realize it, but this person dated a writer for a big newspaper who called him, wrote an article on his concept, and printed it in her paper. That story and his book got picked up on the news wire by many papers and other media and his popularity exploded as a result.

His name is Scott Ginsberg, a.k.a.: The Nametag Guy. One of his books is *The Power of Approachability* and his site, which has a lot of free information and great lists on what to do and not do in certain situations, is *www.hellomynameisscott.com*. He even has the name tag he wears on his shirt tattooed on his chest in case someone rips it off or he goes swimming. He's got a lot of great ideas and has a counter on his site of the number of consecutive days he has worn his name tag. Last time I checked it was well over 3,000 days.

Q. Why fill the pipeline (Rolodex) before I even need it?

You might think to yourself, "I already have a job and know a number of people so I don't have any need for a bigger network now." I had the same thought, and I was wrong. I am giving you the inside scoop in telling you to build it now. Harvey MacKay's book *Dig Your Well Before You're Thirsty* is a great example of the point I am making. His whole theme is to build your network all the time and give to those in your network to solidify your connection. Don't just build the network to have your hand out to get something. Be the first to give others information that is relevant to their business. When you need something, they will be more willing to help you out because you have already strengthened the relationship. The concept of reciprocity rings true when you need them. Always be thankful to them and look for ways to return the favor. Keep them informed about what happened once they assisted you.

Many people do just the opposite: they have a need, so they try to build a network to get assistance with that need. They didn't build the connections before they needed them. I was partially guilty of this because I didn't believe the full value of building a network beyond my immediate needs. Though I built a decent network, it was limited to the industries that I was in. I knew I really didn't want to stay in my main job's industry, but I was so focused on doing more and working hard to move up quickly that I didn't stop and consider a longer-term plan that matched my interests. I was following the traditional mentality and believed my actions would get me everything I wanted in whatever industry I chose. I dismissed the value of a large, diversified network outside of my industry.

As you make contacts, look for mentors as well. Look for business people who have more experience in life and who can take you under their wing and show you lessons they have learned. They can help you avoid potholes they've hit along the way. I am continuously searching for mentors I can learn from. In fact, I often have very satisfying conversations with people who are decades older than I am. They often have a depth of experience and knowledge and may have time to share that wisdom with me. They are usually not as distracted by their Blackberry and the latest e-mail or text message. They view things from a bigger perspective rather than the minor detail level.

Q. What is contact management software?

As you build your network, it is wise to use contact management software to compile a good database with information on each contact. This is where you will keep those tidbits of information that you can review before making your next call, e-mail, or appointment with your contact. You can keep a contact history with what you talked about, when to follow up again, special dates, details about them and their family, pictures, proposals you've made, things you've done to help one another, and the like. You can also set system reminders in your calendar that will remind you when you are to contact them next.

If you are in a marketing or sales role, you should definitely use software to manage your customers and potential customers. ACT, Goldmine, and Outlook can all serve this function. Be certain to include your contact database file in your regular backup so you have this data stored elsewhere in case your hard drive crashes and you can't recover the data.

There are also business-card-size scanners and related software to help you maintain contacts. Unfortunately, I don't think that the scanning software has the breadth of functions that contact management software has.

Most people are flattered when you remember their name, and they are often impressed when you bring up specific things you recall about them. I am fortunate to have a good memory and can usually remember a number of specific things about different contacts from years ago when I run into them. It sort of freaks them out initially, but ultimately they are impressed. People love to talk about themselves and like it when you bring up details about them because it shows you were listening closely. This demonstrates your respect for them.

Don't go overboard and into stalker-level because they may shy away, but it's nice to ask a question or two to show that you were paying attention. Questions like, How are their two boys? Are they still playing volleyball? Have they seen a mutual friend lately? What have they been doing since they graduated from X school? are all good openers. The more details you can include in your questions, the more connected they may feel.

Q. Why should I develop longer-term connections?

Making regular connections keeps the relationships active and strengthens them into longer-term contacts. Developing long-term contacts is the goal because you never know what either of you will do next that may be beneficial to the other. Do something nice for them every so often by sending an article, e-birthday card, job lead you heard about, and similar thoughtful gestures.

Even if you or they move and you get separated for some reason, make contact by e-mail or phone to update your information and keep the contact alive. You will notice that people lose contact for many reasons, and most are unrelated to you. Life gets in the way and people get overwhelmed with other responsibilities. People get married, have kids, relocate, move to a new home, work a lot of overtime, etc. They lose contact so it will be up to you to maintain it. Drop them a note every few months just to see how they are doing and maintain your connection.

I have coordinated all of my high school reunions to stay in touch with friends from the past. Each of us has gone separate ways, but there are lots of contacts and experiences you can learn from them. I maintain a database that gets updated every five years to stay in touch.

I have a friend who followed the dot com boom to different companies in different states, but we have remained in contact every month or so because we connected well a number of years ago. We have met up in different states a few times, vacationed together, and helped each other on different projects. I have another friend who was downsized out of his company after 22 years, and moved several states away to start a new business. He has been there for a few years, but we connect every couple of months to catch up and share new experiences that may help the other. These are lasting connections. Even though we don't talk every day, or even every month, we know the other person is there if we need anything, even if it's just someone to listen.

Q· Why should I stay connected with a jerk?

Avoid burning bridges with any of your contacts, even if you don't get along with them. You never know when you will reconnect and may need to rekindle that contact for some reason. You don't know where they will move, where they will go to work, who they will marry, and other future happenings, so if there is conflict just separate professionally and quietly. If you disconnect quietly, most conflicts will be minimized over time and reconnection will be easier.

But, if you got into a brawl on the floor during the staff meeting, slamming his head into the floor, he may remember it. So forego the temptation; it just may come back to haunt you. Many times, people will mature over the years, and their demeanor, as well as their out-look on life, will change for the better. I was at my wife's reunion and heard a lady in their class apologizing several times during the night to people for being a jerk in high school. She had been through a lot of things by then and had matured to develop a better attitude.

I'm not going to sugarcoat this. You will need to suck it up and grin and bear it to not burn a bridge at times. Be the bigger person and move on quietly and calmly (you can throw things later when you're alone) then avoid contact with the person for a while. There are plenty of jerks out there who take their problems out on others. I am not saying you should maintain a regular connection with jerks, but don't lose your temper and say things that will be hard to take back later.

You can remain in the background and, in rare instances, make a brief contact with them if it seems appropriate. Perhaps you can send an article related to their industry or maybe congratulate them on their child winning the tennis match. Go with something unrelated to your old relationship and you might find the jerk has changed for the better.

Occasionally it may be appropriate to burn a bridge. For example, if you report someone to the authorities, file a complaint in response to discrimination, file a lawsuit for breach of employment contract, etc., it may effectively burn a bridge. Sometimes that is the cost of doing what you have to do to make things right. But, if you have to do it, make it formal, succinct, and don't wallow in self pity, just get it over with and move forward.

Q. How can my family help build my network?

In building your network, look to all of the areas of your life and the groups of people you are in contact with because they all can be good feeders to your network. One often overlooked group that could help is your family. Many family members have jobs outside of the home, have hobbies, go to church, school events, sports events, etc. All of these arenas involve others with their own set of contacts. For example, if you need a contact who works at a particular company, ask around, then ask your family members to ask their contacts, and eventually you will find a connection that gets you inside. You never really know who knows who, so go to your immediate as well as extended family and see if you can reach your goal. If not, don't stop there. Expand your search further. Giving up is the only thing that causes you to fail.

Since you can usually trust your family, they can be your first and best source to get to contacts you need. Even if you are not searching for a particular contact, pay attention at family gatherings and similar events, and take note of the different contact groups each of them has so you know who to reach if you need a specific contact later. Many people don't fully realize the value of a network, don't have much of one, and don't know how to maintain one, so they may need some subtle coaching along the way. The Kevin Bacon six degrees of separation concept demonstrates how everyone is connected to everyone else within six levels of contacts. I have seen this more and more as I continue to spread my contact base wider over the years.

Q. How can my friends help build my network?

Your acquaintances and friends are another group to utilize in building contacts. Notice I didn't say good friends. Many people

A Few Lessons I Learned from "The Street"

An example of a time when a bridge may need to be burned comes from a good friend we'll call Doc, who had a traumatic end to his first "real" job. It caused him to draw a line in the sand and burn bridges because he was put in such a bad position.

He had been at a company putting in more than 50 hours a week for nine years (finding out later he was grossly underpaid for roles he was filling). After four promotions, his last to Chief Operating Officer, and more than five years of successive record growth, sales, and net profit, Doc was fired without notice. The local police escorted him to clean out his offices in different plants while all of his coworkers looked on.

After the shock wore off, he made multiple attempts to contact board members he knew so that he could try to get the termination rescinded. None of them knew the truth about what was happening, and the CEO had fed them a story that blamed Doc for things the CEO had actually done. He was forced to file a formal lawsuit to bring out the truth and get his record cleaned so it didn't permanently taint his young career and employment record. Reporters picked it up, and the soap opera took center stage for awhile, continuing for nearly two years.

Ultimately, after some legal maneuvering, Doc got the board to recognize that he was being used as a scapegoat for poor actions of the CEO. He got the CEO removed along with two other managers that supported the CEO's story. The board agreed to rescind the action, clean his spotless record, formally apologize, and write a letter of recommendation. He resigned formally, and the remainder of his employment contract was paid in full.

Doc had already found a better role where he ultimately became CEO and shareholder and grew this business even bigger. He did have to decide to risk burning bridges to do what he needed to, and had to fight to make sure his record wasn't marred. The moral is that Doc had no idea he was going to need his network so badly by the end of that day, but he utilized that network to get his next role within a couple of weeks. As a side note, you also need to learn to keep your hindquarters covered because you never know when you'll need to use some information you have as leverage to make your point.

have very few good friends and you can usually count on one hand your close friends who will always be there for you. People come and go as life changes. Out of sight, out of mind is usually true. But include even distant acquaintances and people who used to be close but drifted away. Many people make lots of acquaintances over the years, so stretch your network.

Catch up quickly every so often just to see how things are going, what's new, what has changed, etc. It can be especially difficult to maintain friendships after you no longer work together, go to school together, or engage in the activity that brought you together. But with some effort, you can keep that connection.

Something that may surprise you is that friends at your job typically don't remain friends once you or they leave, even if you've been there together for many years. You'll find this to be true even more as you get older. Younger workers at similar job levels do tend to stay in contact a little longer and get together outside of work, but people at higher levels typically don't. In these cases, you will need to make the extra effort to stay connected or you'll lose track of the people. Job search consultants preach about the need to network constantly, especially with prior work acquaintances. You need to understand that you will typically need to make lots of contacts in your network to get one that works for you. You never know who will be willing to help, so do your best to stay in touch.

Q. How can my clubs build my network?

Sports teams, leagues, clubs, gyms, and similar specific-interest groups are other great areas for building your network. I have played at least 15 different competitive sports and have stayed in touch with several people I was playing with and against. Since you have the same interest, it can create a common bond that can gain you other connections and assistance. I am in professional organizations, including the Real Estate Investors Association (REIA) in Toledo with chapters around the state and around the country. That is just one example of a group that can get me contacts around the country based on a common interest.

I've also been in Aspiring Minds of Toledo (young professionals network), Business Network International (trade leads), Jamie Farr LPGA golf tournament (as a scorer), Humane Society (board member and fundraising for animals), Habitat for Humanity (board committee member and volunteer to build houses), board of mental retardation and developmental disabilities events, Junior Achievement (emcee for Grand Prix races and events), United Health Services (french fry booth fundraising), Cherry Street Mission (serving homeless meals), Taste of the Town (food booth fundraising), Rib-Off (VIP bartender), Toledo Zoo (fundraising events), college (attended or taught at University of Toledo, Defiance College, Northwest State Community College, Owens Community College, Davis Business College) and sports and fundraising events for many high schools.

Some other groups I have been a member of include the Women's Entrepreneurial Network, Women and Money, Toastmasters, chambers of commerce, Small Business Centers, Certified Management Accountants, Certified Public Accountants, Toledo Bar, Ohio State Bar, Michigan State Bar, Washtenaw County Bar, and Certified Business Managers. Look at all of the networks and contacts I am or have been connected with just in this area. You can do something similar so start today.

Other niche groups include bird watchers, civil war re-enactors, Red Hat Society, lunar watchers, furniture refinishers, PC makers, cyclists, motorcyclists, NASCAR fans, hikers, and parachutists, to name a variety of the many groups that allow members to form bonds with one another. Look at your different interests and any groups you are in to see how you could further utilize your contacts there. I guarantee you that you can get involved and meet new people if you want to.

Hospitals and hospice always need volunteers and this gets you connected to lots of others; plus, you are providing great services to those in need. You can also be a tutor, substitute teacher, aide or phone answerer for schools and other non-profits. Non-profits always need volunteers who will participate and help spread the word about their organization's cause. You could also step up and form your own niche group for people with a specific common interest.

Many small companies can also use help if you are qualified. You could be on an advisory board or sub-committees of the board. Once you get some education and experience under your belt, you then have something to offer businesses that cannot necessarily afford to pay a consultant or contractor. In the MBA program I was in, we had to consult for no charge with local businesses as part of our curriculum. We provided them with custom business, marketing, and financial plans as well as suggestions for making their company more lean and ways to expand. We also shot a sample marketing video for one company and provided that along with our plan to the owners and board for our final project. All of these experiences expanded my network.

Q. How can my church help build my network?

Another way to make contacts and build some great bonds is through your church and small groups within the church. We have been in a group called Friends in Faith that is comprised of people in our age group. We grew up in similar time periods, have some similar interests, have fun at events together, and are comfortable talking with others in the group about whatever comes up. There are a lot of other small groups as well (men's, women's, singles, couples, college, new members, etc.). There are also classes on different topics like parenting, book-of-the-month, and finances. Be genuine in these groups, though. Don't join them just to get leads. Leads will be an extra benefit that you may get from them, not the primary outcome that you are pursuing.

You can also build stronger connections by becoming an active member of the group rather than simply a participant who attends gatherings. For example, participate in the church activities by being a Sunday school teacher, youth leader, worship leader, singer, musician, reader, communion helper, or volunteer for events. These special roles will get you noticed and connected to a lot of people whose primary reason for being there is spiritual. Most of them work outside the church or have their own businesses and can share in many ways.

We sang in a Christian contemporary band for a few years and made some lasting connections while doing something we loved and enhancing our worship experience. Since then, we've put people we know who were selling their home in touch with the drummer who is a realtor. We've also referred businesses wanting to advertise to the guitar player who worked for a local paper. Remember, building a network provides an opportunity for you to help others, not just a way to receive help.

Q. Can I build my network with online networking?

Social networking sites have millions of members and hits every day. Sites like YouTube, FaceBook, MySpace, and Twitter provide connections to people all over the world. My wife first joined Facebook when her glee club from high school reconnected from different parts of the country. She spent hours on it initially and got hooked on it (it is addicting). I had to have her "put the laptop down and slowly step away from it" before things got ugly one night (right out of *Law and Order*). These sites allow you to stay in regular contact with people you have had a meaningful connection with in the past; for example, with high school and college friends who have moved away. It allows you to continue that connection from a distance when you already have a great bond from the past.

These sites, as well as Internet forums, chat rooms, web cams, and blogs, are other ways you now have to connect with lots of people around the world who share common areas of interest. But, be careful, there are dirt bags (Watched too much *NYPD Blue*) out there that may try to take advantage of you, steal your identity, get you to send them money with promises of great returns, etc. Some web resources allow people to take on fictitious personas, and you may want to use that option at times. You need to balance caution with opportunity and only give information that you would post online or in your profile. Be suspicious until you build rapport and trust.

Do remember that the best connection is a face-to-face connection, so even though there are now many more ways to connect with people from around the world, strong relationships usually require in-person contact. Relationships formed purely over the Internet are more impersonal and can end quickly and easily, so recognize this variable. If you continue the relationship over time, you may be able to make it a more lasting, beneficial one.

Q. What methods should I use to stay connected?

There are so many more ways to stay connected now with less effort. But people seem to have gotten more busy and stretched so far that they don't take advantage of these methods to keep their network alive. With cell phones and smart phones (e.g., Blackberry, Treo, iPhone) that have e-mail, text messaging, Internet, cameras, and TV capabilities, you can do many things on the go, around the clock, without any delays. I would recommend you get comfortable with these devices because technology is only going to get better in the years to come. Additional functions will be added, devices will get smaller and more user-friendly, and they will be more affordable. People will use them anywhere, anytime.

These advanced devices allow you to make contacts and follow-up calls, respond to messages, and complete similar tasks wherever you are. You can then make use of downtime, driving (be very careful), waiting time, nights, weekends, and early mornings. This will allow you to more fully utilize your time to stay connected to your network. Videoconferencing is going to get better and less expensive and is a great way to connect to several people visually as well as by phone in real time. I did an interview recently this way and once you get used to it, you can really accomplish a lot from anywhere in the country.

On the flip side, most people need time to themselves daily. Meditation is a great way to get in tune with your inner self. When doing this type of activity, turn everything off or to vibration mode so you can stay focused on yourself. Find the time to replenish your energy away from these devices or they will take over your life.

I've come to accept that life is not always logical and clearly not fair. Ultimately, you have to learn the game, adjust your strategy, and

A Few Lessons I Learned from "The Street"

I'm going to back up and tell you my occupation search-network story so you understand the situation I found myself in after law school and why I see having a large, carefully chosen network as so important. It was a dark, stormy night in 2001 (OK, at least the 2001 is correct) and I decided to formally assess what role would be best for me next and to use search professionals to help find it. I had passed the Ohio bar exam, was completing the sale of the company I co-owned, and was selling all of the rental homes I had kept for 20 years since high school. I had achieved my goal of becoming a millionaire years before and had no debt, so I was in a financial position where I did not need a specific income and could commit to doing a comprehensive search for a role that would best suit my skills and interests.

Following the experts' advice, I matched my best natural skills to the role, which would allow me to be interested in what I was doing and do the best job imaginable. I wanted to enjoy each day rather than simply do a good job. I had followed the path of doing a good job and getting promoted for the first 20 years of my working life, ultimately becoming CFO, COO, and CEO at multiple companies, but not being truly interested in the companies I worked for. It goes to show that even at the top, you are not guaranteed happiness if you don't find a match for your interests and skills from the start. That is another street lesson you now know.

As a slightly hyperactive, obsessive overachiever, I launched into an extensive occupation search, starting with several assessments to determine about 20 variables (see the table in Chapter 11) that would help to paint a picture of my ideal role. You name the assessment, I took it. Defining these preferences was really important to me for knowing what I wanted to go for next.

I researched executive search firms and for thousands of dollars hired an executive marketing firm to mold and shape me into a lean, mean hirable machine, down to the last detail. I had practiced everything as you are told to and had all of my answers to tough questions down. I was told I did very well with interviews. The purpose of all of this was to make me the top choice because I looked, spoke, wrote, and oozed polished talent

(continued on next page)

(continued from previous page)

with transferable skills that every company would love to have, regardless of cost. At least that's what was supposed to happen. And it did happen for the satisfied customers I spoke with who had previously gone this route, using this company.

I later recognized that my main marketing company primarily found roles in other parts of the country for executives who were staying in their particular role and industry even though they claimed otherwise. Most of their successful candidates had worked for big companies with a specific, big-company network in place. We went well beyond all of the mass and targeted marketing that had worked for many other executives over their 30 years in business.

Three years later, with 35,000 résumés in circulation, more than 25 versions of résumés that were professionally rewritten each time, more than 300 specific cover letters rewritten many different times by many different professional writers, using more than 10 professional services utilizing each of their specific methods, and I ended up with "bupkis" (zero, zilch, nada, zippo, you get the picture) as compared to what my goal was. I even convinced a few services to reimburse me some of their fees because they didn't deliver the outcome they promised even though I followed their process closely. I am confident they firmly believed that it would be easy with my background and were shocked it didn't work. I really couldn't find a good match within a two-hour radius of me (Ohio, Michigan, Indiana). So I continued to do business and turnaround consulting, real estate investing, financial advising, pro bono projects, and personal investing while looking for companies to join, buy into, or start. Yet another strange experience in my life that you get to learn from.

play by the rules on the street to get where you want to go. I also learned that, more times than you'd think, even if you have several years of applicable education and experience under your belt, roles often go to those who have a personal connection to a decision-maker. You wouldn't believe the number of companies I saw *not* select the best candidate for key roles. If you know someone who knows someone who can recommend you to a relative, a school friend, or the like, in a particular company you want to join, that connection will typically be more valuable than your qualifications. This is clearly wrong, but happens all the time.

I ultimately recognized the main barriers to finding my ideal role. I was trying to switch industries (strike one), I didn't have a network in that industry (strike two), and I didn't have specific experience in my target industry (strike three). In the economy and my geographic area, most companies could demand a uniquely-qualified candidate who was willing to relocate anywhere just to get a job. We were and continue to be in a poor job market with high unemployment, with many companies downsizing and going out of business, leaving many mid- to upper-level executives out of work. My geographic area is heavily automotive-based, which makes it even worse, and I wasn't looking for a long distance relocation, so I had multiple strikes against me.

I had many HR executives and recruiters tell me they had received several hundred applicants for the one role I was interested in, and they would not even get through many of them. They could be very picky and select someone who held the same title in the same industry rather than giving consideration to a superior candidate like me with transferable skills and other experience that would benefit their company.

I also learned that it's possible to be overqualified which becomes intimidating to decision-makers. I didn't believe that was possible until I had several tell me that directly. I am confident that in several instances I was a better candidate, but the decision-makers chose to go with someone who was more limited in their abilities and didn't have a background that intimidated them. You finally accept that this screwy reality is the norm.

One good thing that came out of this is that many people told me during this process that my background and experiences had such breadth and depth that I needed to write a book or speak to teach others what I had learned over the past 25 years. So, I decided to complete one of my goals by writing this book and the follow-up *financial habits* books. I also completed additional professional speaking training and have started speaking again, this time for companies, colleges, associations, and other events.

The lesson here is for you to strategically make and maintain connections with people that are in or connected to each industry that you want to be in long-term. This requires you to be a forward-thinker as it relates to your long-term career path. If you assume you'll just end up in a place that meets your needs without making this effort, you will find you need to make these specific connections later in life, which will delay you from getting where you want to go.

WhaT WoULD JEFF Do?
(Fun action steps to try this stuff out)

1. Start building your contact database right now. You can do it manually on index cards if needed, but start building a filing system of contacts. Add little details on the card about them, when you talked last, if you sent them information on something, etc. Use contact management software as soon as you can get access to a package.

2. Schedule weekly and monthly events to attend in your industry and local area so that you can expand your network regularly. Ask for business cards and jot notes on the back so you can update your database when you return. Be willing to give to your network and they will reciprocate. Stay in touch with them every so often, especially when you don't need anything, to build a long-term relationship.

3. As you make contacts, look for those with valuable experiences who can share with you from time to time. Approach an individual that you respect, tell him you respect him, and ask if he is willing to mentor you. If so, set up a first time to talk and have your questions prepared in advance so as to not waste any time.

4. Look to your family, friends, groups, clubs, non-profits, volunteer experiences, church, and social networks to get additional contacts daily. Be in network mode all the time. You don't have to see how that person may be of help to you now, just make the contact and get as much information as possible so you have key items that may be helpful later.

5. Stay in contact with most of your network electronically to be efficient in connecting. Connect with your most important contacts face-to-face as often as possible. Send handwritten notes to certain contacts at special times to make more impact.

Start listening to others whereever you are and you will find lots of options to build your network. Once you've finished these steps, write me to let me know what happened and what you learned at *stories@lifescheatsheets.com*.

Now, think like Nike and Just Do It!

"Many people hear, but few people really listen."

"You can win more friends with your ears than with your mouth."

Discreetly Become a Tech Nerd (Technology Advantages)

I realize that technology is one area that rapidly changes, so it won't be long before some of the information below will be obsolete. Nevertheless, many of the same factors and considerations discussed here will be relevant in making decisions about future technology options that have not even been developed at this point. The key is to leverage your time (get more done than your time allows) by using as much technology as you can to take care of your needs.

Q. What progress has been made in the last 20-plus years?

Graduating high school seniors and college undergraduates have never been in a world without PCs. In 1981, as a high school senior at Gorham-Fayette in Fayette, Ohio, my good friend Tom and I were allowed to set up and "play" with the first two PCs the school ever had because we were both in the top five in the class. They were Radio Shack TRS-80s that did very little compared to today's computers. They were big, boxy units with black and white screens and IBM Selectric-type keyboards built into the unit. We had black and white, dot-matrix printers with tractor-fed, continuous paper feeding into the bottom of the printer from a case of paper underneath the desk. We learned some BASIC programming and programmed some short routines to get it to do some fun stuff. Boy, did we have it made.

Fast forward a number of years later, and we still paid more than $3,000 for a big-box, 14" basic color monitor, processor, keyboard, and mouse. Skip ahead a couple of decades and we paid $600 to $700 for a Dell PC that is several times faster, has lots of memory, huge hard drives, CD and DVD burners, and a much bigger high-resolution, flat-screen color monitor with a lot of other bells and whistles. Think about the speed of the product cycle (time from the inception of the new product until it was produced and then replaced with a newer product) in that industry. Several years ago in my MBA program, I recall that the big computer manufacturers were on a three-month product cycle, which translated into four new, improved versions per calendar year. That cycle time is unheard of in most industries. For instance, at that time U.S. car manufacturers took three to five years from the concept idea until a new car was produced and for sale to the public, which was only a part of the full product cycle.

I am going to focus primarily on Windows-type (a.k.a. IBM-type) computers rather than the Macintosh-Apple side of personal computers (PC). At this stage, most applications work on either platform.

Here's just a sampling of the average increases in PC performance over a couple of decades.

1989	vs	2009
16–32k RAM		2–6 Gb hi-performance RAM
1–2 Mb hard drive		500–1000 Gb hard drive
14" monochrome monitors		22" color, hi-res flat screens
3.5" flexible disk (1.44 Mb)		Ext hard drive (500 Gb–1 Tb)
Int hard drives 25–50 Mb		Int hard drives 500–750 Gb
Single processor running 25–50 MHz		Quad (4) processors each running 3 GHz
No digital pictures/video		Compact hi-res pictures/video
No online activities		Most applications are online

To understand the above statistics, realize that approximately:

1000 characters = 1kilobyte (k)

1000k = 1 Megabyte (Mb)

1000 Mb = 1 Gigabyte (Gb)

1000 Gb = 1 Terabyte, (Tb) and

1000 Megahertz (MHz) = 1 Gigahertz (GHz)

We now assume that most anything we want to do can be done on a particular piece of inexpensive software and usually online. There are very few limitations anymore. Most software handles so many functions beyond what the typical user even knows is possible that much of its functionality is wasted. It's anyone's guess where technology will be in just a few years since it has increased at such a rapid pace over the last decade. The point is to get involved and stay involved because the better you are in using technology to your advantage, the more you can accomplish.

Q. Why should I get comfortable using technology?

You can typically be much more efficient with a PC than using manual processes. This will allow you to get more done quicker and more simply with a better final product.

Realizing the different areas you can use technology in is another challenge. Converting manual processes to electronic processes usually saves a lot of time. You can save and edit information, and quickly reprint the new version. As I mentioned before, when I was in my early years of college, we still typed papers on IBM Selectric typewriters. Some of them had a little memory, but otherwise there was no cutting and pasting without retyping the paper. It was terribly inefficient and the final product did not look nearly as good as it does today. We corrected mistakes with "white-out" which could always be seen.

There is much less handwriting now with the ease of word processing. You should still force yourself to do some writing; otherwise, you will lose some of your ability in that area. I have actually forgotten how to write some letters in cursive because I always print.

With e-mail and Internet connections being so available in most places, you can easily stay in touch electronically. Through online contact managers and autoresponders, you can schedule different messages, holiday cards, birthday cards, and similar notes not only to your friends, but also to your customer base or specific subsets of customers. Let the computer do the work through the week, month, and year.

Q. How do I compare a desktop to a laptop?

When considering a laptop vs. a desktop PC, you really need to examine your uses short-term (several months) and long-term (next few years). Remember that technology becomes outdated quickly. At one time, I heavily used a Gateway desktop that lasted for almost eight years, which is unheard of. I did upgrade it a couple of times and kept it tuned up. Regardless, businesses trade up every two to three years and individuals who regularly use a PC should plan on trading up every three to five years.

Desktops are usually bigger and more bulky, but have several peripherals (mouse, keyboard, printer, etc.) and may be cabled to a network or the Internet. There are usually expansion slots for other devices such as scanners, drives, and multi-port USB cards. Usually you can get faster processors, more RAM, bigger hard drives, and other enhancements for desktops that aren't possible for laptops.

Laptops have made big strides, so they are nearing the speed and performance of the desktop. But you are still limited on expansion and upgrades. You can have peripherals, like desktops, but you need to make certain you have the right connections and functionality. The unit is much smaller, lightweight, and has a smaller screen and a smaller keyboard. Most laptops have a touch pad mouse system or the eraser type, unless you add an external mouse. You will need to get used to these differences because they are significant. I don't like the keyboard or mouse system on most laptops. They slow me down and are less user-friendly.

Laptops are great for people on the road. They are very easy to set up and are easy to carry from place to place. Many students take notes on them, but you need to be able to type quickly on that smaller keyboard to keep up. This typically works much better than manually writing notes and then typing them later. Batteries usually last two hours or more before needing a charge so be sure to plan that into your schedule.

Docking stations are expensive, but can give you the best of both worlds. You can have a full monitor, regular mouse, regular keyboard, backup drive, printer, and other devices plugged into the docking station. Upon returning with your laptop, plug the back of your laptop into the station, and you have use of all of the other devices. You will be using the hard drive and processor of the laptop, but very few other parts of it while it is in the docking station.

Compare prices because you may pay several hundred dollars or more just for the station, and then you need to buy all of the peripherals to plug into it, so you will have more than a thousand dollars sunk into a full set-up.

Ultimately, the choice falls back to use and comfort. I have continued to use a desktop much more than a laptop, but if I regularly had a more mobile role, I would probably use the laptop more extensively. I like to get things done quickly and the comfort and peripherals that come with a desktop allow me to accomplish things the quickest. When buying, shop around because there are a lot of competitors in the market.

Q. How much memory should I have?

In choosing among the options, memory is king and especially RAM. You will want a higher performance RAM type like DRAM rather than plain old RAM. Regardless, get as much as you can afford because more data can be moved faster and tasks can be completed quicker with more RAM. Some operating systems require a significant amount of RAM, and only some computers are built to accommodate those systems so check this specification before buying.

The cost of memory has gone down dramatically and there is competition, so the prices are staying reasonable. Most PCs can easily be upgraded with more RAM, and laptops can now accept additional RAM. I upgrade my own since RAM is a little circuit board that you can very easily plug into a slot on the mother board. You don't need any special tools. You just need to know how to take the cover off the processor.

With the advent of USB or thumb drives that plug into any free USB port, memory and backup options are even less expensive. Makers continue to increase the amount of storage on these drives. Four Gb, then eight, then sixteen was considered big for a few months each and now 32 and 64 Gb are taking their place. The capacity of these drives will continue to increase and will function as many users' offsite backups.

With external backup drives becoming so affordable and able to hold an enormous amount of data for under $100, that is the way to go for large data backups. 500 Gb (.5 Tb) is a medium-sized drive, and a 2.0 Tb drive is available if you need a much larger one. They are small so they can fit most anywhere on or under the desktop. You can schedule backups for times when you are not there, and they will be completed automatically. These have nearly eliminated tape and zip drives. You can just unplug them and take them offsite to protect the backup from a fire, flood, or other catastrophe.

Q. Why is a backup so important?

Having a backup is more important than having the backup offsite, but both are preferred. To convince yourself of this, you only need to lose your data one time due to a hard drive crash, power outage or spike, faulty sectors on the drive, etc. You will immediately understand why having a current backup is crucial. The more data you have, the more critical it becomes. Think of how long it will take to recreate the lost data, if it can be recreated at all. Calculate how much it will cost to re-input a lot of data or rebuild spreadsheets. Compare that to scheduling a daily, every-other-day, or weekly backup and not having to worry about anything.

Develop a schedule that fits your situation and is based on the amount of new data that is added each day or week. The more data that is added, the more frequent the backup should be. If you do an automated, scheduled backup, double check that it did occur and was successful before moving on. Sometimes, with a crash, you can pay a specialized computer technician a lot of money to use software that can recover some data, but don't put yourself in that situation. Just do the backups.

You can also use blank CDs and DVDs to make backups. Most of them are not rewritable, but they are fairly inexpensive, so if that is the main option you have, do the backup on them to have the data in a second place. You can't believe the amount of time you will save by having a recent backup in the event of a crash.

Q. What should I consider for a monitor?

Most prefer flat screen monitors that take up much less space and are much lighter than a Cathode Ray Tube (CRT)or TV/tube-type monitor. They usually have good resolution and can use Digital Video Input (DVI) rather than Video Graphics Adapter (VGA-older style), which makes flat screens even more clear. I usually say the bigger, the better, so that you reduce eye strain and can see more of your data on the screen, but some have gotten so big now that you may not want the biggest. In the store, take a look at them with data on the screen, sitting or standing as close as you would when you use it. Make sure it doesn't overwhelm you. I've used a 24" flat screen, but some people have said it was too big for them. You can also hang it on the wall to conserve desk space, but you better be certain that your desk is going to remain in that place for quite some time.

With a big, wide screen you can divide the screen horizontally (split screen) or vertically (use new window then compare documents side by side) then work on the same or different documents at the same time. I have used both to complete this book and often open two different sections of the book at the same time. See the help function for a few details with each of these options.

I also have a dual screen setup I use for real estate bidding. I have real estate comparable software (shows similar properties that have sold in the area I am researching) on one screen while I enter information into a bid spreadsheet (electronic calculation software that shows what I would bid on the property with lots of variables factored in) on the other screen. This setup has many different uses, and with Vista it is very easy to set up so that the software knows you have two monitors. Dragging the mouse from screen to screen is strange at first, but when you realize you can have a huge amount of screen to use, you'll like the feature. You need to make certain that your video card (rear of the main PC box) has a VGA port and a DVI port because each monitor needs to be plugged into a separate port on the video card.

Like many electronics (VCRs, DVDs, monitors, etc.), there are usually a handful of component manufacturers for many of the internal parts. These manufacturers sell component parts to the manufacturers of the whole unit who assemble all of the components into the final product, such as a monitor. Therefore, you do not need a specific name brand to get a good monitor because there are a lot of companies that buy the same components and assemble the monitors. Just make certain it has a normal warranty and the place you buy it from has been around for awhile so they will be around to support it if it doesn't work properly. I've never heard of the brand name on my monitor and it works great.

Q. What do I need in terms of sound?

Most systems today have a sound card and speaker system so you can watch videos, listen to songs, play video games, hear e-mail notifications, listen to recorded events, etc. I have two systems that have a powered sub-woofer along with five or more speakers to get a surround-sound effect. My old system had a DVD player and integrated surround-sound package that made DVD movies sound good.

How many speakers you need depends upon what you use your PC for. If you are into gaming, you usually want fairly good sound. I bought my speaker system for under $50 (Logitech at Sam's) and it does a great job for what I use it for. I do not play games so you would need to test the system with games to see if it does what you want.

You can use up to six or seven speakers now with great theatre sound, but you will need to make certain your sound card can handle this before getting an advanced system. You might need to upgrade your sound card to get the sound you want, especially if you're after high quality theatre sound or specific gaming sounds. Regardless of the system, I would make certain you add a speaker system so you at least have typical functionality.

Q. What should I know about printers?

First, you need to analyze what your needs are. Since there are so many options now, you need to spend some time on research unless you only want a basic, low-cost, throw-away printer. Assuming you want to have your printer for a couple of years or longer and want reasonable quality at a low cost, you will need to compare brands and models. I tend to stay with brands I know that have been in the printer business for a long time. Hewlett Packard (HP) has been a leader in this area, but there are many other good makers. Canon, Samsung, Brother, Kodak, and others with several models are comparable to one another and very trustworthy.

With all of the digital picture technology and the slew of photo printers that are often included at no cost, it is reasonable to have two printers, one that is for typical work and the other for photos and color, graphic-oriented printing. Most of the photo printers are ink jet printers, which have a much higher cost per page than laser printers. The reason companies give you photo printers with digital cameras and PC purchases is that they make most of their money on the ink cartridges and want you to print a lot on the ink jet printer. The ink jets can print in high quality, but calculate the per-page cost to determine how much you want to use that printer. It may be less expensive to forego the printer and just print your pictures at the local Rite Aid, Wal-Mart, or Walgreens instead. Most of those stores run great deals on photo prints. They also offer a lot of ways to enhance, expand, and print your digital shots.

Dot matrix printers are obsolete. Those still in use are for very low-end, basic printing. Otherwise, you mainly need to decide between laser and ink jet. The cost per page for prints from laser printers, even color lasers, will normally be less than ink jet printers.

Virtually all of the laser printers print at least 300 dots per inch (dpi) and many go up to 600 to 1,200 dpi, which is fine for most uses.

For text print, 300 dpi is fine; you will want higher dpi for graphics or large lettering for signs and similar purposes. You may see some jagged edges on lower dpi prints, but that may be satisfactory depending on your need.

You need to get an actual test printout, see what it looks like, and then calculate the cost per page. Divide the cost of a toner cartridge by the actual number of printed pages in can do under normal conditions (many times around 3000 pages; it tells you on the product). Then divide the cost of the print drum (sometimes separate from the toner cartridge, but sometimes combined) by the number of printed pages (usually a much higher number than the toner) it can do. The paper cost per page is arrived at by dividing the price of the package of paper by the number of sheets included. Add the three cost-per-page figures together to arrive at the total operating cost per page.

To be really accurate, include the cost of the printer divided by its page life to arrive at the printer cost per page. The page life, which tells you how many pages the printer is rated to print over its lifetime, is on the box or included materials.

Another option is a four, five, or six all-in-one multifunction machine. I have used one of these for my copier and fax for several years. But many of these are ink jets, which means a higher cost per page than a laser printer. If a multifunction machine can satisfy your needs, they make sense to look into, especially a laser one. You usually get a fax, scanner, copier, printer, and sometimes a PC fax and phone with an answering machine. Pay attention to the laser vs. ink jet comparison because the laser toner is cheaper per page, and the toner also lasts much longer, so you don't have to deal with replacing toner nearly as frequently as you will with ink cartridges.

I have multiple printers for different uses. Black and white lasers have a very low cost per page and can usually print at least 3,000 sheets per toner cartridge, while ink jet cartridges only print 250 to 500 sheets. Printers have continued to get better and decrease in price, so you can do some high-end printing in your home office that you would have had to send to a printer years ago.

Q. What software should I use?

Now that you have the vital components of your PC system, I'll briefly cover your software needs. You can find software that will do almost anything, and some of it is free. Make certain that you pay particular attention to whether the software is PC-based, which means you load it on your machine; server-based, where your network administrator loads it on the server and not your PC; or web-based, where it resides on a server somewhere and you use it online, but never have possession of the software. We'll assume everything I mention is PC-based unless noted.

An office suite of some kind is a staple for most PCs that are used for multiple purposes. Microsoft Office is the most popular, but somewhat pricey. There are others and a popular one that is free and mirrors Microsoft Office is Open Office at *www.openoffice. org*. I understand this office suite was put together by a competitor to reduce some of the Microsoft Office market share.

Most office software has a word processor, spreadsheet, database, presentation, and graphic design-type package. These programs have many extra functions that most people, including me, don't know exist and definitely don't utilize. One other hint I took advantage of while in college is that many colleges have a school pricing deal with software makers that allows college students, with valid ID, to purchase software dirt cheap. I remember I bought Office Professional for $10 when it was more than $400 at the local stores.

Software packages continue to be able to do more and integrate with others so that they can take downloaded information from one package and use it in their own. Simple graphic design packages that allow you to make cards, charts, signs, and similar items can do quite a bit more, plus there are a lot of large clip art libraries that you can pull from to enhance the design. PowerPoint in Microsoft Office can do animations and other neat presentation functions that it could not when I started using it in the mid-90s.

A quick Internet search for any type of project you have in mind usually returns an available software package. Mindjet Mindmanager software (*www.mindjet.com*) allows you to map out your thoughts step-by-step so you can lay out how to reach goals, complete projects, delegate responsibilities, keep everyone on the team on the same page, and perform similar functions. Since many packages are electronically stored, most software can be downloaded and installed in seconds via the company's autoresponder service, so you can be using it within the hour. I would recommend getting the software on CD so you can reinstall it on a new PC, reinstall it to recover from problems, and load it on a second PC, like a laptop.

Practice and play around with popular software that can help you down the road. Many roles pay more for particular experience with specific software, so the more you know, the better your chances are of getting a different job, contract work, or even coming up with a side business. For example, web design is still very popular and folks that have a graphic arts and marketing background, as well as HTML or PHP programming skills, are very much in demand.

Q. What are my options with digital cameras and video?

Now that you have your system and some software, let's look at some popular additions. Probably the most growth lately has been in the digital camera and video arena. The level of clarity via the number of megapixels your camera has continues to get better every month or two. Meanwhile, camera prices continue to decrease, the physical size is getting smaller, the screen is getting bigger, and the functions continue to grow. Digital camcorders continue to do more, get smaller, and decrease in price also.

Most cameras and camcorders come with their own software to enable you to download, store, organize, and manipulate the images. This technology will continue to get better to the point where you will be able to produce a fairly good movie with special effects without much cost, and then burn it to a DVD and give it away. Many of the current camcorders have large hard drives that you save to directly rather than saving to removable media, such as a mini-DVD or digital tape. They also have still image picture ability where you can freeze an image, save it as a picture, and print it.

With an external hard drive, you can take several weeks of video and download it to the external drive. This allows you to have a custom movie library. An addition to the array of options is "The Flip" handheld camcorder. It's about the size of a digital camera, but it is a digital camcorder that can store 60 to 120 minutes of video. It has a flip-out USB port that can be plugged into any USB drive in your PC so you can download your video clips as soon as you return to your PC. I have one and it works well. This also lets you put your videos out on sites like YouTube quickly and easily. The Flip and competing devices don't have much additional functionality yet, but they do make it very easy to get digital video and put it on your PC as well as on the web and in e-mail.

Q. How can I add a network in my home?

Just by plugging in network-ready components and your high-speed Internet connection into a wireless router, you can add a network to your home or office. You'll need an Ethernet port if your system is cabled, or a wireless network card if it's not cabled. You will also need to follow the initial setup process. This function allows you to have multiple users online concurrently and be able to use network-ready devices that have wireless cards without running cables to the rooms where you need access.

Most laptops have wireless cards in them now so they can be used anywhere in range of the router. The wireless router also allows most new printers to print wirelessly. And you can run an Ethernet cable to printers, PCs, and other devices from the router that will allow you to use each of them as a network device. This capability comes in handy when you want all of your PCs to be able to print to a color laser jet printer and at the same time be able to print to a less-expensive printer for your ordinary printing needs. It basically lets you network devices so they can be used by many users, rather than be slaved to one PC.

With a wireless network card, you can access the Internet (a.k.a. Wi-Fi) in many public places now. You can be inside or outside, on different floors, in different buildings, and still get good reception.

These devices have good range and have a bar meter that shows you the reception level. If you are getting some interference or a bad signal, usually a small move will get you better reception. Just experiment by moving around and watching the meter, similar to a mobile phone.

Q. How can technology help me run a business from home?

Telecommuting has become more popular. It allows parents to stay home with their kids, eliminates the commute to the office, allows people to be more productive out of the office, and offers many other advantages. Because of advances in technology, it is much more affordable and easy to set up a home office and be fully functional there. I completed this whole book and do real estate investing, consulting, and information marketing from a well-equipped home office that I set up years ago and update as new technology becomes available.

The attachment option for e-mail has become a staple for transferring documents and other digital items within seconds. The PDF attachment is commonly used since most PCs can open a PDF file with free Adobe Reader software. The main limitation is that most PDFs cannot be changed or edited without the higher end software.

PC fax to PC fax or regular paper fax has been getting more use and is inexpensive. Some business phone systems can now turn voice mail messages into text messages and vice versa. You can also have the phone system read your e-mail messages to you remotely, so however things are sent, you can receive them in several different media forms. This system is still fairly pricey.

Virtual offices, with specialists subcontracted all over the world, continue to become more widespread. For example, if you had a web site development business, you could contract with a copywriter, editor, graphic artist, programmer, Internet marketer, and marketing consultant to collaborate in putting together sites and do this all online from different parts of the country or different countries.

You can also extend this to a virtual assistant (VA). Your VA can be in another state or country and complete most of the tasks you need her to do. If you can cut down or cut out your office expenses, your overhead will be reduced dramatically, which allows your net profit to increase substantially.

The sites *www.elance.com* and *www.guru.com* electronically bring together a number of subcontractors and potential customers needing their services. Specialists bid on customers' projects, and then the winning bidder and customer work out the details and get the project completed. This is one way to find and try out specialists and VAs for your virtual office without any long-term commitment.

Q. What should I know about smart phones and PDAs?

Another staple of being mobile these days is the smart phone or PDA (personal digital assistant). I have to admit I am a "tech junkie" at heart. When I did the job search assessment I talked about earlier, I noted Sony, Panasonic, Dell, Microsoft, Google, and similar companies I would like to work with. I would love to regularly test the newest devices and actually get paid to play with all of the gadgets. If I did that I would probably have to go through the 12 step program at TA (Techies Anonymous, of course) to control spending countless dollars on every tech device I saw.

I really had to resist smart phones for some time because I did not have a big enough need for them in light of the monthly operating costs. Most of them have a phone and Internet connection, and they allow you to receive and send e-mail with attachments, text message, take pictures and video, and maintain your calendar and contact book. They can even serve as modems for a PC/laptop. Smart phones have a calculator and a database, carry Office suite software to read and edit documents, allow you to listen to music, and set multiple alarms. Some even let you watch TV. They usually have software that allows you to synchronize the data to your main PC so the information is the same on both devices.

In looking at which one to purchase, pay attention to the operating system they run on. Some run on Blackberry, Palm, Apple's system, and others on Windows. Since most people know Windows, this one is the most popular, but I understand the others do have some slick features, so don't eliminate them until you have done your analysis.

I recently tried an Apple iPhone. The phone service was not good in my area, and I understand it is not a very comprehensive network right now. The device is pretty neat, apart from this drawback. It has lots of features and applications written specifically for it. Every one of the applications I downloaded worked well. It is very user-friendly and has a large, colorful screen that is very clear, but it is not the easiest to type on. You can even have your own application programmed for you to work on the iPhone then it can be sold to other users.

Q. What understanding should I have about online options?

As you look briefly into the online world of options, you will see endless possibilities. Always remember, you have not verified the information you see online and it could be erroneous or completely fictitious, so only believe what you can verify by other means. People can put whatever they want on a site, blog, chat room, or bulletin board because most of them have no monitoring or policing to screen out the bad content.

This area continues to explode with different options. Many functions that used to be face-to-face have gone online. Credit card processing, as well as electronic shopping carts and money-handling sites, like PayPal, which is eBay-owned, can automatically handle all of your transactions online through secure sites that protect your personal information. Watch for the closed padlock icon and the "https" on the site address, usually at the top, to ensure that the site you are using is secure.

With e-mail, you can have web-based e-mail, like Hotmail, Yahoo!, and G[oogle] mail, that you can access anywhere you have an Internet connection. If you change Internet Service Providers (ISP) and you had your e-mail address through them, you would need to change your e-mail address if you switch, but if you have the web-based e-mail you can keep your same e-mail address, regardless of ISP.

If you want to have your own site, you need to purchase your own domain. The .com extension is obviously the most popular one, but many of those are already taken so you may need to look at .net and others, which are less likely to be found on a search, but may signify your brand more specifically than hybrids that you would have to settle for in the .com family. You will need to deal with site hosting and servers, at a minimum, if you have a site. If you want to have multiple domain names all lead to your site, you can use a redirect to get them to the same site, so look into that option if you really want to drive lots of traffic to your site.

If you want to build a list of customers, readers, or followers and put out an e-zine, newsletter, sell items, and the like, look into an autoresponder system, like *www.aweber.com*. If you need e-commerce (selling services and goods) options, look into *www.clickbank.com* or *www.1shoppingcart.com* that can manage all of your needs electronically and automatically without your interaction. They can send links for e-books and other electronically downloaded products as soon as they get valid payment, without you getting involved. They also send you your net payment after fees and let you see your account with details online. Some even have affiliate programs included so you can have others selling your goods and split the profit with them through the e-commerce service.

Several other active sites that you will want to get comfortable with are *www.ebay.com*, *www.Amazon.com*, *www.Google.com*, *www.Yahoo.com*, and *www.PayPal.com*. I am confident you have probably already used these to some degree so I am not going to elaborate. It is rare when I cannot find information online about any subject I want to know more about. Just remember, be cautious because the information you are getting may be worth what you paid for it (absolutely nothing). Who knows who wrote it and for what reason. People spend a lot of time writing nasty viruses for all the wrong reasons, so not everything you pull up may have been put there to help.

Q. Do I need to be concerned about becoming impersonal?

As a final thought, please be conscious of becoming so tied to your technology that you lose your ability to complete functions with a personal touch, face-to-face, when that is the best mode to complete them. Some people have become addicted to e-mail. It has become a crutch for some. It is easier to say no, delay projects, put people off, and give uncomfortable information by e-mail because it's not face-to-face and there is no emotion to deal with. Its use has exploded so much that people are lost when it is down.

There are a number of tasks that should not be done through a device. Get out of your comfort zone and do what is needed. Personal contact is much more lasting than electronic contacts. These are the ones that are most valuable in your personal network. People you meet through electronic chat rooms and the like can come and go without any emotional connection, so value them differently. Make sure you spend quality time in person with those who matter most to you.

WhaT WoULD JEFF Do?
(Fun action steps to try this stuff out)

1. Next time you are shopping for a computer, make the bigger comparison I outline to confirm you are getting what is best for you at that stage of life. Use your negotiation skills outlined earlier to get the best deal.

2. Get a backup source and backup your data right now then set a schedule you will follow to do regular backups. You will thank me when you have a crash.

3. Take a road trip and look at several monitors before buying. Go bigger if you are undecided. It cuts down on eye strain.

4. Do some analysis of your needs and compare printers before buying. Truly consider two as I suggest and use them to satisfy specific needs, especially if you do some of your own design and printing.

5. Get an office suite package and learn the basics of the word processing, spreadsheet, database, slide show, and graphic design programs to make you more marketable and build your arsenal of skills. Practice with this software ½ hour each day. Stick with one program until you get a reasonable handle on it then move to the next type until you have practiced each of the five types.

6. Practice shots and features with a digital camera, even if it's on a cell phone. Learn to upload shots to a PC and online (no nudies or sex stuff). Practice using

a digital camcorder, if available, learning its features and how to upload to a PC and to online sites, like YouTube. Take it a step further and find a free or inexpensive video editing package and learn how to edit your videos as well as add sound, transitions, words/titles, and burn them to DVD's. These may be helpful skills at your job or business.

7. If you can use it, add a protected, wireless network to your home so you have the skills and the flexibility. Use the Help function, online bulletin boards, and your local electronics store to get a handle on it.

8. Confirm you know how to use e-mail and attachments for typical programs like Outlook. Also, know how to use a fax and a scanner. If telecommuting and a home office is an option, add it and any of the other options I mention in that section of the chapter.

9. Take another road trip and research smart phones at your local dealers. Even if you don't need one or can't justify it yet, you will have some background on them when you do need one.

10. Bring up GoDaddy.com or another domain seller and buy your name in .com for about $10 a year or less if you buy multiple years right away. If not right now, in time you can use it to build your personal brand, have a store, sell your e-book, and do other things. Also, make certain you are comfortable using the main sites I mention in the chapter for searches and online payments.

Help your family and friends with this area because you've learned something that can help them. Prompt them to go through these action steps to get a basic handle on this area. Once you've finished these steps, write me to let me know what happened and what you learned at *stories@lifescheatsheets.com..*

Now, think like Nike and Just Do It!

Now that we are done with the long sections and heading into the home stretch, I'm giving you a short intermission to get a chuckle. These phrases are actual church bulletin entries or announcements during a service. These gems were shared by Mark Matteson, who provided the Foreword. Enjoy the bloopers.

"Our youth basketball team is back in action Wednesday at 8 p.m. in the recreation hall. Come out and watch us kill Christ the King."

"The peacemaking meeting scheduled for today has been canceled due to a conflict."

"The sermon this morning: Jesus Walks on the Water."
"The sermon this evening: Searching for Jesus."

"Don't let worry kill you off; let the church help."

"Irving Benson and Jessie Carter were married on October 24 in the church. So ends a friendship that began in their school days."

"Scouts are saving aluminum cans, bottles, and other items to be recycled. Proceeds will be used to cripple children."

"For those of you who have children and don't know it, we have a nursery downstairs."

"Please place your donation in the envelope along with the deceased person you want remembered."

"Weight Watchers will meet at 7 p.m. at the First Presbyterian Church. Please use the large double door at the side entrance."

"The Associate Minister unveiled the church's new tithing campaign slogan last Sunday: I Upped My Pledge—Up Yours."

P. Programming Your Mind

A. Accelerate Success with Crucial Skills

L. Life Planning 101

Blueprint to Success System

Section 3:
Life Planning 101

This last section is clearly for everyone. It lays the foundation for a successful and less stressful life. It gives you the tools to get off on the right foot right now. It lets you make plans so you don't have to scurry around and make hasty decisions when you are faced with the challenges I'll talk about in this section.

You will be equipped to handle situations you run into because you have built the appropriate skills and made the decisions that will enable you to handle whatever comes down the pike. These chapters show you how to take control of your destiny before life has a chance to take control of you.

Don't Trade Hours for $ (Build Multiple, Passive Income Streams)

Q. What is my ultimate income goal?

Your long-term income goal is to have multiple streams of diversified, passive income that you can manage with a small amount of time per week. Passive income will free up your time to add new streams, do what you want to do, be with your family, pursue other interests you've put off, pursue your passions, or help with causes that you like. Until you are very well off, I recommend that you spend a significant amount of any extra time that you have adding new investments that increase your income and diversify your investments further.

The extra time that you gain by having income that you passively earn without putting in more time at work will allow you to do things now that you were putting off until retirement. Tim Ferriss, author of *The 4-Hour Workweek*, talks about this concept and suggests taking mini-retirements regularly so you can enjoy your main desires now while you are more physically able to. He defines these as short chunks of time off (a couple of weeks, a month, or more) to complete some of your main desires you might be inclined to wait to do for when you have more money and ultimately retire at age 65. He also gives some specific methods for freeing up your time to be able to get

217

away. He suggests you stop waiting for retirement in 30 to 40 years and tolerating what you don't like during these best years of your life when you can do things and enjoy them now. You need to read it to really wrap your head around his whole concept.

Q. What is passive income?

Passive income is income you receive that doesn't require your regular, active involvement. You can be away from the investment and it will continue to produce net income for you. It does not rely on your daily direction and can operate independently. It produces an income based on the structure and systems that you have put in place, with others assuring that the investment is running correctly. You will still need to monitor it on a regular basis to assure that it is working as planned, but you will only oversee key variables to verify that it's doing well. People in the daily operations will feed you information on a planned schedule that you will analyze to confirm it is on track.

Q. What are some investment areas to consider?

I am going to just give an overview of big areas to consider, but you will need to research them in more depth to really understand the particular areas you are interested in. Real estate has worked for me and many others. If you look up the list of the most wealthy people, the bulk of them are in real estate to some degree. The equity (stocks and mutual funds) and debt (bonds) markets have taken huge losses in the last couple of years, but will probably rebound and can provide good returns for the long-term.

Retirement plans like:
- 401(k)s (for privately-owned companies)
- 503(b)s (only for public/non-profit entities)
- Pensions (typically in large companies usually funded by the company; many are being discontinued)
- Deferred income (second income set aside in a fund, usually for top-level executives to put off paying tax on that portion of income that will be received and taxed later in life)

- SIMPLE and SEP plans (both of these are for smaller companies and for those self-employed)

You should be involved in one or more of these plans as you lay out your investment strategy.

Money markets, short-term certificates of deposit, and other liquid cash vehicles are areas to invest in for short-term and emergency needs. Keeping much money here will severely limit your return.

New and existing businesses, including online (Internet-based) businesses, multilevel marketing or relationship marketing businesses (where you are recruited by someone and start a business then recruit others to start the same business, getting a small portion of income off of everything those you recruited sell. Examples include: Amway, Arbonne, YTB Travel, Pampered Chef and the like), can also provide good investment opportunities. Businesses that produce physical products are usually capital-intensive and require large inventories, so don't get too heavily involved in them without a lot of careful research and advice. Service businesses are usually much less capital-intensive, and some of them need very little money to get started.

Information products (books, videos, webinars, e-lessons, e-books, etc.) are very simple and have great net profit margins since many of them are downloadable and there is no physical product to deliver. Getting them listed on *www.Amazon.com*, *www.BarnesandNoble.com*, video sites like YouTube, and other big, online sellers can really boost sales.

Other Internet-based businesses can also have good margins. Platinum power sellers on eBay with an eBay store and an online site outside of eBay, can be lucrative. I know of some power sellers who have reached several million dollars in annual sales. One of the keys is finding great wholesalers or negotiating a contract to get goods directly from manufacturers, cutting out all of the middlemen markups.

Research the areas you are interested in. I hear something about green products every day. Different energy sources, oil wells and pipelines, high mileage vehicle engines, robotic and automated features, online businesses and services, and electronic devices are all areas that you hear about regularly that offer opportunities for growth. They typically offer stocks. Some have Initial Public Offerings where the public can get stock in the company for the first time. You can join a company like this or help start one that is involved somehow. The point is that these industries seem to be in high demand and will probably become more valuable as they progress so getting in early in their life cycle can be lucrative.

In looking at different possibilities, consider joint ventures with someone who is already in business doing some portion of what you want to do. Look at being an affiliate sales site selling something that is already in the market, but not marketed as far as it can reach. Look at products and services that compliment those that are in place. Look at back-end products that follow an initial book, movie, or game. Also other information products like audio, video, and downloadable goods of the same content as well as physical products like T-shirts, trading cards, and backpacks will typically sell once a "craze" is started on something like Harry Potter or Pokemon.

Consider splitting a business with managers who are the primary operators, but don't have enough money, knowledge, or skill to go forward without you. If these don't work, create hybrid (similar but slightly different) options or come up with another option from reading, researching, and talking with others. There are endless possibilities.

Q. How long does it take to get multiple streams?

Realize that this is a long-term, big-picture view. It will normally take many years to get these in place, but the sooner you start, the sooner they will be in place and you will have more free time as well as the resources to enjoy it. Stay on course and work toward them daily. Always be looking for the right opportunities and find a way to grab them when you find them. Good ones that you can make a significant amount of money from are not available very long before someone else acts on the investment, eliminating your opportunity.

On the other hand, you are not looking for "get rich quick" schemes. Don't be sucked in by fast-talking salesmen who tell you that you must make a decision that day or lose the opportunity forever. If it's truly a deal, you may need to act quickly, but if there is an unreasonable deadline that doesn't give you time to think it through and investigate, it's often better to let it pass.

Never avoid completing your due diligence (detailed investigation, confirming all of the information you are being given from other sources) before fully committing to a new investment. You need to look at:

- Whether it is legitimate
- Whether the claims made by the seller are reliable
- What they are saying in reviews online and forums
- Whether there are hidden risks or costs
- Whether you can afford to get involved
- Whether the terms are right for you at the time, etc.

Get the deal legally under contract quickly so it is temporarily "off the market" during your due diligence period. Make the deal contingent upon the satisfactory completion of your due diligence, giving yourself multiple ways to get out of the contract if you find negative aspects that cause you to not want to be involved. Find a due diligence checklist so you walk through all of the applicable steps in doing a thorough investigation.

Sometimes your due diligence uncovers items that can be negotiated into a revised deal that can still work for all parties. I have done due diligence on a lot of businesses and have found that most of the "deals" ultimately are not deals. You will need to pass on the deal or revise it in light of what you have found. You will look at lots of potential opportunities and you need to select the few that truly fit your target. Remember that buyers and sellers have different objectives and you need to protect yourself by doing due diligence along with the assistance of several trusted professionals (business consultants, attorneys, CPA/CMAs, bankers, realtors, appraisers, etc.).

Q. What should I do once I invest in something?

You should "baby-sit" a new investment until you are comfortable it is running as planned in accordance with your due diligence (if it is a currently operating business, you may hear it called a "going concern"). This assures you that your due diligence process was effective and that there are no areas that need mid-course corrections to assure that it functions as you had planned. Once you have had several reporting periods (usually weekly or monthly periods) and have monitored all of the key areas closely, then you can start to back off and let those assigned to deal with it daily do so, providing you with the reporting or online access you require. New investments will usually take more of your time at the beginning than those that are consistent and have been with you longer.

Q. How do I create multiple streams of income?

You should see if you can come up with additional, related streams of income that can add to the initial or main stream. Sometimes, you can split one stream into multiple streams and have different individuals assigned to growing each individual stream. See how you can continue to build each stream over time or how you can increase the profit margin on the stream by making strategic changes.

One way to look at creating new streams from the same customer base is through additional products or services that are complimentary to the initial stream. For example, a lawn service could be the initial stream of income that includes weed trimming. You could add:

- Edging
- Fertilizing
- Grub control
- Aerating
- Lawn tools and mower sales
- Landscaping
- Mulching and spring cleanup
- Landscaping walls
- Lawn mower repair and warranty work

- Additional mowing crews
- Targeting neighborhood or condominium associations
- Snow removal and salt application, etc.

You can see there may be a lot of related areas you can go into from an initial stream. You need to closely estimate the costs and focus initially on the ones that are more profitable.

Another example is the writing and publishing of this book and others that will follow. Multiple income streams include other products and services with related information like:

- CD sets and CD of the month
- DVD sets
- mp3 and iPod downloads
- Seminars and longer workshops
- Speaking engagements
- Coaching
- Training coaches to coach others on the subjects
- Teleseminars and webinars
- Membership site with lots of content
- Updated versions of the books
- e-books and Kindle/e-reader books
- Newsletters and e-zines
- Radio and TV shows
- Contests, etc.

You can see that some of these generate passive income, while others require an initial investment of time but then start generating passive income, and some require ongoing involvement. The income from these sources is added to the income generated from other streams such as my real estate investments, the stock market, money markets, Internet marketing, consulting, and other business ventures.

Q. Why should I diversify my investments?

If you were heavily invested in the automotive industry in 2009, you would probably understand the need to diversify better than others because you would have lost most of your money. With two of the "Big Three" having filed bankruptcy and the third not in good shape, many creditors to these companies have written off millions and are going out of business themselves because they were not sufficiently diversified.

You've heard the expression "don't put all your eggs in one basket." This is the theme of diversification. Many times, with diverse investments, some are going well, others are neutral, while others are struggling but have the potential to turn around. If you are too invested in one area and that area is down, everything you have is down which will put you far behind on your savings and investment plan and could put your assets at risk for foreclosure or bankruptcy.

By having your money split in different investment types, companies, industries, and countries, you will not be dependent upon any one area or resource so you can much more easily survive a downturn in one area. Some of your investments will be in steady, more predictable areas while others will be in higher risk–higher return areas. Study the history as well as the predicted economic future of the investment you are considering. Also, look into items that offset the one you are looking at. Frequently, when stocks are down, bonds are up and vice versa (inversely related). If you see that one area has some significant risk, see if you can invest a little in something that is more certain that can offset this risk.

I know of some former, current, and retired employees who had most of their 401(k) investments in stock in Owens-Corning and Dana, which are local-based, Fortune 500 companies where they worked for 25-plus years. They lost most of the value in their retirement and stock accounts when these companies filed bankruptcy. A number of them at OC who had not diversified lost hundreds of thousands of dollars. I understand some had more than $1 million invested before the bankruptcy, and they lost nearly everything. In these investors' cases, they made a terrible mistake by keeping their investment in one company (no diversification) and now some have gone back to work to support themselves during their retirement years.

Q. How do I determine how much risk is acceptable?

Each person has a different comfort level that changes over time as your life circumstances change. You should take a couple of risk assessments to see where you fall on that continuum. Many of the financial services companies and banks have these assessments online and in their offices.

Many investments' income will be tied to performance, and many are volatile and fluctuate. Income will usually go up and down, so you will attempt to get the average over the year to be at or above your projections. Understand the typical income range over the year so you are prepared for the good and the bad. If you prefer a more conservative approach, you can make steady income one of your main criteria when searching for investments and rule out many of the volatile ones.

The more conservative you are, the more you will want steady, predictable streams of income that will naturally have a lower potential return. Those folks that have a higher tolerance for risk will want performance-based income because it can go very high, but also very low. The key is obviously to stay involved closely with volatile performance-based investments so you can capitalize on their high seasons and minimize the loss in the low seasons. Keep in mind that the younger you are the greater your risk tolerance can be because you will have more years to make up any losses, while those nearing retirement age would not have this extra time to offset losses.

Q. Do I need to be involved daily?

I am fighting this urge currently and I am restructuring how I get things done. I am forcing myself to outsource (contract others to complete tasks I need done) more as my income grows. I have seen that I can't get as much done without this assistance, and I am constantly pulled in multiple directions when I am too involved in day-to-day operations. Too much involvement typically causes me to count on one primary income stream with minimal additional streams. You will need to resist the urge to stay involved daily if you are like me, because it's the main way to free up your time.

You do need to have trustworthy, competent people managing your investments and running any companies you are invested in. You need to monitor these regularly, getting reports and access to key data that can show you what is happening in each investment. The advances in computers allow you to have streaming, real-time video of an actual site whenever you like if you really want to see what's happening. I know a couple of self storage facility owners that manage sites in multiple states in this manner. I would not get too hooked on watching these monitors, though, or you will not free up your time.

Look for specific types of opportunities that match your availability, desire, need, and risk level. I sold a number of real estate investments that were consuming too much of my time and did not have a very good return. I am continuously searching for different types of investments that can work without me, while providing a good return with a medium level of risk.

Q. How will I reduce the hours I am involved?

With investments that you have had for some time, you need to reduce your time to monitoring only or get rid of them if that can't be done and the return is not substantial. You need to delegate, outsource, trust, and monitor. In *The E-Myth,* Michael Gerber says to work *on* your business from a big picture view, not *in* your business from the daily operations view. You are much more objective, can see areas to improve and grow, and will make changes happen if you are not involved in day-to-day activities. You must realize that you only have so many hours each day and need to utilize the time you allocate to your work and investments on core tasks to grow your income. Freeing up your other time will allow you to allocate additional time to new investments until you have a comfort level with delegating and monitoring to reduce your active involvement.

Q. Won't I have to put in too many hours?

With this whole concept, you need to keep in mind the "hour demon." As you get more years of experience, getting paid X number of dollars for an hour of your time continues to limit what you make because the number of hours you can give is limited. If you really want to free up your time, you need to get away from an hourly paid role unless you can make an un-Godly amount of money per hour or find other ways to supplement your income. Remember to be aware of how much your time is worth.

If you are employed and are earning X dollars per hour, are you making your employer a profit with your efforts? Can you increase the profit, eliminate some overhead, reduce other expenses, and still get the customer to pay you the same fee? If so, you may want to look at opportunities to partner with your employer and implement these ideas to increase profit and increase what goes into your pocket. If that doesn't work, you can consider starting your own business and possibly compete with your employer. These are just a couple of ways to get out of the hour game and exponentially increase the ROI on your time.

I have had a big wake-up call over the last several years with the concept of the hourly rate and hours worked as an attorney. Many people think attorneys make a lot of money when they can charge $150, $200, $250 and higher per hour, but I have learned that this isn't true for most of them. Many hours in a day are not billable to a client. Lawyers can only bill the hourly rate when they are hired by a client for a specific matter. When they are in meetings, listening to potential new clients explain their issue, calling clients who don't pay, taking continuing education courses, attending bar functions, marketing to get clients, dealing with administrative issues, running the firm, etc., they are not billing. This rat race causes many attorneys to work 50 to 60-plus hours per week.

Most attorneys only get paid a portion of what they actually collect, and some clients will not pay what they are billed, so those hours are essentially worked at a reduced rate or free. Once you take out overhead allocations, staff pay and benefits, and the other non-billable time listed above, it can be tough to make a decent amount of money.

Let's say, for example, an attorney pays all of his expenses and he has $75,000 left for himself. He works 2,500 hours that year (50 hours/week times 50 weeks). This works out to $30 per hour even though he billed at four to six times that figure. And this is gross pay before taxes. This is one of many real-life examples. This ignores the risk that he will not have as many cases or as much income the next year and can easily take a decrease in pay.

Obviously, it is difficult for the attorney to work even more hours the following year to generate a higher income. Aside from cutting costs, the attorney can try to gain leverage by getting additional business and hiring someone else to do some of the work while taking part of the profit from that relationship. A better way for him to generate a higher income is to put in place multiple streams of income. Finding opportunities for passive income will be particularly important for someone like this who is already working 50 to 60 hours a week.

Q. Will I have a lot of obstacles to overcome?

I'm not going to sugarcoat this; you will have to take action regularly and will be faced with many difficult decisions along the way. You won't always know the answer. This will often take you out of your comfort zone, and you need to be confident that you can deal with whatever comes your way. Much of this will not be easy and will challenge you mentally. You will need to be a creative and resourceful entrepreneur. Thorough due diligence will uncover many issues, and you need to deal with them during the purchase process so they don't become bigger issues later.

Don't let issues fester over time. Deal with them quickly once you are aware of them. Make mid-course corrections with investments that go off-course, then get back out of the daily operations and see if the corrections work as planned. Each issue will have its own timeframe and associated details so it is helpful to be analytical and have some problem-solving skills. Approach each of these as a new challenge that you will overcome and learn from, rather than just another problem.

Most of the time, you can find specialists who can assist you as needed with whatever issues you face. I recommend that you have these support options in place to call on when their specialty is needed. It's wise to go talk with a few CPA-accountants, attorneys, realtors, appraisers, lenders, financial advisors, bankers, etc., now, before you need them. See who you connect with best, and look for people who you believe have a great handle on what you may need. You don't have to pay to retain them, but just have some relationships started so you know they will be there when you find that opportunity and need them to do their part.

Q. Will I need to invest in risky areas?

Many people will have to increase their risk tolerance and get involved in some higher return investments to free up their own time spent at work. I am currently doing this so I can take advantage of faster growth options. Just make certain that you do thorough due diligence and regularly monitor them. Be selective with people you trust with your investments. Listen carefully to them, ask questions regularly, get good answers, and don't stop until you do. Don't procrastinate about responding to red flags. Follow your instincts and your inner voice. Do your own private investigating if something doesn't seem right. This is your investment, so you have the right to investigate until you are satisfied. If you're not happy, it may be time for a change of personnel or investment.

Q. What if I can't make up my mind and take action?

Be aware of what is referred to as "analysis paralysis." Many people, including me, go through this at some point, and many never make any offers to buy investments. They analyze the deal to death, focus on what could go wrong, and cannot push themselves to actually make an offer. Fear of loss, mistake, liability, and the like continue to hold them back. Fear hinders the achievement of many people's dreams and desires. It just won't let you pull the trigger and take action.

I have struggled with this on bigger, unfamiliar projects because I have seen a number of bad investments in the last several years. This has left me a little gun shy. You need to realize that it is not unusual to look at 50 residential properties (online or in person), bid on 10 to 20, and maybe get one or two. The key is to make a lot of offers regularly with the appropriate contingencies (pending satisfactory financing, inspection, confirming financial statements, and the like). This is also true with other investments. You have to sift through a lot of bad and mediocre investments to find those gems that really shine.

Ultimately, you have to put things under contract, settle on a purchase agreement, and go through due diligence to really be serious about getting these streams in place. If you make no offers, I guarantee that you will not buy any investments, so you must make offers when the time is right to start the process. Many deals fall apart after they are under contract during due diligence for a variety of reasons. Regardless, you need to be serious once it's under contract to make decisions about the questionable factors (and there will typically be some) so you can close the deal and add it to your other investments or move on to a better fit. Don't get too bogged down with any one investment you are considering because there many opportunities out there. Also, act in a professional manner at all times and don't insult anyone or burn bridges because these same individuals may come back at a later time with other options.

Q. What should I do if an investment is losing money?

If an investment is not profitable or is taking way too much of your time, get out of it. Don't hold on to losers. Pull the plug once you have assessed it, tried to correct it, and not had success with it. Pull a Donald Trump and fire it! Factors change, the economy changes, and new developments may change the way things had been working. Changes can make your investment no longer serve your needs or interests.

This is a big reason for regularly monitoring your investments, recognizing issues early, and attending to them once they are noticed. Eliminate procrastination. Don't let one stream monopolize your time. Remember what your time is worth.

It is OK to get involved more in one stream that you are passionate about and want to spend your time in for awhile. If you choose to devote time to an investment that you enjoy, but it doesn't produce the return you want and your other investments are doing fine, that is your decision. Not everything needs to have a positive ROI to be worth keeping. There are other reasons that come into play, and if it is affordable, you can be comfortable with your decision.

Beware, don't get too emotionally tied to one that is losing so much that it is draining your other investments and dragging down your whole investment portfolio. You will have to let it go and get rid of it, or it could sink your whole ship, causing a financial crisis.

Q. How can I learn more about this concept?

Do some research and read materials from a number of established folks in this arena. Robert Allen is the one who laid it out clearly to me many years ago in his materials. He has multiple books, courses, coaching programs, etc. on investing and building multiple streams of income. I have been through some of his materials as well as a few three-day workshops, and they have a lot of good content on real estate, Internet businesses, stock market investments, company investments, and so on.

Robert Kiyosaki of *Rich Dad, Poor Dad* and Donald Trump both have multiple streams of income working for them and encourage that diversity. "The Donald" is heavy in real estate and development, but has a number of other interests like the rights to the Miss USA pageant and *The Apprentice* show that he has expanded upon with celebrities. Loral Langemeier is another spirited investor who has done a lot with her Cash Machine concept. She has helped a lot of investors grow and diversify their investments into many different areas through her "Big Table" system. Harv Eker has good materials on training your mind for financial success.

If you move toward the online world, Jim Cockrum is someone I have connected with and have read many of his materials over the past few years. He started in eBay 10 years ago and has the highest selling online book called the *The Silent Sales Machine.* He has put out several updated versions with the latest one focused less on eBay and more on models for growing online businesses. He has many online and some offline income streams that work without much of his active involvement. He does a lot of outsourcing and spreads his risk very wide among a number of projects.

Yanik Silver, Ryan Lee, Joel Peterson, Joel Comm, and Ryan Deiss are additional online entrepreneurs who I have read and listened to extensively. They have been heavily into online businesses for several years and have helped many people get into the business. One of my goals is to get more heavily involved online and mirror some of the things they have had success with. They all have multiple passive income streams and enjoy a financially free lifestyle.

WHaT WOULD JEFF DO?
(Fun action steps to try this stuff out)

1. Look at all of the areas I mentioned above and determine areas you are interested in. Research them now and see if you can afford to get involved in one or two areas right now, even if it's only a small amount. This will give you a taste of that area and help you determine if you want to be more involved.

2. Get a comprehensive due diligence checklist and modify it for the areas you are specifically interested in. If you find an opportunity, you will be ready to investigate it further. Also find the professionals you want to assist you with due diligence and secure that connection now. Interview them to make certain you are confident in your relationship.

3. Get a sample of the commonly used real estate purchase contract from a Realtor so you begin to get a feel for what is covered in a purchase contract. It will need

to be modified for other types of purchases. An attorney is usually the best person for these other purchases or someone like a Realtor or broker that specializes in the area.

4. Once you have invested in something, baby-sit it and learn as much as you can about the investment and the industry. This will reduce potential surprises and may uncover other areas you may get involved in.

5. Take a couple of risk assessments and determine your level of risk tolerance. The younger you are, the more risk you can typically afford to take because you have decades to make up losses. Also determine what type of income you want from your investments.

6. Calculate what your time is worth right now. Determine ways you are going to increase that value daily and put time into those tasks, eliminating some time wasters. If you are in a smaller company, is there a way to partner with the owners in some way to earn much more? Is there a company you want to start? If so, write down a detailed business plan to get it started.

Share this information with your family and friends because you've learned something that can help them. Once you've finished these steps, write me to let me know what happened and what you learned at *stories@lifescheatsheets.com*.

Now, think like Nike and Just Do It!

"Ideas won't work unless I do."

"If there is no wind, row."

"The door of opportunity won't open unless you do some pushing."

IT'S NOT WHAT YOU MAKE, IT'S WHAT YOU KEEP AND WHAT YOU DO WITH THAT (FINANCIAL PLANNING 101)

For this chapter, assume there will be no Social Security, no Medicare, and no Medicaid available for retirement income or benefits when young adults get to a typical retirement age. With the political climate, the poor economy, increased foreign competition, and the like, who knows if there will be any replacement or supplemental system by then? You should not count on it as you build your plan now. As a country, we have increased our national debt by trillions (1 trillion = 1,000,000,000,000 = 1,000 billion, that's a lot of zeros) with all of the bailout and economic stimulus packages. There is still no viable plan to pay it down and eventually pay it off so the country has just become much more indebted primarily to other countries. I have written this and the follow up book so that young adults will be successful and financially secure so they will not need any bailout. It's my long-term anti-bailout solution. Maybe I should sell it to or go to work for the federal government?

Seriously, I believe we have entered some very scary territory with the growth of the country's debt load and no good way to monitor the use of the money being doled out. The financial institutions wasted their money, in part, on big bonuses and still got billions of dollars in bailout money. But the country and the economy are counting on

235

you (young adults) to run your life wisely, get financially savvy early, and not depend on the government to take care of you as you age. With so many people living longer due to new advances in medicine and health care, it is up to each of you to fund your own retirement and health care because it will simply be too costly for Uncle Sam (a.k.a. government) to take care of you.

Q. Does this really apply to me now?

You may think, "Why would I do any financial planning when I'm young and really don't have much money or income right now?" Everyone needs to start getting a financial education in high school and continue to build on that knowledge throughout their entire life. If retirement seems too far away, consider other long-term goals that may help you stay motivated.

- Do you want to buy a nice car (or just drive a clunker)?
- Buy a house (or keep renting a puny apartment)?
- Take nice vacations (or none at all)?
- Have a boat (or a little remote control one)?
- Have a nice wedding (or get married by Elvis in Vegas)?
- What kind of lifestyle do you want for yourself and your family?

In order to get the material things that you want to have, you need a plan. You need to know how you are going to generate income, how you can limit your expenses, how to save, and how to get good deals. So if "financial planning" sounds dry and boring, think of it as "getting what you want." Isn't that more exciting?

Over time, you will probably continue to earn more money, you may go to college, you may have kids, your kids may go to college, you will take on debt, buy a house, buy cars, etc. Learning about these areas now will allow you to know your options and have the proper tools when you need them.

You won't have to get stressed out and hope that you know what to do when the time comes. You will already have researched, studied, and learned about these areas by the time you are faced with them.

You can then set a plan and carry it out, being confident that you have a reasonable grasp of the issues. Many times, you will solicit the assistance of an advisor who specializes in the particular area you are getting involved in, and you will be able to assess whether he knows what he is doing by having this base of knowledge. You will then be confident in your advisor or know it's time to pull a Trump and fire him!

Part of your planning will involve a personal strategy to increase your income and save what you need to in order to reach your goals. You will also learn to compare investment options, account types, returns, and other features, do your own banking, set up accounts, reconcile them, and manage your money. Don't wander aimlessly like many do and think you'll get to it later. Eventually, later becomes too late, and procrastination takes over. You will be scrambling when the need arises, usually guessing at what to do and not having sufficient knowledge to be confident that you've made the best decision. It's much better to think ahead, learn what you will need, and be confident when the time comes. Like it or not, you will be faced with these subjects eventually, so you need to grasp them before that.

Q. When should I put a plan in place?

Everyone coming out of high school should get a plan together. If you have already graduated, it's not too late to start right now. Develop a plan that is in sync with your goals, and start funding it right now. It should be written with reasonable detail and with specific timelines so that it can be measured and adjusted along the way. The amount of dollars and complexity doesn't matter as much as getting something in place now and building good habits (remember Nike and Just Do It). You will continue to monitor your plan and revise it as things change. Once you have a basic plan in place, you can always add to it and make it more complete. You may piece one together using the model I've included in this chapter or get one from a financial planner in your area. Many banks and credit unions also offer assistance with financial planning and can give you a good model to follow.

Q. How do I go about building a plan?

Turn to the pyramid exhibit in the Appendix and study it for a minute. (Go ahead, I'll wait. Yes, that's Jeopardy music playing) You can probably see that you start from the bottom, which is the foundation of the structure. Like building a house, you start with the footer and foundation that will support the rest of the structure. Most financial firms use something very similar to this to illustrate the levels of your planning. As your resources grow and you gain more income, you advance to the next level and so on. The higher you move on the structure, the more the risk grows, as well as the potential return, and the greater the fluctuation in returns.

Make certain that you stay diversified as you move into the investment sections that are higher in the pyramid. It is usually recommended that you never have more than 5 to 10% in one investment category, depending upon the structure. Following this method, one investment may be up, another down, and others neutral, so they will average out to your target return. With this allocation, big shifts in one investment category won't significantly affect the value of your entire plan.

Q. What are the typical areas in a plan?

Most financial planners have a big questionnaire. Some call this a fact finder or personal survey which they use to cover most areas of your life that could be included in a complex financial plan. Many of them will not apply to your situation starting out, but they will be more applicable as time goes on. Don't eliminate these areas; just store them in your mind for the future when they may apply. I have seen fact finders that are 25 to 30 pages long, so some are very specific. The better picture your financial planner has, the better her recommendations can be.

Areas typically covered include:
- Identifying everyone in your family and extended family
- The job or business that you have
- Short- and long-term financial goals
- Retirement and pension plans

- Education plans
- Your financial statement
- Potential inheritances
- Your tax situation
- Risk management/insurance
- Basic estate planning
- Risk tolerance
- Your current budget

The budget will tell them if you have extra money to fund financial plan needs that you have not already taken care of, or if you need to "sharpen your pencil" (add income/reduce expenses) to increase your net income. Your advisor's objective is to help you fund your plan's needs now as well as meet your overall life goals.

Don't freak out if they recommend products in many areas of your plan. They show you what the perfect picture looks like, but realize that many people cannot afford to allocate all of the resources needed to have the perfect plan. It will probably be necessary to prioritize and put off allocating resources to contain items that are lower in your hierarchy. You will want to put all of the areas in a hierarchy of need, assuming you cannot fund everything and still have the resources available to complete your highest-priority goals.

Since many of the first steps are insurance policies that reduce your risks, you can determine which risks are higher and start with those. If you have a job, your employer may already cover a number of them. For example, some people locally (while in college and after) worked at UPS part time (four-hour shifts a few days a week) because all employees received good benefits. They could get most of the insurance they needed without any out-of-pocket cost while earning a second income.

Q. Should I care about an emergency fund now?

Right when you start building your foundation, include an emergency fund as one of your first priorities. It is not listed in many of the pyramid charts, but should be added and can't wait until you get to the follow-up *financial habits* book where I explain it in more detail. One of the causes of all of the foreclosures and bankruptcies is that these families didn't have an emergency fund to fall back on.

Believe me and build an emergency fund now. It is recommended that you save six months of living expenses in this fund. If that is impossible right now, start with one, then two, then three months and build it to six months over the following six to twelve months. You can also determine how much to build in the fund by conservatively estimating the time it will take to replace your main income stream, if it were lost. If that is less than six months, use that number.

The fund will serve as your backup plan. You rarely know in advance if you are going to lose your job, if the company whose stock you own is filing bankruptcy, or if you will have a serious sickness or accident, which will eliminate your main income stream or savings. It usually happens on short notice, and it usually takes some time to replace it. I had this happen on my first job without any notice and fortunately had already built my fund to live on while getting over the shock and picking up the pieces.

Even though you may not currently have the need, don't fall in the trap of believing you can hold off on saving for the fund. Preplanning avoids panic. I am betting you personally know someone who has been in foreclosure, lost their job, filed bankruptcy, or had a car repossessed in light of the vast number of people who have been affected in these areas. Without the emergency fund to buy you time to solve the problem, you could experience these same issues.

In 2009, I received an e-mail at Christmas time listing 35 store chains that were closing hundreds of stores after the holiday season. This meant tens of thousands of additional workers were losing their jobs soon. (Merry Christmas, damn it!) Do you think they had their emergency accounts funded or were they panicking because they put it off? (Most fell in the latter category.) Without a crystal ball, you can't predict the future so this account needs to be funded.

Q. What are the first items I should look into?

As reflected in the pyramid, short- and long-term disability, health, life, property and casualty (P&C) and vehicle insurance, along with liability and long-term care insurance, are the typical insurance products that make up the foundation of a financial plan in addition to the emergency fund. I am not saying that you need all of these things, but you need to assess whether, in your particular situation, the risk vs. reward analysis determines that you need them and can afford them. I cover details of each of these products in the *financial habits* follow-up book.

I hope it is obvious that health, P&C, vehicle and liability coverages are really not optional unless you don't have a house or car. You should consider them required. The risk is far greater to go without them than they currently cost.

Once you get past the insurance and emergency fund level, you move into the basic savings and investment level. This involves liquid or short-term investments, like Certificates of Deposit. They will typically not earn a good interest rate and the interest is taxable so you don't want to invest a lot of money in these areas for a long period of time, but you can get to the money quickly if you truly need it. You can even cash them out before they expire with a penalty if you have an emergency and need the cash, whereas many other investments lock the money up longer.

Cash accounts (checking, savings, and money markets) are usually taxable so the interest you earn will be reduced by around one-third, and you only keep the net amount. For example, let's assume you earn 3% in money market savings. Reducing it by the one-third tax nets you 2%, yet inflation is 5%. You just lost 3% on your money. This illustrates the importance of earning more than inflation. This basic savings and investment level is primarily used for operating money and short-term savings to cover your regular budget expenses.

Once you have enough income to satisfy the insurance, emergency fund, and basic savings and investment levels, you will move into income and growth areas where you can earn more on your money and let compounding really start working for you. But keep in mind, higher potential reward is accompanied by higher risk. As discussed earlier in Chapter 16, do your due diligence and test the investment with a smaller amount until it has a track record you can count on. You can also start getting into real estate, which is one of the main areas I have concentrated on and would recommend that you look into. In the Appendix, I have included a list of real estate investing areas you can consider and some of the experienced investor-instructors I know in each of these areas.

Q. What if I am not good with money?

As you get into the details with your plan, I am certain many of you are wondering, "How am I supposed to do this if I am not good with numbers and money?" I have heard this from many people and I think it is mainly in their minds. I happen to be comfortable with numbers and can do many number-related functions in my head. Most of the numbers and functions we are talking about are very basic math calculations, and the ones that are not can be done with any basic financial calculator. Once you do them a few times, you will learn the key functions you need, like calculating a loan payment, and you will be able to whip right through them. If you just write down the few keystrokes, you can do what is needed.

I have worked with a number of math-phobic people who shove those tasks off on others. If this describes you, work on getting past it now. Take baby steps and practice some typical calculations that you need to be able to do the basic functions. Ask someone who is good with numbers to double check your work and help you if you are confused. Review your work after you have put it away for several hours so you can look at it with fresh eyes. You will find that you can catch errors better if you check your work after a break from it. Even if you have an advisor, you need to be knowledgeable in this area and able to work the typical calculations. The more you work with them the better you will get, which translates into more confidence.

Q. Should I hire an advisor?

Since I have mentioned an advisor many times, I want to share a little inside knowledge about my experiences with financial advisors, planners, representatives (I will refer to all three as advisors here) and their related companies. After many years of being asked to join financial services companies, I decided to research the area and "test the waters" after law school. Based on what I have learned as a financial advisor and as a client, I recommend that you visualize a big yellow caution flag being waved, like at a NASCAR race, in dealing with this area. If you want to understand my experiences more, read the shaded box that follows this section.

Studies show nine out of ten advisors (actually above 90%) leave the field, and most leave in the first year. So you may find yourself dealing with someone who has training, but lacks the experience to counsel you about your investments or who may not know you at all because your initial advisor left. The high turnover may leave you without an individual who is committed to your financial success once the company has your money. I'm amazed that companies and the industry as a whole hasn't changed the model to severely reduce this pathetic rate of turnover.

Most advisors work 100% on straight commission, so the company incurs very little cost to hire advisors. Companies then take a significant cut of the income the advisors bring in. As a result, most newer advisors feel pressure to sell rather than advise. There are also minimums at some companies and if agents don't meet them, they can get terminated. Therefore, advisors may be motivated to recommend something that will increase their commission, rather than suggesting what is best for you, the client. Compliance standards are not supposed to let that occur, but I've seen it happen.

Realize that you won't see what they get paid for each of the products and services that you purchase through them. They get paid annually for some items, monthly on others, and every time you make a payment on others, so make sure that you are getting the service you are paying for. The business model is built on advisors building a large amount of passive income from the products and services that you purchase.

The SEC, FINRA, and others continue to regulate the industry, but the regulations often have unintended consequences. They have become so restrictive that they stifle newer, motivated advisors and prevent them from aggressively building their client base. Ultimately, the restrictive compliance standards that were intended to help consumers actually tend to drive newer, good advisors out of the industry. Many products can be purchased directly online now, which has further affected the number of reliable advisors.

A Few Lessons I Learned from "The Street"

I had five poor experiences as an advisor and client which set the stage for my comments. I had decided I would only start as an advisor if I took over a book (group of existing clients) from someone who had left or had too many. I knew it took an average of five years to get to a reasonable income if you started from scratch and I wasn't going to commit to this new role if it would take me that long. So once I got all of the licenses and became an advisor, I targeted advisors who were planning to retire to expedite my timeline. I found someone retiring, had verbal agreements, actual and projected financial statements, and a written purchase agreement. I was partnering in the purchase with two other advisors I already knew there. But after almost two years of delays I was cut out of the deal for a still unknown reason (strike one).

While working this first deal, I earned the highest security licenses (Series 7 and Series 66), plus health insurance, life insurance, and annuities licenses which were all needed to do what clients might want. I got these through another financial company and the week after I completed the last one, that company closed the office and terminated our advisor contracts (strike two).

I put together a database and sent out a glossy mailer to more than 200 advisors to try to find an available book. I talked with 20 (10% response was good) different manager-advisors I heard from to see if any of them knew someone leaving where I could buy and service his book of clients.

(continued on next page)

(continued from previous page)

I found the independent ones were in fear of losing their finite pool of clients so they didn't take action to grow (mistake) and the bigger ones only had entry-level roles (not for me).

I ultimately accepted an offer from a large company's local office because the manager gave his word that he would help get my marketing plan past their strict compliance department to build a book much more quickly than was typical. Compliance disapproved every marketing method I was trying to implement, and the manager was not backing me. I agreed to give their antiquated phone call book-building process a try. After cold-calling off group lists where I knew someone in the group to the tune of 40 phone calls a day and getting nowhere, I ended my trial with them. Later I found out managers get bonuses for advisors joining them with all of their licenses completed (strike three).

Out of a later response to the above mailer, I thought I had finally found one that was a good fit. She was a 22-year veteran agent who had gotten hurt and wanted me to take over her practice with four staff and a good volume of business. She said she had not been able to service her regular clients for nine months, but they normally only have an annual update so I realized that was not a problem.

With all of the experiences I already had, I did my typical due diligence investigation to confirm her story. I found she had been evicted from her office, lost all of her licenses, moved her stuff into a storage unit, and that unit was being auctioned off for non-payment a few days from then which would eliminate all of her client files. I put together a purchase agreement to buy her book and worked out a deal with the storage company to buy the physical contents for a portion of the back rent, but had to clean it out in two weeks. I broke my foot the next day. The agent said the purchase agreement was good, but wouldn't return calls in a timely fashion and ultimately didn't get the agreement signed or pick up the records. I never heard from her again and the records were destroyed. I found out when cleaning out the unit that she had a drug problem, had been taken to jail previously, and the clients had moved on because they had not been serviced in two to three years (strike four).

(continued on next page)

(continued from previous page)

I have also used multiple advisors personally as a client and have never had a good advisor that serviced me and gave me good advice on a regular basis. I have tried several because of this lack of service after the initial meeting and not found one (strike five).

So, I was zero for five with financial services. I did talk with the only other option I considered viable, but because of my experiences to date, I could not convince myself to sign on with another company. It is still an option.

Even after all of this I still am interested in the industry and continue to look for a good fit independently or with a small, entrepreneurial firm that truly "gets it." You may need multiple advisors, specializing in each of the areas you need, unless you find one that has all of the resources in-house. Consider established agents and those newer agents who are closely supervised and actively mentored by experienced advisors. After reading the draft of this book, people have talked with me about being their advisor, but I have put their request on hold until I know I have found a good place that will be supportive of me for my clients.

Q. How should I find a qualified advisor?

There are good advisors out there; you just have to sift through them to get to the one who works best for you. Advisors must be licensed, and getting licensed is not easy. They usually have some industry training, have to pass several exams, are required to get more training by their specific company, and attend continuing education.

I suggest that you talk with at least five candidates before deciding on someone. Get recommendations from trusted family, friends, and coworkers on advisors they have used for some time. Find out how they know them, what they use them for, how long they have used them, why they like them, do they advise them, if so, how often, or do they just provide products, and what services and products they offer. You need to interview them, like them, and believe they are competent and will look out for your best interests, rather than sell you the product with the highest commission.

Realize that some of the products are company-specific (you may hear they are a captive agent). If you don't care for your advisor once you have purchased one of these products from him, you usually cannot change the product without penalties. The penalties can be severe so keep this in mind as you select products to buy.

Q. Do I need an understanding of the options?

Do your own homework before meeting with advisors so you have a basic understanding of the different options. Go to online financial sites, read some brochures, and visit the library or bookstore to gain enough knowledge to catch glaring inconsistencies and poor advice. Use the same questions for multiple advisors and see if you get consistent answers. If not, follow up with additional questions and make sure the advisor knows what she is talking about. If you know an advisor personally and can trust her, ask her about commission rates on different types of products so you know what items pay the most and see if they become recommendations. Don't roll over; take an active role and make certain you are getting what you are paying for.

Q. Do I need an advisor, planner, or what?

I consider financial representatives to be primarily product salespeople, and they are usually the lowest level of advisor. The terms financial advisor and financial planner have also been used in settings where they primarily sell rather than advise, so you need to be careful you know who you are getting. Investigate their credentials, rather than their title. If you see Certified Financial Planner (CFP), they have attended advanced courses and usually are more knowledgeable. This is probably the most popular, advanced credential. There are other special designations with estate planning, long-term care, life insurance, stock trading, etc. Regulators are trying to standardize all of this, so the meaning of titles may be clear soon.

For the long-term, you need an advisor, not a salesperson. Many times, once you have accumulated some wealth it is advisable to hire a fee-based advisor rather than an incentive-based/commissioned advisor. They can then be more objective and won't be compensated based on what product or service is sold. If you hire someone on a fee basis, make certain that you utilize her because that will be a fixed cost that you will pay regardless of use.

If the person is truly an advisor, he should do a comprehensive needs analysis (a.k.a. fact finder). He will use analyzer software to create a plan with details and reasons for taking certain actions. The advisor should review this in detail before meeting with you and make certain he agrees with the plan or adjusts it as needed. The plan is a good start for understanding a long-term strategy for your particular situation. Life changes and so should your plan.

Another key to choosing an advisor is whether they have a good, licensed assistant. This provides the agent with immediate backup and helps you get the paperwork through the system quickly and accurately. Does your advisor work with other advisors who specialize in areas they do not? Most advisors tend to specialize in a couple of areas, then partner with other advisors in or outside their company who specialize in other areas so they can offer everything with a high level of competence. This is the better way to go because the products and regulations frequently change.

Look for an advisor who has been in the business a number of years, or someone you know personally and whose skills you have confidence in. You will find that some folks who go into this field later in life are more matured and committed. Look at their whole situation and find someone likely to build a solid, long-term relationship with you to help you set and attain your financial goals.

Q. Should I deal with an advisor in a bank?

Most banks and credit unions have advisors, and many offer private client banking with senior advisors for higher net worth customers. In general, some bank products have more fees and lower returns because of their regulations and the overhead they carry. This also limits their variety and flexibility with non-traditional products (REITs, partnership shares, private company stock, stock options, puts and calls, and the like). But they usually have more support for their products, and primarily have traditional, very safe products because these institutions avoid risk of loss heavily. If you move into the private client section, you usually get more advising and strategic advice, which may carry an extra fee, but it could be worth it.

Another generality is that bank advisors are usually paid a base salary, and then get a small amount of commission or bonus pay on the volume of products and services they sell. This typically means they are not quite as "hungry" as 100% commission advisors are to get your business, unless they are new and really motivated. On the positive side, this makes them not as concerned about which products pay the most commission so they may be more likely to help you get what you truly need. They usually can get you what you want, but there is not much planning until you move into the private client arena.

Financial and insurance products that banks offer, on the average, are conservative investments and fit well into many plans. I have used them personally and everything was done accurately and on time. One potential reason that I have not received much planning advice from them is because most of the ones I worked with knew my background and assumed (right or wrong) I already knew what I should do.

Q. Should I work with a big or small practice?

You may also be wondering if it's wise to go with a bigger or smaller company advisor. The answer is not black and white. I have seen better and worse advisors in each type of company. The same is true when comparing captive agents (those who have to sell their specific company's products) with independents (who can sell many companies' products). This is more a matter of personal choice once you have considered all of the variables. You need to try the actual agent out and see how that connection works. You need to believe he is working in your best interest. I think any financial planning company can work out if you have the right agent with backup resources in the areas you may need assistance with but he doesn't focus on.

Advisors and companies that have been around longer tend to have a better handle on the profession and the industry, but I am familiar with several newer, small firms that formed because of problems with the bigger companies they were with. I have found that bigger companies can be bogged down by fear of a compliance audit and such strict compliance standards. They believe they are bigger targets for the regulators that believe they have deep pockets. They are more risk averse because of the fear of being made an example. Smaller companies may be more flexible and can get things accomplished quicker on a more personal basis because their fear of this is not as great.

Q. Do I want a local advisor or is one online OK?

With online purchasing and online business portals, conceivably you can do some of this online. I would be cautious in doing so unless you know there is very good phone support by someone you can understand (normally someone from your same country) who is able to help you resolve issues easily. Otherwise, I tend to want someone local I can meet with. I can talk with the advisor's assistant when he is away if needed. I can work through examples that illustrate why I should do one thing versus another. I do firmly believe you need to be able to get someone qualified and licensed on the phone who can help you to understand all of the ins and outs, get clarity, purchase or sell items as needed, and the like. To get a handle on the complexities in a full financial plan you need interaction beyond text messages and electronic chats.

Talking with your advisor's other clients is usually helpful, though the advisor will need to get confidentiality waivers to make that happen. Overall, you do not need a local advisor for products that are sold like a commodity ("one size fits all") anymore. Term life insurance is an example that could fall in this category. But to complete your plan and acquire more complex products and services, a local advisor is helpful. Once things are set up and you have become a client, you can use online systems and support to get answers to many of your questions and to complete transactions.

Q. Do I need to know about their Broker-Dealer?

When you move into the investment arena with variable products (those that vary their return rate based on how the market is performing so there is no fixed rate of return), mutual funds, individual stocks, etc., you need to understand that most companies have a third party company called a Broker-Dealer (BD) that actually completes the transactions when you buy or sell. If you do trading, you will want to understand how long it takes for them to complete a transaction. This other entity has to follow a lot of SEC security regulations that are very rigid, and there are huge fines if they don't follow the guidelines closely. They, and not your advisor's company, are usually the custodian (holder) of your money.

I would suggest that you do a little research on the BD for complaints, fraud, lawsuits, time in business, volume of business, number of entities they service as BD, and similar factors that could throw up a red flag. Ask your advisor about the advantages and disadvantages of having this BD. Normally you wouldn't even know they exist if you didn't get statements with their name on them. I wouldn't spend a lot of time with this, but if you have any concerns do a little snooping to resolve those concerns.

Q. In light of this, what do you suggest I do?

I recognize I have painted a more truthful, slightly negative, insider picture different from what the industry might want you to see, but I want to throw up cautionary flags as you enter this area because of these glaring issues I recognized in the industry. Do your homework; get familiar with the areas that you have a need in, and the typical products that can fill your needs. It's your hard-earned money, and it's important for you to allocate the time needed to learn about ways to preserve your assets and generate more income for you and your family.

Meet with several potential agents in different companies, take good notes, verify that what they are saying is accurate, follow up with questions, see how they respond, and choose someone you trust. If you don't like what she is doing or is not doing, express that to her. You have no contract for a specific term with your advisor. Remember that you need to see them perform to continue to keep your business. You should have no problem finding many potential advisors to use. There is usually an abundance of them circling (for prey) for potential clients, so be selective and interview them for the job since they play an important role in your planning.

WHaT WOULD JEFF Do?
(Fun action steps to try this stuff out)

1. Start building your plan now. Get a template from a local bank or financial services firm or one online from a financial source and get something drafted on paper. It will continue to be modified so get the basic plan in writing.

2. Double check that your plan has the main parts of the pyramid's base level. Use the different items at each level of the pyramid to assess options for your plan.

3. Complete a fact finder from a financial planner and use that to more fully complete your plan. Remember that a number of the items will probably not apply right now.

4. Set a plan and start building your emergency fund right now. Waiting is like going without a data backup for your computer until it crashes without any notice.

5. Do some research to understand the basic options in the plan. Make some calls to find a few financial advisors that may be a good option for you. Ask questions to screen out candidates, and set appointments with those that make it through your screening. Let them know your needs and see which one seems like the best fit. Select one and work through a fact finder and a draft plan for you. Decide which products/services you want now, if any, take action to put them in place, and monitor them.

6. Don't just sit on your assets. Monitor the level of service you are getting from your advisor. It is OK to have a couple of advisors and compare their products/services and how they interact with you. You can always terminate your relationship with an advisor if she is not filling your needs.

7. Get involved and stay involved. It's your hard-earned money and you want it to grow quickly.

Share this information with your family and friends because you've learned something that can help them. Once you've finished these steps, write me to let me know what happened and what you learned at *stories@lifescheatsheets.com.*

Now, think like Nike and Just Do It!

"Professionals built the Titanic, amateurs built the Ark."

DeterMine Who gets Your Stuff When You kick It (Estate Planning 101)

Q. When should I do basic estate planning?

Every legal adult (18 years old; fortunately for some not gauged on maturity) needs to do basic estate planning that complies with his state's laws. It's unpleasant to think about, but accidents happen and you simply never know if you will be incapacitated, unconscious, in a terminal state, or dead by the end of the day (don't get paranoid). You can't predict when your time on earth will end. An estate plan is like insurance: it's better to be prepared and not need it than to need it and not have it. Estate plans can also help you protect your assets from creditors and lawsuits, take care of your charitable interests, reduce taxes, and get nursing home assistance through Medicaid and Medicare while retaining some of your assets.

The key to this whole area is to follow Nike's theme and Just Do It, NOW (I'm not kidding; put this on your schedule). You need to get these forms properly completed and do it before you run your next errand, watch a sports event, go to sleep tonight, do any additional travel, or take your next vacation. You never know when something unexpected will happen to you. Your number may be up today and you won't have any notice to plan ahead, which is why you need to step up to the plate and Just Do It, NOW.

The Terry Schiavo case in Florida highlights the importance of planning for your eventual death or a potential disability now, while you still can. Terry was a young lady who suddenly found herself with a severe health issue that put her in a vegetative state with no prior warning. Conflicts between her husband and her parents about whether to end life support turned into a long, publicized court battle. She stayed in a terminal state for many years while the battle continued in court, causing trauma to the whole family. Had she completed these documents according to Florida law, they would have spelled out her wishes and avoided the dispute. No one would have incurred millions of dollars in medical and legal expenses. Don't put your family through that. Let them grieve and follow your wishes when your time comes.

I got rid of my motorcycle because of the dangers caused by others on the road. I couldn't justify taking the chance of having my 850 pound GL1800 Honda Gold Wing come crashing down on me while skidding down the pavement. Someone's apology just doesn't cut it at that stage.

Within a span of just a couple of months, I had three close calls that convinced me to listen to my family and friends and sell the bike. First, a young girl (we'll call her "doufuss") on a cell phone nearly cut directly into me because she wasn't paying attention. Then a big Labrador Retriever darted into the road from the side of a house, nearly running into the side of my front wheel. The last straw was when I drove by some kids playing baseball at a park near the road and narrowly dodged two baseballs laying on the road.

I've had a lot of hair-raising (or hair-losing) experiences involving motorcycles. Any one of those incidents could have left me severely injured and possibly in need of my estate plan documents. Obviously I wasn't planning on that when I left for a ride. Most people don't wake up and think, "Gee, today would be a good day for a devastating head injury leaving me in a permanently vegetative state." But sadly, it can happen.

Even though I sold my bike, I continue to encounter risks daily in my SUV. Did you know driving or riding in a vehicle is more dangerous than most daily activities? Your chances of being severely hurt or killed in a car are many times greater than while flying. Yet many people have a fear of flying and think nothing of riding in a car. You never know when someone else is not paying attention because their kids are fighting, they spilled something, they are on a call or text message... and they cause an accident. You might just be the victim of a freak accident; have you ever seen the *Final Destination* movies? The point is, even if you aren't skydiving, racing motorcycles, swimming with sharks, or participating in other risky activities, you should still plan ahead in case you are seriously injured, or worse, you bite it.

Q. Can I do an estate plan if I'm not yet 18 years old?

You can do a basic estate plan before you even turn 18. There may be some conflicts with parental rights and guardians for minors, so you should consult with an estate planning or family law attorney in your state if you need to know those details and are concerned your parents might not follow your wishes. Even if a minor's estate plans (not implying it's a minor estate) can be overruled by parents, it is important for your loved ones to know your desires. Get them written on paper, signed, dated, and witnessed so your intention is known in the case of your unexpected death. For example, if you and your brother had a great baseball card collection and you were killed in a bicycle accident, you might want to make certain your brother got it. Make sure you get your intentions on paper and filed in a place where your loved ones can find the documents.

Q. Who should do this basic estate planning?

This applies to anyone who wants to determine how his property will be handled if he unexpectedly passes away or becomes incapacitated. A Last Will and Testament (Will) is one basic estate planning document that you should complete now (see details later). Decide who gets what rather than allowing the state to make that determination in the absence of a directive from you. Regardless of what you have, you should be the one deciding what to do with your stuff. You also don't want the court to name a guardian for you, if you are incapacitated. You name your guardian in your will. The court-appointed guardian may not act as you would want him to, or may disagree with your significant other or family on your care. So all adults should complete the forms described in this chapter now.

Q. What is probate?

No, it's not what really skilled fisherman put on their hooks to catch lots of big fish (get it?). Probate means to prove the validity of a Will. The probate court determines whether your Will was executed properly and, if it is valid, uses it to distribute your assets after death in the manner you have outlined in the document. As a general rule, try to keep as much from the probate process as possible. This will reduce costs, expedite the transfer of your assets to beneficiaries, and keep most of your affairs private. Many items can be transferred directly at your death if you make arrangements in specific documents while you are of sound mind (before anything occurs that would make you legally incompetent). While you are living, assets such as real property, bank accounts, investment accounts, retirement accounts, and insurance policies can all be set up to transfer to your beneficiary immediately upon your death, outside of probate.

Q. Does my estate have to go through probate court?

In Ohio, each county has a division of the common pleas court called the probate division (check your government website for your specific one). This court has a probate judge. Larger counties also have magistrates who handle many of the tasks that don't require the judge. The court oversees each case to make certain the Will is authentic and followed properly. The probate court also confirms that all debts, taxes, and other financial affairs are paid, and then the remaining assets are distributed to those who are legally entitled to them.

Technically, if you have no probate assets, you would not have to go through probate. But virtually everyone has personal property, accounts, or other items that have not been held in a trust (explained later), are not already in someone else's name, or have not been directly transferred via one of the methods explained earlier. Accordingly, most estates have to go through the probate process for at least a portion of their assets. In Ohio, if your estate is $35,000 or less, you can take an expedited route (since you ain't got squat they put you on the fast train out). If your surviving spouse is getting all of your assets, this amount increases to $100,000.

The probate process can easily take six to nine months or more since creditors' claims can be submitted up to six months after your death, and federal tax returns are not due for nine months. It is common to experience delays along the way, and your beneficiaries need to follow the court's timeline. Attorney costs can be 4 to 5% of the estate value in Ohio. The Executor (person you appoint in your Will to work with the probate court, oversees getting your bills paid, gets your heirs what you left them, and completes any remaining loose ends) can also get up to a 4% payment for their services. The process is open to the public and your beneficiaries lose control of the timeline by having to go through the court system. This can elongate the grieving process and can get annoying since there are a lot of forms to be filed to get through the whole process.

Q. Does my family need a lawyer for this process?

It is not necessary to have an attorney to file in probate, but it is highly recommended since it is a detailed, paper-intensive process. There are a lot of interim deadlines, forms, and fees to work through. My grandmother's process took more than two years with additional tax payments being made to finally resolve it, and we aren't the Rockefellers or Kennedys (super rich dudes). The more wealth and complexity, the longer it can take, even with complex estate planning. Thus, you should try to keep as much of your property from going through probate as you can so you reduce costs and hassle.

Q. What estate documents should I complete?

The basic documents are a living will (LW), healthcare power of attorney (HPOA), financial power of attorney (FPOA), and a written Will. A more detailed explanation of each of these follows. You will also want to consider trusts once you have some assets so that you can avoid probate, keep more of your affairs private, and do more complex planning.

Q. What does a Living Will cover?

An LW allows you to pre-determine your wishes as they relate to life support treatment (a.k.a. "pulling the plug"), artificial feeding and fluids, cardiopulmonary resuscitation (CPR, a.k.a. "the paddles"), a do not resuscitate (DNR) order, and anatomical donations (giving away body parts).

This document only applies when you are terminally ill or permanently unconscious and cannot make or communicate healthcare treatment decisions for yourself. If you are expected to recover from your illness, this document does not apply and the HPOA usually applies (see below). Therefore, it is wise to complete both documents at the same time. In many states, the LW trumps the HPOA; therefore, your wishes in the LW are followed prior to those in the HPOA if you have executed both and they are in conflict.

An LW allows you to designate a person to make certain decisions for you if you are unable to do so. You can, and should, name multiple alternates in case the first person you designate is unable or unwilling to accept this responsibility. You need to completely trust these individuals to follow your treatment wishes, regardless of their opinions. They step into your shoes to assure that what you have authorized occurs if you are unable to make those decisions for yourself. You are the only one who can change this document, but you can make changes at any time while you are still competent. Many states have an accepted LW available online. In Ohio, you can get one at *www.ohpco.org* (Ohio Hospice and Palliative Care Organization).

The medical and bar (groups of drunks? Oh, you mean legal entities) associations worked together to create this one, so it is trustworthy in this state.

Q. What is a Healthcare Power of Attorney?

An HPOA states your wishes for healthcare when you are unable to do so, but unlike the LW, you do not have to be in a terminal condition to have this apply. If you have not written specific care instructions you want for a current health condition you have and you are incapacitated, the person you name to make these decisions for you (your attorney-in-fact) will need to make them, but they must be consistent with any previously expressed wishes they are aware of. So, if you have specific thoughts about how treatment should or should not occur in different scenarios, spell it out in this document so those wishes are known. This document becomes effective when you cannot make your own decisions regarding your treatment.

In Ohio, you can also get the HPOA online at *www.ohpco.org* (Ohio Hospice and Palliative Care Organization). This is another trustworthy document put together by the medical and bar associations. Since October, 2003 in Ohio, there is an optional "Declaration of Mental Health Treatment" document that can accompany the HPOA to specifically address mental healthcare. The HPOA covers both physical and mental healthcare, but there may be specific issues you want to address in more detail. If you want more information on this, go to the Ohio Bar's site at *www.ohiobar.org* then to "public" then "resources" then "law you can use" then scroll down to the article on declaring mental health treatment.

If you follow the instructions completely, you can complete both the LW and the HPOA on your own. If you are uncomfortable with that decision, get legal counsel to confirm you are doing it properly. Recall that if you have an LW and an HPOA, the LW trumps the HPOA, if care and decisions conflict. However, it is wise to have both because the HPOA covers many other situations that are not covered by the LW.

Q. What is a Financial Power of Attorney?

Once you have executed an LW and an HPOA, you should complete a Financial Power of Attorney (FPOA) authorizing an agent, who you name, to take care of your financial affairs if you are not able to on your own. I have seen many different versions of this so you will probably want one from an attorney. You can also institute an FPOA for a specific time or for a limited purpose.

For example, when my grandfather retired he would go to Florida for the winters. He would execute an FPOA giving my mom authority to handle his affairs while he was in Florida. She would pay utility bills, property taxes, and receive income from his sources during this time, essentially taking care of all of his local affairs while he was gone. I have used these when I was out of town and needed to bid on a property at auction or close on a property.

This document can be tricky and should be instituted with the assistance of legal counsel so it does specifically what you want it to do and nothing more. It can cause problems if you inadvertently give your agent more authority than you want. The Ohio law on this subject has been updated so it outlines normal actions and prohibits specific actions like gifting the principal's (what does my high school principal have to do with this? Oh you mean the owner of the assets) assets while acting as his agent. Make certain you check the laws in your area.

This document can be customized specifically to your needs. It should clarify the specific authority and powers granted, as well as any limitations. It should state when the authority starts, or what triggers it to start, and when it ends. It should give you, as the principal, the power to revoke it at any time. It should also specifically state whether the agent can act when the principal is incompetent or disabled.

Q. Who should I designate to handle my affairs?

When completing these documents, be very careful about naming your fiduciary (person you trust and name to take care of you and your affairs). This person is required to act in your best interest and should be held to that high standard. Make certain you can trust this person to carry out your wishes, regardless of his opinion. If you can't, don't name him (kick him to the curb). His role is to follow your set of instructions when you are not able to act for yourself. You should also name an alternative person as a back-up in case the person you originally select is unable to serve in that capacity for any reason. Keep in mind that some decisions may require them to use their discretion. While you will provide instructions for a number of scenarios, you should name people who will use sound judgment (no "doufusses") when you are not available or are no longer capable of making decisions on your own, and your documents don't cover the particular situation.

In deciding who to name to make your decisions, you do not have to limit the thought process to your family. Neither your physician nor the administrator of the healthcare facility or their employees can be named. But others outside of your family can fill this role.

Q. What should be included in my Will?

Complete your written Will along with the LW, HPOA, and FPOA. A Will can be simple, or more complex provisions can be included. It should be comprehensive, so include typical sections even if they don't currently apply at the time you execute the document. Remember, you want to plan for the future, so consider potential scenarios and decide how those should be addressed. If you forget to update your Will and a section that didn't apply at the time you executed your Will suddenly becomes applicable by the time of your death, you can eliminate a potential conflict by specifying your desires and including that section in advance. For instance, you may not have any children at the time of execution, but you would want certain property to pass to your children at the time of your death, so include the section on children when you execute the Will.

You should also have legal assistance with your Will from a lawyer who does them regularly, not from someone who dabbles from time to time. For example, in Ohio there is a specific way to execute Wills to make them valid, so you must follow that closely or a disgruntled family member could contest it and have it declared invalid because of a simple mistake. I recommend that each page of each original be initialed and numbered "1 of 10," "2 of 10," and so forth, so it is clear that all of the pages were seen and are there.

Your Will should include provisions that give particular items to specific people (a.k.a. specific devise). For some reason, many of those I have seen tend to leave out this important section. This section assures that property is allocated as the decedent (the person who dies) would want it. When this section is skipped, heirs (usually children of the decedent) have to decide who gets what, which can lead to bitter fights. I know of several cases where children have "raided" the house very soon after the last parent died to get what they want or believe is coming to them. Obviously, it really causes resentment, at a minimum, when the children who arrived at the house later discover that their siblings took cherished possessions.

So if you want any specific items to go to specific heirs—such as a particular watch to your oldest nephew [name], a certain vehicle to a specific sibling [name], etc.—have these bequests clearly written in the Will. If there is a chance the bequest can be interpreted differently, give serial numbers, model numbers, etc. to clear up any possible confusion. I have included in the Appendix an example of the form that I use for specific devises in my Will that you may want to adopt. Most Wills have a catch-all or "rest and residue" section worded something like "all the rest and residue remaining will be divided among..." that picks up anything that is not specifically mentioned and disposes of those items in a generic way.

I dealt with a case where a child had the locks changed on her parents' home right after the last parent died and changed the alarm code so only she knew how to get in the house. She wanted first dibs on the valuable items of the estate. Her siblings got a Temporary Restraining Order (TRO) placed on the sister to try and stop her from taking anything from the home, and the feud took many months to resolve. The interesting part of the story is that there was not much to fight about, yet each sibling had her specific thought as to who should get what and none would budge. The court and attorneys had to get involved to legally resolve the feud. This fight used up a good portion of the estate money on attorneys that would have been inherited by the siblings. If the parent just had a Will that laid out these things in detail, the entire problem might have been avoided.

Another case I dealt with involved a man who had an expensive watch that he was given upon retiring after 40 years from a Fortune 500 company. His only grandson loved the watch and collected watches, so the grandfather wanted to give it to him. He forgot to enter that specific devise in his Will, and the watch became part of the overall estate that was split among all four children, who had eight children among them (seven granddaughters and one grandson). They had a problem because not all of the children agreed to give the watch to the grandson.

To illustrate my point further, let's now assume it was a $20,000 diamond-encrusted, gold Rolex watch. Are all four children going to give up the watch voluntarily realizing it is worth at least $5,000 to each of them? Can the grandchild come up with $15,000 to pay off the other three uncles/aunts? I think you can see how basic mistakes and omissions in Wills can easily cause family disputes that can create long-term problems among the heirs. I know of cases where siblings have not spoken for decades after similar situations.

Some Wills also omit wishes about the burial and cremation, funeral and visitation, cemetery plot, casket, etc. There are a lot of decisions to be made in a day or two when someone passes away. If all of these decisions are made previously by you and included in this written document with instructions, it dramatically reduces the pressure on your loved ones while they are grieving. It is a great gift to provide to your family and allows you to choose how things are handled after your death.

You should also look at including provisions such as:
- Naming the probate attorney (if needed)
- Naming an Executor and at least two successor Executors

- Naming two or three levels of beneficiaries, especially for specific devises (If a beneficiary has died before you, then the property will go to the next in line.)
- If married, details about how your spouse is involved
- If previously married, details about how your ex-spouse is involved and any involvement from children from the prior marriage
- Children and grandchildren and how they are going to be involved
- Simultaneous death (What happens if both parents are killed in one accident? Clarify who will be considered to have died first so the chain of title to each of their goods passes through both Wills as you wish and beneficiaries get what you want them to.)
- Debt forgiveness (If someone owes you money at your death, do you expect them to pay your estate or will you forgive the debt?)
- Disinheritance of specific people (Do you want to make certain someone specific does not get anything? If so, spell it out in the Will.)
- Nieces and nephews (How are they and more distant family included?)
- Any trusts (Refer to the specific trust document so it can be followed.)
- Devises to minors (Do you need a guardian or trustee to make certain the minors are taken care of properly? What are their duties and responsibilities? Who should that be? Also, name a successor to this person.)
- Organ donation (Which ones and to whom?)
- Charity donations (Which ones and how much?)
- Prenuptial agreements (These cover property that an individual owned prior to marriage that is not included in marital property. A prenuptial can trump Will bequests, so include a reference to the agreement.)

- Ability to reject devises (Occasionally, a beneficiary may want to decline to accept something given to him in a Will, particularly if there are costs associated with the property so it will go to the next beneficiary in line.)

Q. Can I change my Will once I have completed one?

You need to review your Will regularly (briefly each year) and revise it as your life changes so it reflects your current wishes. Additions or changes can be made to a current Will. These amendments are called codicils. Codicils leave the original Will in place with the sole exception of the newly adopted changes. Codicils still need to be executed in accordance with the specific guidelines of your state to be valid.

If the Will is available in a word processing document, it is more typical to create a whole new Will incorporating the new changes. This would be printed and executed according to state law. Language in the new Will outlines that it replaces all previous Wills and Codicils so it overrides the old one. A Will remains effective until it is formally revoked by the maker or it is purposely destroyed by the maker with the intent of revoking the Will.

Q. Should I tell people that I have a Will?

You should inform your Executor that you have named them to administer your estate. You may also wish to tell your beneficiaries who you have chosen as your Executor and make it clear that you expect them to comply with directions you have given to the Executor and with the terms of your Will. If you believe it is likely that someone will try to take certain items without authorization after your death, you may want to inform them that no one is to take anything before checking with the Executor and getting her direction.

The court and the probate attorney will provide direction to the selected Executor. The Executor typically has personal liability if she does not follow the court's decisions and Will properly, so the "t's" have to be crossed and the "i's" dotted before there is a final distribution to the beneficiaries. This makes certain all liabilities of the estate have been paid before giving the remainder away.

Q. What happens if I die without a Will?

If you die without a will, you die "intestate" (no it's not the organ your food travels through) and must follow the statute of descent and distribution (a.k.a. intestate succession) for your particular state. This is a state law that lays out how your estate will be distributed and who gets what, once all claims, debts, expenses, and taxes have been paid. You have no power to determine who gets what; state law takes over, as interpreted by the local probate court. As you can guess, you really don't want to go this route because you give up your ability to distribute your possessions as you would like. If you die intestate, the court appoints an Administrator who takes the place of the Executor. This is usually a surviving spouse or one of the closest relatives, but may be a professional advisor to the decedent or family.

The law is reasonably logical and gives most assets to those people who are most closely related to the decedent. But that may not be the manner that you would have chosen. The spouse and children get most goods when this happens. When there are second and third marriages with kids mixed in, it gets messy, and there is a better chance your assets will not be distributed how you would have wanted.

This process involves the probate court much more heavily, and it may take longer for many different reasons. The heirs will need to follow the court's schedule, and it may be more expensive because of costs to find relatives, find assets, get assets appraised, hire an Administrator, etc.

Non-probate assets (those that skip the probate process) are those that are directly transferred at death (see section below titled "...stay out of probate") to a named beneficiary or are jointly owned with rights of survivorship. This survivorship titling means two or more people own and are listed on the title to a property and the decedent's (person that died) ownership portion gets turned over to those that are still living and are on the title right when he dies, so the remaining, living title holders now own it completely without the deceased person. Normally, both probate and non-probate assets will be listed in the inventory even though non-probate assets will not go through the probate process.

Q. How can I learn more about estate planning?

One way to get more knowledgeable in this area is to go to a few of the free estate planning seminars that are often held by estate attorneys. Some are held in conjunction with a financial planner. It is helpful to get opinions from both professionals. I've personally given a number of seminars on estate planning, trusts, Medicaid and financial planning, and my experience as an attorney and a financial planner allowed me to offer both perspectives on these planning techniques.

Compare the presentations, handouts, and other information given. Take detailed notes at the seminar and jot down any web sites they recommend. Many offer free consultations, which I would accept if you have any interest in working with that person. The consultation we offered included an examination of the individual's circumstances and showed him specific strategies that could be put in place at that time to save him money and hassle upon his death or incapacitation. For example, many clients wanted to save their house and vehicle as well as some personal goods for their family while still qualifying for nursing home assistance through Medicaid, if they had that need. We showed them a strategy to make this happen, and how it had to occur five years before the event under Medicaid guidelines.

You should also find out how long they have practiced in this area, their credentials, and whether they have partners for backup if they leave or cannot be available when you need them. Assess whether they seem to know what they are doing, and ask for a quote and a time frame for having them do your estate planning. Make certain you have a clear understanding of what they will be doing for their fee and clarify whether that charge includes any assistance in the case of your death or incapacitation.

Doing your own due diligence will make you more confident and prepare you to ask good questions that will fill in gaps in your knowledge. Become familiar with these documents and do your own research. Look at their sample documents to see if they appear comprehensive. Once you are comfortable with this area, decide how you are going to get the documents completed (by yourself or with an attorney) and do it. Overcome any procrastination.

Q. Can I use free forms that I find online?

Since these are very important documents, don't just search for forms online that you can get for free. You need to be confident they will hold up to court scrutiny if you need them. If you choose to use prewritten forms, make certain they are from a reputable source that knows your state laws and has a sound legal background. I don't recommend these types of forms from most sites, though state sites with these documents may be used to have something in place.

Otherwise, I recommend that you spend a small amount of money to get the basic documents completed and executed properly. For example, in Ohio, you have to be at least 18 years old to make a Will, then have two witnesses, not named as beneficiaries in your Will, see you sign your Will, then they have to sign your Will in your presence. They must believe you are of sound mind when doing so or it may be deemed invalid, if contested. You don't want to go through preparing a Will then screw this step up and have it thrown out after you pass away.

Q. What is a trust?

Another item to consider adding to your estate plan is a trust. Trusts, in general, avoid the probate system because the trust owns the assets, not an individual. The individual dies, not the trust, which is considered a separate entity (like a company). The trust lives on and won't die until is it revoked or terminated in some manner.

Trusts are private; therefore, the probate court is not involved. Trusts generally are not delayed by the death of the maker because they are established to hold assets and transfer them in a specific manner. Many times, the death of a beneficiary doesn't change the trust and it continues to operate for a specific purpose.

Whether or not assets in the trust are counted as part of your estate and taxed depends upon the type of trust and how it is set up. You need to get an attorney who works in the estate planning area to give you guidance in this area.

There are a lot of special types of trusts for many purposes, and some can get very complicated, but two of the most common and less complex trusts are the revocable living trust (RLT) and the irrevocable life insurance trust (ILIT).

Q. What is a Revocable Living Trust?

With a Revocable Living Trust (RLT), you can be the maker of the trust (the person who starts the trust), the Trustee (the person who manages the trust for the beneficiaries), and the first-level beneficiary (the person who is going to get the contents of the trust first) at the same time. RLT assets are still considered the maker's assets for Medicaid qualification purposes; therefore, you would need to permanently transfer ownership before Medicaid would not consider them. But, once the assets have been transferred to a trust, they do not go through probate and are not public because the court does not consider them owned by the trust maker, but owned by the trust entity. This is one of the simplest and most common vehicles to put many of the assets that would otherwise be in your Will in, keep them all private, plus save all of the probate fees.

Q. What is an Irrevocable Life Insurance Trust (ILIT)?

Generally, in an Irrevocable Life Insurance Trust (ILIT), an irrevocable trust is established that owns a life insurance policy on the maker. The maker cannot change the trust, does not own the assets, and is not a beneficiary. The maker gifts enough assets to the trust to make the payments on the life insurance policy that the trust owns. The beneficiary is either the trust itself, or someone else. The maker must give up all ownership rights. This is usually used for tax benefits, avoiding estate tax, and increasing the size of the proceeds that are distributed to beneficiaries of the maker. This is fairly simple also, but there are particular details that must be followed to set it up correctly, so see counsel if this concept seems to fit your need.

Q. How do I avoid trusts and stay out of probate?

The most common mechanisms for directly transferring your assets at death without a trust while avoiding probate include:

- Naming beneficiaries on life insurance policies, pensions, and retirement accounts
- Titling bank accounts and other similar ones "payable on death" to a beneficiary
- Deeding real estate, securities, and vehicles "transfer on death" to a beneficiary
- Owning property joint tenancy with rights of survivorship (surviving owners automatically own it fully after one owner dies)

These methods avoid probate entirely so if you can do this with all of your assets, you avoid the need for a trust. It is usually advisable to designate a bank account with some operating funds in it titled "payable on death" or joint tenancy with rights of survivorship to a surviving spouse or child who is going to be your Executor to be able to pay some bills before the estate account is opened and functional. You can read books or other materials to learn more about these methods, but you should at least be aware that you have many options for estate planning to accomplish your objectives.

Sometimes people want to do specific things with assets like give a life estate (which gives someone use of a property while they are living), providing an allowance to a child who can't handle money well, taking care of grandchildren in specific ways, paying for advanced schooling, etc. A Trust or a very detailed Will is typically necessary to accomplish those goals since the direct transfer methods above won't fill those needs.

Q. What should I do with these documents?

Once you have all of these documents finished, you need to get them to the right people and keep them in the right places so they are readily available when needed. With the HPOA and LW, I recommend that you make five copies and give them to your spouse, two trusted family members, your physician, and attorney. With the FPOA, make four copies and give a copy to the first and second agent named, a trusted family member, as well as your attorney.

With your Will, I generally recommend that you make three originals and two copies. You should keep one of the originals and give the others to the Executor and your attorney, while the copies would go to your spouse and a trusted family member. This is just my preference and can easily change based on your particular situation. All of your originals would go in your offsite safe deposit box or someplace similar, while copies would stay in your home, with you and your spouse knowing where they are kept. Mark the versions "Original" and "Copy" so it is clear. Make it very simple to find your copies and get to your originals upon your death.

You need to determine who you want to see your Will in part based on who is named as a beneficiary and who is getting what. Maybe it won't matter in your family, but it may cause some issues you don't want to deal with while you are living. Depending upon your family relationship, you may want to talk it out with your close family members so you and they know where you stand on your Will and distribution. It can alleviate problems if you explain why you are doing what you are doing, and you may be influenced to change your Will based on what comes out of this meeting.

Otherwise, you should at least let your family members know that you have a Will and inform them who they can contact after your death if you don't have a spouse, significant other, or child to handle this. This person may also be a lawyer. Or you may keep your Will in a bank that has a lock box or other secure location. In many states, the original Will is what really counts while copies are not official and may or may not be deemed valid if the original cannot be located. If the original and copies are different, you have a legitimate Will contest that could get messy.

Q. What instructions should I leave to use upon my death?

Your spouse/significant other and Executor (depending upon your situation) need to understand where to find these key documents upon your death. Sit down and walk through this with them now so there is no procrastinating. They will be going through enough after your death. They don't need to panic and experience additional stress trying to locate these important items. They also need to know which attorney (if you've selected one) is going to do any needed probate work.

They should know where to find your bank documents, insurance policies, safe deposit box, copies and originals of all of your important documents, budget items (like income and expense files), pension and retirement files, and related items, so they can pick up the ball in case of an emergency. They should also have instructions on whom to contact if there are questions about any of these things and be able to get direction from the probate attorney on banking details during the probate process. It is best to draft a detailed instruction sheet, to go along with the Will, that outlines all of these details and contacts with phone numbers.

Funeral, funeral home, and visitation details are needed so scheduling can be accomplished quickly. It is important for your spouse or Executor, if no spouse, to quickly contact out of town family and friends you want notified. They need to write the obituary (but I recommend you write it yourself) and any other newspaper submissions and forward them for print. If you were still living in your home before passing, they may need to clean up the home or secure it, if there is no surviving spouse or others living in the home. They may also need to deal with bills or utilities so services continue during the transition. The more detailed the instructions, the easier life will be for those who will be picking up the pieces.

Q.   What should I know about estate taxes?

One last area to be a little familiar with is estate taxes and how they affect estate planning. Through 2009, the federal tax exclusion value (amount of one's estate that does not get taxed by the federal government) of an estate has risen to $3,500,000 while the top tax rate has decreased to 45% for federal estate tax (highest tax rate that could be charged on the portion of an estate above the $3.5 million exemption). In 2010, the tax is repealed, so there is no federal tax on estates if you die during 2010 (so pick 2010 if you have a choice). But, as it is currently written, the exemption amount and tax rate will revert to their previous values of $1,000,000 and 55%, respectively, in 2011. This proposal is under scrutiny by Congress.

I realize that many young adults may believe these levels are very high, but you need to remember that your estate includes everything that you have an ownership interest in. Proceeds from life insurance policies, retirement accounts, pensions, properties, personal property, etc. are all included, so it can add up quickly. Many estates have been exempt from federal estate tax with these increased amounts over the last several years, but will be taxed at very high rates in 2011, if nothing changes before then.

Earlier in this chapter I explained what a Revocable Living Trust (RLT) is. A common pair of RLTs known as an A-B trust (a.k.a. "marital trust") are two related trusts that allow a married couple to get double the federal estate tax exclusion amounts. If your estate is above the current exclusion amount, you can establish this pair of trusts that allows you to get the ($3.5 million) exclusion twice for your combined estate. These trusts must be in place before the death of the first spouse to take advantage of them, but this is a great option for an estate that exceeds the exemption level.

In Ohio, there is also a state estate tax. Ohio estate tax exclusion is $338,333 of the value, and then the remainder of your estate is taxed at approximately 6 to 7%. Many estates would still owe state estate tax, even if it is excluded from federal estate tax. In 2006, Ohio's estate tax receipts were nearly $273 million so you can see that this is a very important issue in most states and at the federal level because it generates so much income for the state and federal governments.

If you want to avoid this whole chapter, just decide not to die, right? I realize some of this may seem pretty advanced, but hopefully this information will prompt you to get these documents in place now. You can learn more about these topics in my *financial habits* follow-up book, which will outline crucial shortcuts to wealth.

WhaT WOULD JEFF Do?
(Fun action steps to try this stuff out)

1. Stop and give some thought to who or what agency you would like to get your stuff and jot down those details on paper. Let it drop for a couple of days and go back and revisit your list to make certain you still agree with your initial wishes. Also, make decisions about burial or cremation, viewing, writing your own obituary, guardian, etc. and write them down.

2. Find the standard Living Will for your state and complete it now, making the appropriate copies and distributing them as I suggest.

3. Find the standard Healthcare Power of Attorney for your state and complete it now, making the appropriate copies and distributing them as I suggest.

4. Locate a typical Financial Power of Attorney for your state from a trusted source and complete it now, making the appropriate copies and distributing them as I suggest. Make certain it does what you want it to and only when you want it to. If you are hurt seriously, you want someone set up to take care of your finances for the time being.

5. Give some serious thought to your fiduciary and his backups. Make certain you are very confident that he will take care of your wishes if it is really needed.

6. Spend some time and a little money to get a good, comprehensive Will completed and executed. If you don't want to use an attorney, although I suggest you do go to an estate attorney, get a recent edition of a "How to" book at the library

or bookstore and follow it to complete a Will now. Make certain it is a book written by an attorney recently and for your state. The more complex your life and financial situation gets, the stronger my recommendation is to get legal assistance.

7. It is your call as to whether you share the contents of your Will, but I would make certain the appropriate people (Executor, significant other, parents) know it exists and where to get the original as well as copies so they can be found in an emergency.

8. Don't die without a Will.
(or I will haunt you.)

9. Find a couple of estate planning seminars in your area, attend them, and go to a free consultation to learn more about the area and your options. You will also be able to decide if the person giving the seminar is someone you might want to work with. (No, I'm not doing them right now, but thanks for asking.)

10. Do a little research on the two trusts I outline and see if they apply to your personal situation. They may not right now, but may down the road. If they do apply, ask about them in your consultations to determine whether you should put one in place right now.

11. Use the techniques for avoiding probate that I outlined so applicable assets can directly transfer to the beneficiary upon your death. Complete the paperwork right now.

12. As you complete your Will, write the "instructions upon my death" document at the same time and let the appropriate parties know where it is.

Quiz your family and friends on these topics because you've learned something that can help them. Suggest they do the same. Once you've finished these steps, write me to let me know what happened and what you learned at *stories@lifescheatsheets.com*.

Now, think like Nike & Just Do It!

Conclusion (You Just Completed Your First Goal)

Give yourself a hand! (Go ahead, I'll wait, let me know when you're done.) Great job on making it through the whole book. You probably never thought I would shut up. I know this is a lot of information to take in. Please see this as some of the least expensive schooling you will ever get, not as another assignment. If you did not do some of the action steps as you finished each chapter, I would go back now and complete them. I would reread each chapter as you apply it to your life so you have that material fresh in your mind. Use this as a reference throughout life.

Now that you are done, send me your comments on the content and let me know how I can improve the book for revised versions. Also, if you have additional real-life examples that relate to any of the subjects I have covered, please forward those to me.

Remember these are foundational skills and each of them can be enhanced with further reading and practice. The key is to take action and put these new habits in place right now so they start enriching your life daily. I ask you to pay it forward by showing others your new habits so they can grow also. You will reinforce these habits as you teach them to others so you both benefit. You will be amazed at how these habits will get you what you truly want in life. That's a wrap.

Sign up for Jeff's e-zine at *www.lifescheatsheets.com* to get free materials to apply these concepts and to get advance notice on the follow-up *financial habits* book as soon as it's available.

Appendix

Chapter 3: Limited Thinking Answer

Most people assume a mental perimeter around the nine dots and limit their solutions accordingly. But you can see that the answer lies outside of the self-imposed perimeter. This is an example of what you need to do to open your mind up to life's real possibilities. Eliminate the barriers and think big!

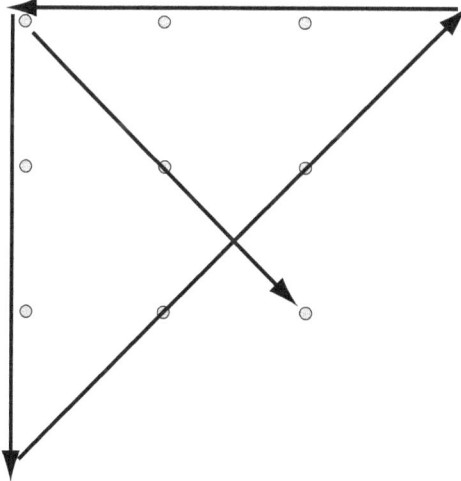

Chapter 11: Sample Young Adult Resume

JOE SCHMOE
1234 Schmoe Lane, Toledo, OH 54321
(999) 999-9999 x101 • joeschmoe@abc.com

OVERALL ROLE/POSITION TARGET
[Network Administrator, Head Chef, Branch Manager, etc.]
Strength Area1 – Area2 – Area3 – Area4 – Area5

Like your longer elevator speech. Outline your strengths in a few sentences followed by your biggest 2–3.
• Led ...
• Directed ...
Additional core strengths include: (some samples included here)

Due Diligence	Lean Management Culture	Real Estate Savvy
Expansion/Diversification	IT Overhauls	Turnaround Proficiency
Business Negotiations	Process Reengineering	Entrepreneurial Instinct
Hands-on Leadership	Business Law Competencies	Creative Problem Solving

PROFESSIONAL EXPERIENCE

Company A   20XX-Present

Title
Strong action statement about what you did and accomplished there.
• Strongest accomplishment.
• Strongest accomplishment.
• Strongest accomplishment.
• Strongest accomplishment.

Company B   20XX-20XX

Title
Strong action statement about what you did and accomplished there.
• Strongest accomplishment.
• Strongest accomplishment.
• Strongest accomplishment.
• Strongest accomplishment.

Company C (oldest experience)   19XX-20XX
Title
Strong action statement about what you did and accomplished there.
• Strongest accomplishment.
• Strongest accomplishment.
• Strongest accomplishment.
• Strongest accomplishment.

CREDENTIALS
University of...
Master of Business Administration, GPA X.X, Awards

...College
Bachelor of Science in Finance, GPA X.X, Awards, Clubs

DESIGNATIONS/AFFILIATIONS/VOLUNTEER ACTIVITIES
Certified Public Accountant, AICPA Member,
Habitat for Humanity, Humane Society dog walker

Chapter 17: Financial Plan Model Pyramid

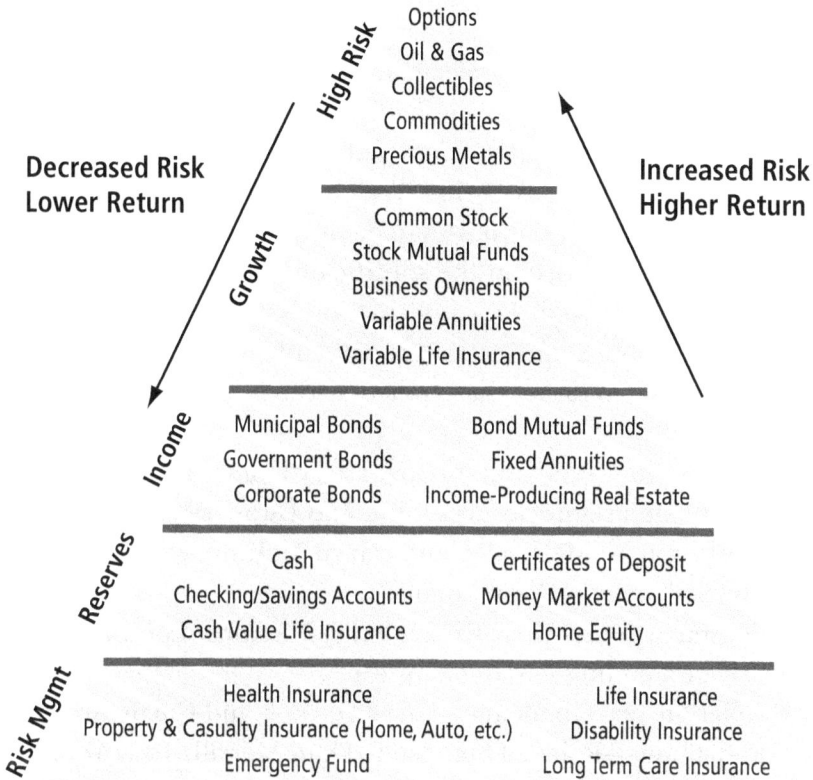

Decreased Risk
Lower Return

Increased Risk
Higher Return

High Risk

Options
Oil & Gas
Collectibles
Commodities
Precious Metals

Growth

Common Stock
Stock Mutual Funds
Business Ownership
Variable Annuities
Variable Life Insurance

Income

Municipal Bonds   Bond Mutual Funds
Government Bonds   Fixed Annuities
Corporate Bonds   Income-Producing Real Estate

Reserves

Cash   Certificates of Deposit
Checking/Savings Accounts   Money Market Accounts
Cash Value Life Insurance   Home Equity

Risk Mgmt

Health Insurance   Life Insurance
Property & Casualty Insurance (Home, Auto, etc.)   Disability Insurance
Emergency Fund   Long Term Care Insurance

Chapter 17: Real Estate Investing Resources

I enjoy and have been in real estate since 1981 in high school. More recently I have researched different areas to see where I wanted to go from where I have been. I have been to lots of workshops and boot camps now and have a reasonable handle on a few of the mentors and coaches that are in some of the major categories that are available today. This is not a complete list.

I recommend you look at this arena as you diversify your investments and choose your businesses to be involved in. You will need to do further due diligence on the specific ones you are interested in and the people involved. This information is regularly changing. It is helpful to choose someone that is currently investing in the area they are teaching in rather than someone who is solely teaching now.

- Wholesaling—Vena Jones-Cox, Larry Goins, Than Merrill
- Short Sale/Preforeclosures—Bill and Dwan Twyford
- Bankruptcy—Mark Klee and Caryn McKinney
- Buy/Sell Notes—Donna Bauer
- Online/Systems—Kris Kirschner, Jeff Adams, Lou Brown
- Private Lending—Alan Cowgill
- Seller/Owner Financing—Larry Harbolt and Curtis Brooks
- Rehabbing—Robyn Thompson, Than Merrill, Tony Youngs
- Rentals—Jeffrey Taylor "Mr. Landlord"
- Mobile Home/Parks—Ernest Tew, Lonnie Scruggs, Doug Ottersberg
- Multi-Units Apartments—Dave Lindahl, Scott Scheel

Chapter 18: Specific Devise Form Example

Note: Some sample distribution items are listed below for example only. I've also filled in some of the first, second, and third level fields for some of the items just to show you how you would complete the form. The first line has Wife, Dad/Mom, Sisters for the three distribution levels, but you would fill in the appropriate parties that you would choose for each of your items to complete the form. The notes at the bottom are also just examples of ways you can utilize this form to do what you want.

Item	1st Level	2nd Level	3rd Level
Home Office Equipment	Wife*	Dad/Mom	Sisters
Home Furniture	Sister [name]	Nephew [name]	Niece [name]
Home Artwork [name]	Sister [name]	Sister [name]	Wife's Parents
Lawn/Snow Equipment	Bro-in-law [name]	Bro-in-law [name]	Nephew [name]
Power/Hand Tools	Wife*/Parents	Sisters	Nieces/Nephews
Bicycle	Sister [name]	Brother [name]	Oldest Living Nephew
Garage Goods			
Home Appliances			
Jewelry-Wedding Ring			
Video Equipment			
Home Theatre System			
Pictures/Albums			
Sport Equipment			
Ball Card Collection			
Wardrobe			
Luggage			
Book Collection			
6' x 12' Box Trailer			
Personal Memorabilia			
Music/Video Collection			
Phone Equipment	**Local Startup	Wife	Sisters
Mutual Funds-[where]	Wife (PNA)	Parents	Living Sisters
Soc. Sec. Retirement			
Life. Ins.—with no beneficiary	[Normally houses, vehicles, and monetary items like these are included in a Will or Trust specifically so they are not listed here.]		
Stock Options—[where]			
401k			
IRA's			
CD's/MM's/Savings/Chkgs			

PNA = PreNuptial Agreement between Testator and Wife

*Devise conditioned on the requirement that she must personally keep and use the item(s) or she must concede them to the other beneficiaries at her level or they must automatically pass to the beneficiaries at the next level below her as if she did not survive Testator or rejected the devise.

**Donate the item(s) to a local, startup business that has a strong business plan and a promising long-term product or service.

NOTE: All items devised to sisters can be shared/given to her spouse so long as all devisees at that same level agree and the sister is married to and living with the Brother-in-law at the time of death of Testator and distribution of the items in this chart.

NOTE: All multi-person devises within one level are intended to be split reasonably equal in value or quantity, but is left up to all of the devisees at that level. If ALL devisees cannot mutually agree on the split of the item(s), a mutually agreed upon, non-relative will be selected to decide on the specific split. All devisees must agree upon this third party prior to selection. If all devisees cannot agree on an independent third party within thirty days of the distribution day of the other items in this chart, a mutually agreed upon, local attorney/mediator will be retained to try to mediate the split and if that is not successful, the attorney/mediator will arbitrate the matter to a binding decision.

Next in the School Never Taught You Series:

Life's Cheat Sheet:
Crucial Financial Habits School Never Taught You

This book's topics include: planning to get what you want (budgeting), income from your job/your business, pay-yourself-first savings plan, and early retirement planning. It outlines your typical expenses and how to deal with them, including: credit/debit cards, housing and utilities, transportation, spending money, meals, insurances, education, wedding, children, and taxes. It concludes with financial and estate planning to build on the skills introduced here.

This is a must-read to follow the *Success Habits* book. You really need both sets of skills to be successful today. Go to my site (www.lifescheatsheets.com) and get on the e-mail list, or send me an e-mail (see next page) with your information and read my monthly e-zine so you will get the earliest notification once the book is available.

Additional Suggested Topics for the *School Never Taught You* Series:

A) More Advanced Financial Planning 202:

Diversifying investments / active investing / dollar cost averaging

Real estate investing/rentals/commercial

Qualified and non-qualified investors with offerings

Business investing/management / partnerships / LLCs

Stocks-bonds-mutual Funds [like Investools]

Online businesses/internet marketing

Net worth / goals / updating periodically

Advanced investments-REITS, oil, pipelines

Short-, mid-, long-term planning

Self-directed IRAs, 401ks…

B) More Advanced Estate Planning 202:

Estate taxes and exclusions

Trusts—charitable / generation skipping / A-B marital

Detailed instructions to trustee/successors/heirs

Detailed distribution directions

Education and charitable funding

Long term care / self-funding insurance

Analyze life insurance need / charitable life insurance…

Please e-mail me with other topics you would like to see included in the series at info@lifescheatsheets.com.

Index

Prestige Publishing Instant Order Form

Order Date: _____

Name: _____

Address: _____

City/State/Zip: _____

Telephone: _____

Email Address: _____

Postal Orders: Prestige Publishing, P.O. Box 350986,
                      Toledo, OH 43635

Phone Orders: 1-866-475-4675 or 1-419-842-8112

Fax Orders: 1-419-842-8113

Email Orders: info@lifescheatsheets.com

Please send the following books/materials:

_____

_____

_____

Have your credit card ready. We will contact you for payment information once we receive this order or you may order it direct from our web site at *www.lifescheatsheets.com*.

*We will add 6.75% sales tax to orders shipped to any Ohio address

*Shipping is approximately $4.00 for the first book

Please send me additional information on the following items:

☐ Other Books   ☐ Speaking   ☐ Coaching   ☐ Consulting
☐ Publishing   ☐ Partnership   ☐ Volume Purchase   ☐ Other

www.ingramcontent.com/pod-product-compliance
Lightning Source LLC
Chambersburg PA
CBHW070340090426
42733CB00009B/1241